FAMILY SECRETS

BY

BILLIE JEAN YOUNG
AS TOLD TO HER BY JAYE PEAY

To Sister Brenda Miller,
Keep the faith – Enjoy
your Retirement –
Peace,
Billie Young

WESTRY BOOKS
MASSACHUSETTS · NORTH CAROLINA · WASHINGTON

Westry Books
an imprint of Westry Wingate Group, Inc.
www.wwgpress.com

Credits and Acknowledgements:
Cover design by Mali Cayetano
Special thanks to my sister friend writers who read the early script:
Kathy Engel, Alexis DeVeaux, and Barbara Smith

ISBN-10: 1-935323-08-3
ISBN-13: 978-1-935323-08-2

This book is dedicated to my son,
Keith Allen Young (July 12, 1967 – June 2, 2010),
who always believed.

1

I find Creole bread in the breadbox and begin to slice it to go with the cheese and marmalade, add new water to the kettle and open a tin of milk to prepare a warm beverage for the kids. It is a quarter of six. In just over an hour, we will head down the lane away from our house for the last time. We must go south to Rivertown toward the school, which is where Bea will come from. I have instructed Bea to come early, pass our house, turn around, and head back toward town, as she cannot look as if she has come for us. Amite may be in the yard when we leave, so we must simply flag down the vehicle and hop aboard as if we were lucky enough to catch a ride and not have to wait for the bus this morning. It had to be perfectly timed, so Bea and I had synchronized our watches last night. Otherwise, Amite might have reason to be suspicious.

The water in the pot begins to boil. Amite asks if there is fresh tea. I quickly pour tea and serve him and Taiji and return to the kitchen. Amos is yelling at Nefertiti, telling her she is spending too much time in the bathroom. He is particularly disgruntled this morning because he does not want to go into town with me. I have insisted that today is the only day for him to take the comprehensive exam to obtain placement in technical school. He finished high school two years ago and has spent most of the time helping his daddy on the farm, so he is no longer used to having to dress to go to town with me. He considers doing so today as an inconvenience of my making. But it had been the only excuse I could think of to include him in the escape. And I have to take him with me. I cannot leave him with his father. He will simply have to understand later when he knows the truth. Finished with breakfast, I leave the kitchen and the men, go to check on the children and ready myself for departure. Nefertiti can set the table later and make sure the littlest one finishes his breakfast. Amos can fend for himself.

I am scared. Today is scary. I have never been so scared in all my life. I am leaving my husband of twenty-two years, running away. What will today bring? The uncertainty terrifies me. Disobedience. My heart is beating fast. I can feel it thumping, loudly, it seems, in my chest. Will Amite see it? No. He is too busy talking to his friend Taiji, who came last night. Up early, they have taken scant notice of me, even though I have passed through the front room where they are seated three times since I arose. Good. I walk around in my bedroom. It is now 6:00, and the tropical sun is a half hour old. We will leave here just at 7:00. We will walk down the lane to the highway at five minutes of seven to catch the bus. Only we won't take the bus. Bea will be there for us in a vehicle. Perhaps a taxi. I look out the window. What lies over the horizon for me?

I can hear the birds whistling outside, see the mist rising from the mountains in the distance. Every day, the mountains hold a different face for me. Some days they smile and on others they frown. Today, with a touch of the golden sun, they smile. Are they happy to see me go, my constant companions as I washed clothes in the sun? The mountains used to play games with me smiling on one side and crying on the other. They are symbolic of what Largo means to me: a bittersweet place that is beautiful but does not value life. Today, you are a queen; tomorrow, you are a slave.

Facing the mountains, I repeat the prayer my sister gave me, my own personal prayer—three lines long. I am only able to remember the first lines today: "The Lord is my Shepherd, I shall not want. My soul doth magnify the Lord, for He hath..." God, I cannot remember any more words, but you will say them for me today. You know what I mean. My mother, I wish I had obeyed you. You always said, in time of fear, say: "The Lord is my Shepherd." What are the words of my mother? What has the Lord in store for me today? I am leaving a husband whom I promised to love, honor, and obey until death. Will death come today? I am taking away the man's children, his children whom I could not even take to the doctor without his permission, or even send to school for that matter.

Mother, you predicted that I would leave here. Today, it comes true, I hope. Thinking of my mother, I smile. She was good at foreseeing the future. When she gave all of her daughters a gold bracelet, and mine was stolen in Largo in the town of Mayonne, Mother said I would get it back, not to worry. Five years later, I found my bracelet on the arm of a student who sat down next to me on a crowded bus in Rivertown, sixty miles from Mayonne! I had squeezed my uncooperative seat mate to let

2

the woman sit down, looked at her arm, and there was my bracelet, come back to me, just like my mother said.

My eyes fell upon my mother's rose bush, at the front of the house. It is as beautiful as ever, its sole blossom dangling on its languid stem, bright red, a survivor rose that Amite had been unable to kill. I had planted many of them and Amite had just as relentlessly dug them up because "they were in the wrong place," or had been trampled by the bulldozer "by mistake," or "they don't form a straight line." Amite always had an answer though: "Jaye, I will plant another one for you one day; why are you upset? I can always plant another for you when the weather is right."

"But why do you destroy it before you plant another?"

"Don't you have confidence in me? Do I ever lie to you?"

Does Amite ever lie to me? Does Amite ever lie to me!! Does he ever lie to me? Lie. Lie. Lie. The words echo in my head and threaten to drown out the litany that has formed there already. "The Lord is my Shepherd; I shall not want. My soul doth magnify the Lord for he hath...."

Amite and Taiji are talking again. "Dem women dere forget dem place inna de world ...."

It is the same conversation I heard last night when I dropped off to sleep. So many memories in this house wrapped up in here. The times that seemed to be happy and the times I made myself happy. Was I happy? I had convinced myself that I was. Our little house built from concrete blocks sat forlornly beside the road like a little box, its unfinished roof rising into the air to reveal a crude attempt at uniqueness that resembled turrets. Amite considered himself an architect, so the house had been erected pretty much according to his whim, changing styles as he went along, similar to the way he had ruled and shaped us.

How can I leave the little house? What will Amite feel when we are gone? Will he be sorry for what he has done? Angry at us? Will he come after us, try to stop us? Where am I going? What am I doing? What confronts us in a world without Amite to protect us? Is there safety after Amite? Was there safety with him? Did I love him? Will I miss him?

The last three days have been the longest and shortest of my life. Saturday morning I had begun to slip things out of the house to take with us. That was the day I made the final decision to leave Amite. Today is Tuesday, three days later, May 9, 1989. How do you move a family of five within a few hours, in secret, never to return again and without their knowing they are moving? Why must I bear this burden alone?

Amite passes through the room, our bedroom. I look at him. It is hard to believe that I am leaving him. I stifle the impulse to give up, to tell him what I am doing—to seek reconciliation. It is too much, too hard to break a twenty-two year old habit. Amite gives me a disinterested and impersonal look, similar to how he looks at any of his belongings, as if he is just checking to make sure I am still here. Perhaps he wonders what I am doing as I have left the kitchen and am unavailable to pour more tea. I glance at his face, half scared that he can see through to my thoughts, but he has dismissed me already to return to the living room. I follow him back out to the kitchen and put on vegetables to cook, hoping that Amite will stay in the house until they have finished cooking —anything to slow him down a bit before he follows us to the hospital.

Amite and Taiji are still talking. Thank God for Taiji. I forget the inconvenience of his former visits, and thank God for the timeliness of this one. With Yala in the hospital, I slept in her bed last night. Taiji slept in my bed next to Amite. God must have sent him last night. I had been saved the fear of sleeping with Amite, the certainty that he could read my mind and know what I was planning to do. I am sure he still heard my heart beating from the next room. Taiji will go to the hospital with Amite when he goes to see Yala to bring her home. Taiji is slow to get dressed and Amite slows to his crawl whenever Taiji visits us. That should give me the head start I need. *The Lord is my Shepherd.* He sent Taiji for me.

Presently, my youngest daughter, Nefertiti, comes to the doorway. She is ten, gangly, sharp-witted. Mornings, she is quiet, busying herself with thoughts of school, which she loves. Today, she looks at me questioningly, and I realize that, caught in my reverie, I am holding Yala's sheet music for her guitar, wondering at the same time, why I bother, since the guitar always seems to stand there between Yala and her father anyway, connecting them, to the exclusion of me. But Nefertiti does not notice what I am holding; she simply moves on down the hallway to ready herself for school, giving up only a quiet, "Morning, Mom," as she does. I respond, though not audibly. Nefertiti does not react; she is a practical child.

Hannibal, my youngest, appears in the doorway. He is still a baby at six, and having just started school a few days ago, he is unused to the morning routine. The older ones have awakened him, however, and he is trying his best to wake up. Will he remember this? Any of his life here? His father, on whom he dotes? Is this best for him? Of what will his memories consist?

Amite, Jr.—Amos, we call him—rumbles through the house. Voice gruff from having just awakened, he is disagreeable and is, as usual, aiming it at the little ones. He takes out his frustrations with his bossy, domineering father on the rest of us, particularly the children. How I wish I could tell him what we are doing! But I cannot. At nineteen, he is anything but an adult. I have not been able to confide in him about our planned escape. He would foul the whole thing, so fearful is he of Amite and his power to control all of us. Amos would be afraid to cast his lot with me, since, practically speaking, he knows that I never win with his father. And he would, therefore, sooner or later, have to come face to face with his father's wrath. No, it is best that I have not tried to confide in Amos. This must be borne alone. For us. For the whole family, but most of all, for my daughter, Yala, who is in the hospital in town, and whom we must still collect from there to go with us.

And what of Yala? She is the main reason for all of this. What will she say? Will she resent me? Refuse to go? What would/could I do if she does? Force her? Hog tie her onto the plane? Will she try to run away, back to her father? She loves him so. And she is stubborn, opinionated. Will I be able to stand up against her, this miniature of her father's creation?

I shake myself. Fear notwithstanding, I must keep moving. Time is running out. I choose a favorite dress, one with multicolored stripes, which Bea brought me from the States. I don't want to leave it here. Amite had been resentful when she gave it to me. He never wanted me to have anything that he did not provide or that he did not see me scuffle for. Receiving a gift from someone was an act of defiance in and of itself; taking the dress with me somehow completes the act.

Quickly now, I fold a few changes of clothing for Hannibal and put them into my book bag. He will need them the most, being the youngest, I reason. The rest of us can make do with whatever we have until we can get more. I had sent a small bag out with Mrs. Orlando on Saturday. She had taken it to Bea's house and it is the only suitcase I will risk carrying. Whatever I carry out of here today will have to look like school things, the everyday load of books, lunches, and other school paraphernalia which I normally carry with me. So little space in which to pack so much time, so many years!

Putting aside the "packing," I collect myself and enter the kitchen again. The clock on the wall says six thirty. The kitchen extends to the dining/living area where Amite and Taiji are at the table relaxing over morning tea, still talking. Amite enjoys Taiji's visits immensely, as they give him the opportunity to try out his various theories on a man. Their conversations are always peppered with women, how women are forgetting their role in the family, and the resulting disintegration of family life. This morning is no different. Without their noticing, I turn off the vegetables, as I do not want them to cook too much before I leave.

Back in my room, with my heart in my mouth, I realize how unnerved I have become in Amite's presence. The fear that he will somehow read my thoughts and stop us is overwhelming. I sit down on the side of the bed to steady myself. I am trembling, coming unglued. Where will I ever find the nerve to leave my husband, my home and hearth? I have to. I rise and dress myself, remember the locket my mother had given me just before she died, and frantically begin to dig into my dresser drawer to find it. Just as my fingers close around the locket, Amite appears in the doorway. Guiltily, I look up to see him watching me.

"Do you want Hannibal to wear his runners to school or his sandals?"

Relief washes over me. I can hear Hannibal quarreling with Nefertiti about letting him wear his sandals, but she is insisting that he wear the sneakers. Without straightening up or removing my hand from the drawer, I respond almost in a whisper, "the runners." If ever there was a day he might need to be sure-footed, today is it, I think, as Amite turns and goes back to settle the argument. I grab the locket and quickly slip it over my head, underneath my clothes, out of sight. Having done so, I feel better. It is my good luck piece and I will need all the luck I can muster today and for some time to come.

It is now fifteen minutes to seven. Only ten minutes left. Nefertiti is used to the morning routine and timing, and has begun to gather up her books and pencils, and ready herself to go down the lane with me. In the living room, Hannibal is trying unsuccessfully to get into his father's lap. He is still a baby, I think, as I encourage him to hurry up. His father is absentmindedly fending him off, telling him to be a big boy and go to school as he continues his conversation with Taiji, but Hannibal wants a hug. *Hug him, please*, I think, *it may be your last time. He needs a hug from you.*

I escape to my room again, look around at the various memorabilia that I have managed to collect in twenty two years of marriage and moving around: The prints from Africa, the little sculptures I never found a permanent place for, the drawers full of carefully hoarded linen so hard to come by in this remote outpost, my shoes, my school uniforms from eight years of teaching in Largo. I walk through the house. It would be so easy to cry, to give up, pretend I never made these plans, act as if everything is normal, "come to my senses," as Amite would say. So much easier than what lies ahead. Why not? I could just go to school today and forget about leaving now, wait for a more appropriate time when I could make better plans. Why not? Everything is in disarray; and there must be a more orderly way to do this. Nobody knows that I am leaving today except Bea and a few necessary others. Bea would be upset, but she would respect my decision, and that would be that. The others? Can I trust the others? But could I stay? I don't want to walk out on my life; I want to stay. But I must go. The only way out is to walk out—forward—without looking back. In the kitchen, I remember to turn the vegetables back on again, and having done so, I walk to the front of the house, past Amite and Taiji, remind Amite to tend to the vegetables, call out to Amos to hurry, and walk out of the door, out of my life, with a plastic bag in each hand, heading for God knows what.

Hurrying down the lane to the highway, I pass by the various trees we have planted to make the ten-acre site more hospitable. The house is situated on what had been an open field. The trees are young and still somewhat small but sturdily growing. There are citrus, coconut and cashew; and the cashew trees had even begun to bear fruit a few years ago. I remember now how, with so much pride, I had shown Bea the fruit of the cashew tree and how thrilled and appreciative she had been to discover that a lone cashew sat atop the apricot-looking fruit that the tree yielded.

"No wonder they cost so much!" She had exclaimed.

How much these trees represented for us! I had envisioned my grandchildren visiting me on the farm in my autumn years. But it is over now.

Looking up, I see that we have made it down the lane to the highway, having covered the one hundred fifty or so yards in my reverie with the trees. Just a little more, I think. Will Amite come out of the house? No. He is busy talking. Can he see me? If I stand about here, the cashew trees block his view of the road. Thank God for Taiji, for his timely visit. He had kept Amite occupied last night, giving me precious moments to gather myself and prepare for the journey this morning. Otherwise, I would have, as usual, been expected to find time to sit with Amite, to rehash the day, listen to his musings or just be on call for him. I had kissed Amite as usual when I left the house, moving automatically, saying the usual things. Most mornings, he would have, at least wandered outside the door to see us off. But Taiji had come, was there to hold his attention. They had both remained seated when we departed. Amite is not likely to come outside now. That is my rational side. But the fear of what I am doing, actually taking this step to leave Amite, still makes the hair stand up on my neck. It is as if Amite will pounce on me out of the air any minute with an "Aha!" I hear a vehicle, and look up to see a blue, rather beat up van headed towards Rivertown. It appears to be going slow. Reason tells me that it is Bea with the vehicle. I hasten to flag it down. It is. By now, the children and I are at the roadside. The van halts for us. We board. It is Bea, smiling a good morning, quickly moving out of the passenger seat up front to let us board from there.

The driver is Mr. Santos, a local shop owner who also owns a taxi service. He has come in his personal vehicle. Good. No telltale signs of a taxi to arouse suspicions in case Amite is looking. I wonder if Mr. Santos knows what we are doing. Reason tells me he does not. Bea would not have confided in a man for the simple reason that she knows no man in Rivertown or all of Largo for that matter, would knowingly participate in helping a woman leave her husband, no matter what the reason. Breaking up a man's family is the way he would view it. No, he couldn't know. As if reading my thoughts, Bea motions for me to take over, leans in to whisper: "He knows nothing. Tell him what to do."

We are now rolling towards town which is six miles away. I tell Mr. Santos to take us to Rivertown. The children, though surprised, are happy to see Auntie Bea, and beam smiles at the seeming coincidence of finding her in a van which we have flagged down to catch a ride. I sit back, breathe a sigh of relief for one brief moment but decide to tell the children right away. We are in the back away from the driver. I break the news simply by saying that we are going on holiday. Smiles. All around.

"When?"

"Now."

"Today, Mom?"

"Now?" It is Nefertiti.

"Yes."

"No school?" Practical Nefertiti.

"No school."

Nefertiti settles back. Amos is more analytical, aggressive. He frowns, face clouds over.

"Dad doesn't know?"

"No."

"Mom! He is going to be angry at me!"

"No. OK."

Amos scowls, a worried, frantic look on his face and for the remainder of the ride to town, vacillates between happy thoughts of frivolity and escaping the drudgery of life on the farm outside Rivertown and the fear of his father's ire. He is a fickle boy. Soon as we close in on Rivertown, he begins to worry out loud again. I tell him not to. He is quiet.

My mind is racing. It is in the hospital with Yala. Will she be surprised? Of course, she expects me to go to school today, and that her father will pick her up and take her home after she is dismissed from the hospital. Somehow, although I am aware of how hurried and unplanned this is, I feel that I must take her from the hospital, that I must not allow her to return home again, or we may never escape.

I confided this to Bea last night, when she ventured that we should perhaps wait until Wednesday instead of today in order to allow us more time for organizing.

"If we leave at all, it must be from the hospital," I had answered.

Something told me that if I waited for Yala to go home, we would never leave. So, Yala does not expect to see me this morning. Will she resist going with me? I honestly don't know. So many times I had gone to her and arranged things that she would resist with all her might—her continued schooling, my opposition to her going to the farm/bush with Amite alone, her refusal to take a separate blanket for herself when she did, her refusal to be involved in women's group matters—all these things she would resist until she had discussed them with her father. The results were inevitable:

"You are pushing this child, Jaye, and if anything bad happens to her, it will be your fault!"

Experience tells me that Yala will want to wait for her father and when I insist that she leave with me instead, will she? Amite has a strong hold on Yala, one which he refers to as a "special bond." Maybe I can't get her to leave! What, then? We will be exposed. What will Amite say, do, then, when he discovers that I have tried to run away? No, I mustn't think about that now. Of course, she will go with me. I am her mother. She must, mustn't she? How did she become more Daddy's girl than Mama's daughter? I look over at the little ones and my eyes linger on Nefertiti. No one will ever control her, I think. She has her own mind. She is her own girl. Amos is frowning. Bea is silent. Hannibal and Nefertiti are all smiles at the thought of going on a holiday and not understanding the consequences, they are perfectly content, although I sense the practical side of Nefertiti may be wondering at the impracticality of my actions in leaving so abruptly. But she says nothing, has ventured no questions beyond her initial queries.

We are now approaching Rivertown. I lean forward to tell Mr. Santos that I must go by the hospital. He looks puzzled but puts on his left signal that will take us around the riverside to Rivertown Hospital. Bea leans over to tell me that Mr. Santos started this journey thinking he was driving her to the air strip. We are playing it by ear with him, one step at a time.

A few minutes later, we are at the hospital, a single, white frame structure that sits bravely by the sea, reeking of disinfectant and old age. Quickly now, and without a word between us, Bea and I alight from the van to make our way to the entrance. I tell the children to sit tight, that I will be right back. It is now seven fifteen. We must be at the airstrip by seven thirty to take the small plane Bea has chartered to carry us to the international airport in Capitol City. Timing is crucial. On entering the hospital, we encounter a ward nurse, and request to see the nurse in charge. I remind the head nurse that Yala is scheduled to be dismissed by the doctor and I have come for her. She says the doctor is not due until ten o'clock. I ask to see my daughter. Fine. We enter the ward where Yala is one of two patients in an open area of six beds with curtains being the means of privacy. Yala's curtains are open and she is sitting up on the side of the bed, talking to Sister Deer who is a nun and co-worker in whom I have confided about the planned escape. Nuns are highly respected in Largo so I have asked Sister Deer to be here to enhance my credibility should anything go amiss. In this largely Catholic country, anybody would think twice before daring to question the rightness of anything Sister Deer is involved in. She had understood why I wanted her there without my saying it.

Sister Deer looks up, smiles a beautiful smile: "Well, Good Morning! I told Yala to go ahead and get showered and dressed, and pack her things because I may be able to give her a ride before I have to go to school."

She sounds so normal! Yala has complied with everything save getting dressed. Her clothes and toiletries are in a bag, but her jeans and shirt are still neatly folded atop each other on the bed, as she is stubbornly refusing to get dressed. Yala speaks up rather petulantly, to inform me that she must wait for her father to come for her after she is dismissed by the doctor, a trace of the thinly disguised annoyance she is feeling coming through in her voice. I begin to tell her that I have come for her, to take her for treatment; she must get dressed so we can go. She begins to argue back.

Bea interrupts: "Yala, go put on your clothes like your Mama asked you to, so we can go."

Abruptly, without another word and with wind in her cheeks, Yala grabs her clothes and heads for the bathroom. As she departs, Sister Deer seizes the moment to tell us that Yala had been adamant about not getting dressed until her father came even though Sister Deer had told Yala that I was coming for her soon. Yala had been hospitalized on Friday with excruciating pain in her stomach caused by what the doctor thought might be a possible womb infection. Antibiotics have helped to ease the pain but the infection has not totally cleared up. When Yala was admitted on Friday, I spoke to the doctor:

"Womb infection? Why do you think it is a womb infection? Isn't that related to sexual activity?"

The doctor had nodded, "In a way, yes. She has reported to me that she has been sexually active and that she has had sexual intercourse within the last week."

Sexually active? Intercourse! Who? Yala? During the last week? But she has no boyfriend. She spends all her waking hours with me or her father.

Out of the bathroom, dressed now, Yala is visibly angry but does not again object to leaving. Ignoring her anger, we gather her things and head out, encountering the head nurse again as we do. Bea and I have neither rehearsed nor planned any of the details of this part, so by way of explanation, I again ask the nurse what time the doctor is due.

"Ten o'clock," she replies, looking first at Yala, dressed, then at us. "I will return then to get a prescription for the pain," I say and turn to leave without signing Yala out of the hospital or waiting for a reply. Bea is nearest to me, headed out. Sister Deer is in the lead, ushering Yala out of the door. At the doorway, I turn back to the nurse.

"Oh yes, and give that message to my husband, too, when he comes."

We depart. Nobody speaks as we cross the hospital yard to the van. Having delivered Yala to the van, Sister Deer tells us she will meet us at the airstrip; she must run by the convent. In the van, Yala discovers her brothers and sister and in spite of her anger, her face lights up. She has not seen them since Friday, almost five days since she entered the hospital. She is happy and surprised. Of course, Amos immediately tells her that we are all going on holiday. Yala responds quickly:

"When?"

"Now."

"When, now?"

"Now."

"Right now?"

"Yes."

This colloquy is between Amos and Yala. Bea, I and the little ones have been silent. Yala turns to me, having just as quickly grasped the situation:

"Mom, what about my dad?"

"What?"

"Does my dad know we're going, leaving?"

"No."

"Why?"

No answer. Yala is silent.

"Mom? Why?"

"We are getting you out of here for medical help. Don't worry about your father; he will be all right."

"Mom? Will the police pick up my dad?"

I do not answer. I tell her again not to worry; we are going for help for her.

My fear, never far away, returns again, now. Yala is quite angry. What if she tries to escape, to remain here with her father? While Yala and I are talking, Bea has directed Mr. Santos to take us to the airstrip. I have sat beside Yala, so I have to turn now to look in her face. Her jaw is set. She is so angry it seems her eyes are flashing. I keep my hand on her arm. I cannot risk her running away. What would I do? All would be for naught. The fear is washing over me in great waves. Yala does not want me to touch her and though I feel it, I hang on. We simply must get away. This is my child, my girl child I have so much hope for. I cannot let her go. I hold onto her. We arrive at the airstrip. It is now seven thirty. Only fifteen minutes since we arrived at the hospital. It seems like an age. The little plane is not in sight. I look at Bea.

"It will be here any minute now," she says.

Yala listens, but says nothing else. We sit. Long moments pass and Sister Deer arrives, looking for all the world like an angel of mercy in her nun's white shirtwaist dress and matching kerchief. I want to hug her. She starts toward us and I think of Mrs. Orlando, who promised to be here and is not.

Out loud, I say to Bea, "Mrs. Orlando didn't come. She promised." Bea says something must have prevented her.

"But she gave me her word!" Bea does not answer but instead moves to take the suitcase Sister Deer brought. They quickly redistribute the few items from the suitcase I had slipped out with Mrs. Orlando on Saturday and the plastic bags and school bags we brought this morning, giving us two half empty suitcases now and presenting a modicum of respectability for a family of five traveling to another country. Finished with the packing in the van, Sister Deer gathers us together for a word of prayer. I fear closing my eyes, still thinking Amite will show up any minute. I manage to close my eyes out of respect for Sister Deer but keep my ears peeled, alert for any sound. Yala had become even more sullen, angrier, wooden, refusing to smile or even speak again. She looks caged, caught, trapped, surrendered. I stay close to her as Sister Deer prays. The little ones are curious, inquisitive. Amos is irreverent, his daddy long ago having inculcated in him that God is a foolish idea best forgotten and that there is only Man and Mother Nature. During the prayer, Yala exhibits nothing.

As Sister Deer finishes a beautiful prayer with, "God, please take care of this family; go with them, provide safety for their journey. Put your loving arms around them and protect and keep them from harm, Lord. In Jesus' name we pray, Amen," we hear the drone of the little Cessna coming to get us.

2

Emerging from the van, I see that Casey, the boy who helps Bea out around the house, has arrived on Bea's bike. Mr. Santos is standing at the back of his van looking for all the world like he wishes he were not here. We see the little plane land and as it does so, Casey and Sister Deer heave our bags on it. We begin to board. Hugs all around. Rushed. Every second is important. Anything could happen. It is now a quarter of eight, forty five minutes since I left home, time enough for Amite to reach town easily should he have become suspicious when we left. Hurry. Bea is talking to Yala, holding her arm lightly. "...And Yala, listen to your mother. You may not think she knows what she is doing, but she does. Stop treating your momma like a child. She is a grown woman and she knows what is best for you. You may not think so, but she does; listen to her. And remember that I love you. All of you."

Yala is silent and Bea hugs her. She does not respond, instead keeping her arms dangling at her sides until she is released. I board the plane behind her. Amos is irreverent and silly to the end, trying to give Casey a message to give to someone about his leaving even though he is well aware that we are slipping away.

"Can that!" I snap to Casey who already knows better anyway.

Everybody is strapped in, the pilot revs the engine, and we clear the land, headed to Capitol City. Amite did not catch us here. I breathe a little easier. We don't have passports or visas for everybody, but we are one step closer to getting away.

On the plane to Capitol City, I open my hand to reveal an envelope that Bea had pressed into it as we boarded the plane in Rivertown. As I open the envelope, a check falls out. Without looking at it, I slip the check inside my purse and read the note:

Dear Jaye,
I am praying for you that all will be well. I know it is burdensome but God is Good. God is Good! Don't forget. God will not put on you

more than you can bear. And remember that "THIS TOO, SHALL PASS." You will be fine with your family—whatever happens. Know that I am here for you and that I can do more for you in the States than I can here in this foreign country. If this check is of any help, show it (to immigration authorities)... Keep your chin up. I visited Yala. I think she knows that I love her—all of you. Please see to it that she has some kind of therapy. These things only seem to go away. They return (when untreated) to haunt us. So please try to seek help for her. Try not to think too far ahead. "One day at a time," the AA people say. So take it slow. We will all reach." I love you. Am praying for you. God bless and keep you. See you soon. Peace and God's blessings. Bea.

There was a line of X's and O's for kisses and hugs and a smiling face drawn below that. Then a p.s.:

Please read the 91st Psalm. It will comfort you. Keep your Bible open to that spot and read it each morning. And, pray, my dear. Prostrate yourself to the EAST each morning right after your shower while you are clean. Ask HIM and HE will protect and provide. I love you!

When did she find time to write me a letter? With everything that was going on last night—the calls, preparations, our collective fear— she had written a note to me. Bea? Bea and her God. As blustery and irreverent as she could be, her GOD was never absent from her; and for all her sophistication, she was never shy about reminding people, anybody, that her God was in the plans. Thinking of Bea made me smile. She is something of an enigma, even to me. She is a Black American who had come to live in Largo four years earlier. I was constantly amazed by her. She is a scholar, an activist, a person of tremendous abilities, and renown, even in the U.S. I always marveled that she had become my friend. I thought back to those first days of getting to know her, my reticence to respond, and what can only be described as her naturalness.

I first met Bea four years earlier at a reception given for her in Rivertown. She had been the guest speaker for a women's group and typical of Caribbean hospitality, Rivertown had held a community get together at the home of one of the women. After formal introductions and with the party in full swing, Bea drifted towards me and struck up a conversation.

Family Secrets

Before that, I had known absolutely nothing about her. My impression was that she was "different." When I tried to define different, I realized it was in relationship to the stereotypical American Black I had in my head. My knowledge of American Blacks was pretty much fashioned on those who were most visible—the ones in show business —Diana Ross, Nancy Wilson, Sammie Davis—all of whom had white spouses at one time or another. The latest megastar, Michael Jackson, was seeing some white movie star. So I had felt that American Blacks were always sucking up to whites, looking for some commendation from them to make them feel like they were somebody.

This one was different all right. Bea seemed downright condescending in her manner toward the whites living in Largo who were now attempting to place themselves in the limelight as someone who had something to do with the success of her visit to Largo. I had convinced Amite to go with me to hear her speak and surprisingly, he had nothing disparaging to say about Bea. I was one to keep a low profile at such functions as Amite was the lead talker. I spent more time worrying about when it was time to leave and whether or not I was behaving/acting/comporting as I should. I was surprised that Bea kept coming back to talk to me at the party. I soon realized, however, that I provided a good escape port whenever she wanted to get away from conversations she didn't find to her taste.

Before long, I was party to a number of out-of-the-corner-of-her-mouth, under-the-breath-statements that I found most amusing, frank, matter-of-fact, and devoid of maliciousness. Most unusual. It was easy for me, as shy and socially inept as I was, to respond. I started to trust her then without fear or judgment. When she said she was happy to have met me, I believed her. It was not hard to get to know her. Her honesty was disarming, especially for me, being raised in the Caribbean, where decorum is taught and false modesty is an innate characteristic.

Imagine my surprise at the party when Bea leaned over to me after dancing and said, "You know, I perspire a lot. I don't smell in this tropical heat, do I?" After the initial shock, I found her freedom enticing, delightful, and when Amite and I went home that night, we talked about her and agreed that she was indeed, "different."

It was a good evening, a beautiful memory, and I went away thinking that I would never see her again as she was only scheduled to be in Largo for a few days. But fate would not have it so. Bea returned after four months and lived in Largo for two years. We became close—best friends—and even though I was originally from another Caribbean country, Bemi, I found that as expatriates in parochial Largo, we had a lot more in common than I would ever have imagined. Although Bea returned to the States two years ago, she would come back twice a year for extended visits, and our relationship had remained intact.

My friend, I thought. Even the sound of the word was precious to me. Amite did not like having people around, did not like for us to mix with the Largotians even, let alone "fast" people from the States, so my friends were few and far between. Besides that, we had moved around so much, it was hard for the children and me to cultivate lasting friendships, especially since we always wound up in remote rural areas, wherever we lived.

Feeling the small five-seater descend toward the runway at Capitol City International Airport, I am jerked rather unceremoniously out of the past and into the troublesome reality that is the present. Has Amite made it to the hospital in Rivertown and discovered us missing? Will we be able to get on the plane? Suppose Amite discovers us missing and takes the eight thirty commercial flight to Capitol City? It was only fifteen minutes by plane so he can get here before we are scheduled to take off at ten o'clock; and the flights out of Largo are always late! As we touch ground, my eyes fall upon the open space surrounding the little block building and warehouses that make up the airport. Yala could get away from me here if she wanted to! Will she try? The pilot taxis to a stop, opens the doors, and we alight, our little family on the run: me, Yala, Amos, Nefertiti, and Hannibal. Without Amite, we seem small. Grabbing Hannibal's hand, I enter the doorway of Capitol City International Airport, my heart in my mouth, wrapping itself around the words: "The Lord is my Shepherd; I shall not want. My soul doth magnify the Lord, for he hath ...."

And I add the words fresh from Bea's letter, words she had said to me so often, especially in the last ten days: "He will not put on me more that I can bear." I cannot bear this burden alone. The Lord will provide.

We walk into Capitol City International Airport and I immediately look around for Therese, the woman from the Largo Rural Women's Group. Not seeing her, I try not to panic. But what if she doesn't come, had not been able to get the passports for my two little ones? My God, what would we do? Go back to Rivertown and face defeat? I can just see Amite's face, see him gloating, asking me how on earth I could have ever thought that I could do such a thing. I look at the children.

Yala has begun to loosen up a little with the one hundred mile distance between her father and us. She is really afraid of her father, I think, which, of course, reminds me that I am equally afraid of him. Amite would never get physically violent with us, I reason. He is just always so logical, so right. He could talk refined sugar out of molasses bread. And it would all make perfectly good sense, always. We had been under his rule for so long—I for twenty six years since I began to take guitar lessons from him at age thirteen, the children a lifetime—that to deviate on such a scale was unprecedented for us all. I talk to Yala about our official "reason" for going to Canada, and try to prepare her for interrogation by the immigration authorities: She is sick, cannot get adequate treatment in Largo and we are going to Canada to put her under the care of a doctor.

Both Yala and Amos were born in Canada so their birth certificates will provide easy admittance for them. I had lost my permanent residency in Canada years ago when we left after our initial ten year stay, but I still have my old passport. The two little ones were born in Largo and it is they who need passports in order to travel. I and both of them will need visas. It is now almost eight thirty. I search the airport, frantically scanning each face for Therese or one of the women from the women's group. Nobody. Nobody? Where are they? I go to the counter to see what I can do. We have reservations and tickets because Bea has talked to Therese and gotten the women's group to purchase them for us.

"But how can I get tickets just like that?" I had protested to Bea when the tickets came and she told me what she had done.

"Hell, I don't know, Jaye. Just take the tickets. If it makes you feel better, we can call it their Abused Families Program or something. You've got to go. Stop worrying about it. Take the tickets and run, gial." She had said, lapsing into her version of Creole on the last word, trying to allay my apprehensions about taking something for nothing, a hand out, I called it.

I approach the counter, clutching the manila envelope which holds our tickets, my old passport, and birth certificates for Amos and Yala. The envelope is worn and a bit damp from my sweaty hands. I know I don't have everything but I have to do something. Sitting around waiting is beginning to drive me insane. I approach the light skinned

Creole woman in the red, white and blue uniform behind the counter of Tecumseh Airlines.

No help here, I think. *I can't even be lucky enough to get an African at the counter*. Glancing around, I see that there is nobody with dark skin working and even though the woman is Largotian, the airline is from El Salvador anyway and they save all of their favors for their own.

"Help you, Miss?" The woman inquires as she sees me hesitate even though I am next in line. I decide to plunge ahead, dump my goods onto the counter and extricate the tickets, hand them to her. She checks the five tickets, then inquires about the passports. I hand her my own passport and the birth certificates for Yala and Amos. She checks them and inquires about the visas for me and the two children.

"We're expecting them to arrive any minute now," I tell her and hold my breath.

"I'm sorry, Miss, I can't finish processing you until I have the rest of your documents. I have you on the manifest but I cannot check your baggage until I have the rest of your documents. Come back to the counter when you have them, OK?" I thank her and move off, back to our little group, after giving the airport another once over for Therese. No one in sight. We begin to wait.

Soon, a man approaches us selling sculptures made of Largotian wood, one of the many hawkers who trouble the tourists for the last time at the airport, and convince them to buy that one souvenir they forgot. This one is wearing a thin, light colored shirt and I glimpse American dollars in his pocket. Seeing the U. S. dollars, I suddenly remember that most of my money is in Largotian dollars, worthless in Canada and the U. S. Yesterday, I had gone to the bank in Rivertown and took out the balance of my savings, leaving behind a hundred dollars for Amite until he can get on his feet. I seize the opportunity. "How much is that bird?" The seller points proudly to a carved pelican and begins to give me a spiel about the mahogany wood that it is made of. I cut him short.

"I will buy it if you can get me some American dollars—$500.00 worth and I will throw in an extra $20.00 (U.S.) for your trouble."

Stopping short, and sizing me up for the first time, he nods his head, whirls around with a "rat chere," and departs. Soon, he is back, signaling me to join him. Walking towards him, I marvel at the ingenuity of the Largotians when it comes to making deals, join him, and complete the transactions in hushed secrecy—money exchanging among the unlicensed is illegal in Largo—and return to the children. It is now nine fifteen.

Can we get out of here? It seems impossible. Where is Therese? I didn't actually talk to her again myself but Bea had and it was my understanding that she would be here when I got here. What if there had been a mix-up? There is always a mix-up in Largo! Bea was fond of saying that Murphy's Law originated here—if anything can go wrong, it will—and she had long ago learned to prepare herself for the inevitable mishap that was certain to occur in Largo even in her best laid plans. Well, these plans are not very well laid at all; where is our backup, Bea? How in the name of God do we correct this if something goes wrong? And something has definitely gone wrong. Therese said she would meet me here with the passports and visas. It is now over an hour since we landed. How could anybody be late on a day like today? That white woman over there—Mulatto, Bea would correct me—is from Rivertown. Just what I need. If I turn, she may not spot me; but she already has. Her name is Mrs. Estes, a taller—for Largo—than usual, very light skinned woman who sports her whiteness like it is a badge of honor. She has a long, birdlike nose, and now she is pointing it in our direction, flapping over to us.

"Mawning, Mrs. Peay. Looks like you going on holiday." Just now, she spots the rest of the family. "And the children, too! How lovely," she cackles, glad, it seems for having caught me. She is someone I never talk to in Rivertown so why is she coming over here now? Nosy.

"Yes, we are," I manage to say with just a hint of civility, hoping she will fly away. There is an awkward silence, so I feel obliged to continue, as she seems to have nested on our spot. "And you, too?"

Triumphantly, having forced me to make conversation, she answers.

"Yes, I going to Miami to see me daughter. You know she living over there now many years. I go every summer to spend time with my grandchildren and just to get away from this place. You visiting family over there, too?"

I answer, a bit tightly, "yes, family," and cut my eye at the children lest one of them should pipe up and volunteer up that we are going to Canada.

I need not have worried. They are all mute, looking noncommittal, letting me have the lead. *Thank God for well-behaved children.* Although they are a part of family discussions, they have been trained to let the adults have their conversations with outsiders, but you never know. Nobody says anything. The woman begins to fidget a little nervously, but she is looking at us even more closely, and I do the same. With a start, I realize that I am wearing my customary school teacher's uniform—white cotton blouse and gray polyester a-line skirt. Yala is wearing the jeans and blouse she wore to the hospital and Nefertiti has on her burgundy school jumper and white blouse. The boys are in everyday nondescript clothes as well.

As if reading my observations, Mrs. Estes ventures further: "And don't you all look perfectly lovely!"

"Thanks," I answer her dryly, knowing full well that we are not exactly a replica of the spruced up family on its way abroad, but what the hell?

Who is this nosy woman anyway? A party favorite of the present right wing government who acts as a stoolie for them, she is typical of the so-called politician in Largo: suspicious of anybody foreign, labeling all dissenters as communists or communist sympathizers and spying on the opposition. Therese herself is labeled a communist or at best, a sympathizer because of her work with women's groups, I think. Wouldn't it be just grand if Therese chooses this moment to turn up with papers in hand? What wouldn't this small minded woman conjure up to explain that? I turn my head quickly as if I have spotted someone to talk to and Miss Nosy gets the message. "Well, see you later. Have a good trip," she tweets, and flaps away.

I breathe a sigh of relief, but immediately become concerned that I will run into others who aren't leaving today, and who may have occasion to spread the word back in Rivertown about seeing us leave. But we will be gone! I immediately add, *I hope. My Lord, please send Therese. The Lord is my Shepherd; I shall not want. My soul doth magnify the Lord, for He hath....* I move the children to the tiny alcove that passes for a refreshment area and busy myself getting cool drinks for the kids. Anything to get out of that fish bowl. The airport is small so I know Therese will have no trouble spotting us even in here once she arrives. I stifle the urge to close my eyes and put my head on the counter as I am tired. Instead, I toy with the straw in the orangeade wondering once again why it is so hard to get packaged orange juice in a country overrun by orange groves, and why, when you do find it, you have to pay an arm and a leg for it.

I try to think pleasant thoughts but my mind is obsessed with the immediate situation. Anyway, the past few days are beginning to run into each other. Was it just yesterday that Bea and I went to the American embassy to try for visas to the U.S.? I recall the partial sneer on the face of the American consul at the embassy when I made application. Bea and I had taken the eight-thirty commercial flight from the Rivertown airstrip that morning and waited around until ten o'clock when the embassy opened for business. Even though we both knew that most Largotians' attempts to obtain visas to the States met with failure, Bea had been optimistic. Because I traveled to a Caribbean island each summer as an examiner for the region, and usually had to stop in the States, I had a multiple entry visa, so I could go whenever I pleased.

Besides, she reasoned, I have a secure professional job to come back to Largo for, so maybe they would believe us when we request a visa for a holiday for the children. I didn't share Bea's optimism but I had no choice but to try. We approach the guard house—a tiny cubicle that always sits in front of the homes and offices of important people in Largo, which are sneeringly referred to as doghouses by the Largotians—sitting about fifty yards from the embassy building. A Largotian man in a U.S. Immigration uniform, light blue shirt, dark blue trousers, and hard hat, stops us, searches our purses, and waves us on. Covering the distance, I realize that the encounter has affected Bea's optimism, even.

"Jaye, why do I feel like I just stole something all of a sudden?"

I had grinned. "It's your country, girl," I responded teasingly.

We walk up to the smallish rectangular building and enter the embassy. The waiting area is perhaps thirty feet wide and forty feet long. Entering through the glass doors, one faces two barred windows that have those little metal speakers built into the wall which serve as microphones. On the left is another, larger, but otherwise identical window behind which we can see three people milling about, chatting to each other, one of them on the phone. These clericals include one U.S. white and two light-skinned Largotian Creoles. We walk to the desk, stand. Nobody moves or looks up even though we know they are aware of our presence there. We look at the sign, figure out what to do, and finally pick up an application form for me to fill out. We turn away from the window to search for seats among the maybe thirty chairs in the room, most of which are filled. Finally, spotting two empty seats together, we thankfully sit down. I am clutching the papers and the tickets in my hand. Bea is looking around. "Damn! Mirrors in here, like a store. What are they for? There is nothing in here to steal?" Bea is muttering this under her breath through clenched teeth.

The embassy has two way mirrors in the front and back corners of the waiting room. The atmosphere is so hushed that even though Bea's remarks are so low as to be unintelligible to all save me, several people look around to see who is being brave enough to utter sound. In truth, except for the seats and applications, there is literally nothing in the room. No coffee table with outdated magazines, not a single potted plant or flower, nor even a picture on the wall. Nothing. Save air. And the air is stifling. Even with the air conditioner cooling the place to the frigid temperatures the Americans insist upon, it is hard to breathe in the embassy. The air is unnatural, sated as it is with everybody's fear. Mixed with my own, I find it uncomfortable, heavy, burdensome. I proceed to fill out the application, read and sign the statement about 'knowingly falsifying information,' and take it back to the counter, push it under the slot and stand waiting. The clerks are still talking. I check myself for again inviting insult, and return to my seat next to Bea who is being uncharacteristically quiet. A sign on the wall advises Americans traveling abroad that they now need visas to get into Mexico. "Wonder what they did to the Mexicans this time to make them take so drastic a step?" muses Bea, a comment really, that neither of us perceived as requiring an answer.

Occasionally, we hear a voice crackle through the microphones on one of the small, barred windows, calling out someone's name in the nasal accent of the Americans. An elderly woman rises, hurries to stand at the window. Although it is hard to hear the questions being asked, listening you can tell what they are because the applicant has no privacy and is scant feet away from the rest of us seated, listening.

"No, suh. I never been dere before, suh."

"Yes, suh. Me dahter libe ober dere twenty five years. I going for medical treatment."

"Job? Me nuh work. Me no able. Me going for doctor care."

"No, suh. Me no habe money inna bank."

"Six months. Tek at least six months."

"No, Suh. I no habe doctor statement fum heah. I nevah habe one doctor heah. I going fuh try dere to see doctor inna States."

"Yes, Suh. Me no habe money inna bank. Me dahter, she di send for me."

"Tre months, den?"

"Six months. I di make application six months ago, Suh. Rat chere."

One or two people, looking like Saint Peter gave them entry to the gates of heaven, move away from the counter, refrain from any physical or oral demonstrations of emotion, gather up their satchels and papers, and scurry outside before Peter has a chance to change his mind, rush home to exult with family and friends over their good fortune. They got the nod from behind the closed counter. Most people, ninety-five percent, at least, walk away dejectedly, shoulders slumped, determined not to audibly display their disappointment and pull themselves together enough to get out of the place. Each time, we waiting onlookers are all wrapped up in the decision of the voice behind the bars. Will we be one of the blessed few, or part of the rejected multitude?

A visa to the States was considered, for most people, a passport to prosperity. While tourists flocked to beautiful Largo to experience the serenity of its undisturbed waters, the beauty of its flora and fauna—in a word, the tranquility and peace Largo represented—the majority of Largotians would give their eyetooth to trade places with them. On my own island of Bemi, the same had been true years earlier when I had lived there—people wanted to get away to the U.S. or Canada. Bea often remarked that it is similar to the way, years ago, black people in the States had begun migrating from the South to the North running away from the farm in search of jobs and security. The only difference is they had no embassy holding them back. All they have to do is get the ticket and go. They have long ago found out that their "north" is not Mecca. Here, you might visit this embassy every year for four or five years before being given a visa, and sometimes people just gave up, after realizing they were never going to get one. So hard was a visa to acquire that many people resorted to "going through the back door." This sometimes meant bribing your way through Mexico, usually over land where it was easier to get away with phony papers. Largotians still speak of the old days of coming to California, smuggled by the Mexicans in trucks, and being held on arrival, in huge trucks, and fed like animals inside locked cages until relatives could come up with the money to pay off the Mexicans and retrieve them. The voice had crackled again, spitting out my name: "Jaye Peay! Jaye Peay!"

Breaking into my thoughts now, Hannibal is asking to go to the bathroom, snapping me out of my remembrances of yesterday. While I am asking Amos to take him, I spot a young woman hurrying toward me. But it is not Therese! The woman heads directly towards me anyway, so I steel myself for some disappointment. It is someone from the Largo Rural Women's Group. Therese has sent her to find me and she has the passports in hand. I glance at the clock. Ten minutes to ten! Luckily, I had been so absorbed in thinking about the embassy debacle, I had not realized for a few minutes just how close we were cutting it. The young woman, Lourdes, explains that she had been to the airport earlier, found that the lawyer who was supposed to meet her there had gotten mixed up and thought he was to meet her at his office, so she had had to go back into town to his office to pick up the passports. The passports are fresh off the press. Another woman, Marcella, is at the desk talking to the officials about our transfer in Miami since we still have no visas. She has a third woman in tow, Vernice, who is now quickly placing our two lightweight bags at the counter for checking. Marcella walks over, explains that she has paid the officials extra money to put a guard on us in Miami to make sure we will not slip into the States while we are changing planes for Canada in Miami. Marcella has also brought a few extra U.S. dollars for me. I look at the passports for Hannibal and Nefertiti. They are indeed new, and sure enough, contain samples of my photography work. On Friday, I had surreptitiously taken pictures of Hannibal and Nefertiti, to be used for passports since there was no way I could get them anywhere to have regulation passport pictures made.

***

The trip to the U.S. embassy had been a complete fiasco, a waste of time. Once I got to the counter and asked for permission to take a holiday with my children in the States, I had received a flat no.

"But I have a home and property here in Largo, a husband and a job to return to. Of course, I plan to come back."

The consul had been adamant. "That has been tried before. You cannot have a visa at this time."

No amount of pleading with him would make him change his mind, even reminding him that I had a multiple entry visa myself, that I go to the States each year, and always return. His answer was no. Bea and I

26

had decided earlier that if I were turned down, perhaps it would be best to tell the truth, to appeal to their human side, let them know that I had to get my daughter away from her father, seek treatment for her outside the country. I pulled out all the stops. This time, the consul became even firmer in his denial.

"Why should you come back? No. If that is the case, go to the authorities here. That is not our problem and we can't get mixed up in something like that. We don't want anything to do with it!"

And so saying, he had closed the window behind the little bars, terminating the interview. Bea and I walked outside, stopped to reconnoiter before looking for a cab back to town.

"Jaye, you're going to have to go to Canada to your family."

I didn't want to go to my sisters, to face them. "But I can't get into Canada. The French handle the Canadians' business here and they say getting a visa will take at least three weeks. Besides, I don't want to go to my sisters, you know I don't. They can't stand Amite. How can I go to them in shame?"

"Jaye, they are your family! They might not like him, but they love you. Family is family! What do you care if they gossip about it a little? It's all family business. You can always go to family. Your family loves you. Call them and tell them what is going on. They will want you to come to them. You'll see."

I had finally acquiesced, and Bea and I rushed from the embassy to the telephone exchange to try to figure out what to do next. Bea got in one of the booths and I in the other. Telephoning was cumbersome, as there were no street phone booths. You have to talk to the operators and try to place your call at the offices of the telephone exchange. After thirty minutes of trying, Bea emerged to say that she had reached her Largotian lawyer and he had agreed to facilitate getting the passports, pull some strings overnight so we could leave this morning. She had also called Therese and Therese had agreed to work with the lawyer to get the passports to us this morning. I had managed to call the French embassy again and been told the same thing about visas to Canada. Bea went to the airstrip to take the two o'clock flight back and I went to carry the film to have them developed, promising to meet her as the two o'clock flight was the last commercial flight of the day back to Rivertown. There was no one hour service for film developing, so I had to leave the film and pray that someone would pick them up for the passports. Everything fell through; I missed my flight back to Rivertown, and in the process, realized that I had not taken any money out of the bank in Rivertown to travel with today. I rushed to the airstrip, chartered a two seater, and arrived just in time before the bank closed. I found Bea pacing in her living room, happy to see that I had enough money with me to get home without having to make the trip on the evening bus, a four hour deal that would have put me in Rivertown long after everything was closed. Besides, Amite had assumed that I was teaching school. So I would have had all that to try to explain. Bea and I talked fast, and I left to go to the hospital to see Yala, asking Bea to go by to check on her later. Before I left, I told Bea I had drained our bank account save the one hundred dollars I had left for Amite.

She sucked her teeth, saying only, "you're such a good egg!"

We finished making plans as best we could on such short notice, worrying together about the passports, wondering if we were wasting money to charter a plane when we might get to Capitol City the next morning and find that we didn't have passports, be unable to leave. We decided that we had to chance it and synchronized our watches for this morning's rendezvous with the taxi. I also gave Bea Elsie's and Lena's phone numbers in Canada, told her to call them and say only that I'm "on the run," and to expect me Tuesday evening. I told Bea how scared I was, how it seemed so much to try to bear up under that night by myself. She suggested that perhaps I could solicit support by confiding in Amos, but agreed with me when I pointed out that Amos wasn't mature enough and just might tell his father. Finally, I went by the hospital to check on Yala, took the last bus home, and began to try to gather myself to travel today.

***

I am relieved to see Therese's emissaries, though disappointed that her calm spirit is not here for me. She is well known in Largo and had asked the women to let me know that she felt she might be too conspicuous along with me at the airport. I quickly listen to their instructions, offer our thanks to the three women, bid them farewell, and get in line to go through customs. After what seems an interminable amount of time, the children and I board the plane. Yala and Amos are having an argument, and as I tune in to it, I am pleased that she has returned to at least that much normalcy. On board the plane, I spot Mrs. Estes who is smiling like an old friend, and make a mental note to try to avoid her when we arrive in Miami. We find seats, get the children situated, and on sitting down, I breathe a mental "whew!" and glance at Yala. She has chosen a window seat, thank God. Then I catch myself. I guess it doesn't really matter; there is no chance of her running away once we are in the air. The business of taking off occupies us for a while, getting seat belts fastened, making sure the seats are upright, and taking the declaration slips from the flight attendants to be filled out. As I glance at the form, I have the urge to write in: "One frightened woman and four children." That's about all we have to declare! Pushing such a thought aside, I occupy myself listening to the flight attendant describe safety measures as the plane is taxiing down the runway. The plane speeds up and seconds later, we are in the air. I can't believe it! We have actually cleared land! Amite can't catch us now. I look at the rest of the family. Hannibal is grinning, Amos is looking uncertain but finally smiles, Nefertiti manages a grin, but Yala is cool, turns her head to glance down as the plane continues to escalate. I settle down, want to go to sleep, but force myself not to. Instead, I try to imagine what lies ahead. What in the world will we have to face next?

3

Back at the small, five room cottage on Mango Lane that had been Bea's home abroad for four years waited two very anxious and very nervous women, both friends of Bea and by extension, Jaye as well. One was an African American from the states, the other a Largotian of Sarawee descent. Jeannie, the Sarawee woman, was walking back and forth in the open space nearest the front that was a living room, which fed into a dining area, an open area of perhaps thirty feet long. Jeannie would walk to the screen door that yielded a view of the sea a hundred or so yards away, with Beachfront Road and an open field in between. Tethered horses grazed in the open field, occasionally stopping to look at the sea as they munched contentedly on the various herbs and grasses that managed to grow there even though young boys regularly trampled the area in their daily afternoon games of soccer. Standing in Bea's doorway, Jeannie had a clear view of her own tiny house on the left and Miss Em's larger, more ramshackle house on the right. Bea's house sat in between, a bit back from Beachfront Road and on the corner with Mango Lane, so that the three houses formed the "V" of a triangle with Bea's house being the bottom of the "V". Jeannie was listening intently lest her telephone should ring and she not hear it. Bea had resisted all such modern conveniences so any distress call from or about her, Jeannie figured, would come to Jeannie's house. Ever since Jeannie had called the taxi for Bea at six o'clock and watched her climb into the beat up van with Mr. Santos at six thirty to go for Jaye, Jeannie had been unable to sit still. She had finally given up and gone over to Bea's house to be with the African American woman, Bonita, a close friend of Bea's who used to live in Rivertown, but who, like Bea, had gone back home to live in the States over a year ago.

Fortuitously, the two women had arrived in Largo from the States for visits a few weeks ago and Bonita was now spending time with Bea. Jeannie had found Bonita up and worried but looking fairly calm.

Not knowing each other very well, they had, nonetheless, begun to talk vigorously this morning, in their worry and fear over what the possible outcome of the daring feat in which they were all engaged would be.

"Bonita, you think they going to make it, girl?"

"Of course, Bea knows what she is doing. We just have to keep the faith, Jeannie; everything will go all right. They've got a plane; he can't overtake and stop them."

"But suppose he gets suspicious and heads them off at the airstrip before they can get on the plane?"

Bonita did not want to think about such a scenario and looking at Jeannie wearily, she checked in with herself. In truth, she was scared. More fearful for Bea than for herself because Bonita too, had experienced altercations with her own Largotian boyfriend eighteen months ago, and when the law had been brought in on the matter, had been astounded at the few rights she had in Largo as a foreigner but most especially as a woman.

Her daughter had been an infant when her Largotian father, trying to gain back Bonita's affections, had begun to try to physically tear the child out of her arms. Bonita had, after countless such encounters and failure to reason with the boyfriend, Musa—a Sarawee man—gone to the police department to explain the situation and seek help.

The captain had appeared mildly unconcerned about Bonita because, after all, the child belonged to the man and if she wouldn't go with the man and the child, the man had a right to his child. It was up to Bonita to stop him from taking the child.

"But he is snatching the child from my arms!"

"Don't let him have her if you don't want him to."

"But I can't let the man jerk the child in two; he won't let go! Why can't you make him leave me alone?"

"Man have a right to come to his house to be with his child."

Bea had been with Bonita and had, at that point, intervened: "But it is not his house. He doesn't live there, never has. It's her house. Why can't you make him stop coming to her house, bothering her?"

The Captain had looked around at Bea who was being her assertive self now, unimpeded by the ingrown servility that kept most Largotian women in their place.

"What! Man love his baby. Man have a right ...."

"What about her rights? I know she is American, I know nobody cares about her, see? But what about the baby? It is Largotian-American. Doesn't the baby have rights even if its mother is from the States?"

Bea was being sarcastic now, expressing just how fed up she was with being an alien in Largo and therefore, second-class, something which always surprised newly arrived black expatriates and was often discussed among them. Most American blacks came with starry-eyed hopes and belief in an all-embracing, pan-Africanism, hopes which were quickly dashed in their everyday encounters with the Largotians.

Bea, realizing that the Captain was giving her some attention now, continued: "Don't you see, she doesn't want the man. You're telling her to hold on to her baby and let the fool snatch the baby in two?"

Bea had called Musa a fool before she had realized it, treading upon dangerous ground! Just as the captain, a Sarawee man himself, opened his mouth to respond, Bea continued: "Remember Solomon and the two women fussing with each other over just who owned the baby? The real mother refused to have the baby cut in two, because she loved it. Man may love his baby, but this woman loves it more—enough not to hold on to it and let his daddy snatch it in two!"

Bonita, as upset as she was, almost smiled. Where in the world did Bea get these analogies? She had just resorted to a Bible story now. Bonita watched the captain. He was beginning to waver, look a little less sure of himself, so Bea pounced on him again, "Don't you think she is right?"

The captain floundered. "Well, indeed, it may be true...."

Just at that point, a blue unmarked pickup truck, an aging Chevrolet that the police department owned, backed up to the gate leading into the courtyard surrounding the station, sped backwards for twenty five or thirty yards to the door of the station and stopped, kicking up sand as it did so. A gaggle of excited people came with it.

Bea, the captain and Bonita had been standing just inside the station, their conversation, particularly Bea's uncharacteristic and unwomanly outburst had been providing entertainment for an assortment of men inside—a couple of policemen, the desk sergeant, and various others standing around—most of whom, including the captain, quickly disbanded and ran outside to see what the commotion was about.

Bea and Bonita had remained inside near the doorway at the counter over which they had been conversing with the captain. Soon, the truck was entirely surrounded by men, women, and children, a virtual horde of Largotians. Bea and Bonita looked at each other, then outside again at the truck. They could see two policemen on the back of the truck who were now nudging a handcuffed, reddish looking man, his long kinky hair sunburned to blond in places, trying to get him out of the truck. He was standing uneasily, looking about at the noisy crowd that was inches away, some of them leaning over the truck to peer inside, pointing at him, and at the truck bed. In the truck bed on the floor, prone, was what looked like a twelve or thirteen year old child, completely covered with an old blanket. The policeman finally got the man out of the truck and walked him into the station, now vacant, save Bea, Bonita, and one clerk who was leaning over the desk to peer outside. The man, who was barefoot and wearing sun faded cutoff jean shorts, made it just inside the door with some from the crowd having elbowed their way past him to turn around and stare.

Suddenly, a wild, caged animal-like look came into the man's eyes, and he appeared to try to run, only to slip up in his own excrement that was now running all over the front of the police station, a smelly brown liquid, the remnants of his bowels that looked like mangos. Bea had been able to eat only popcorn for a week after that and she gave up mangos for that season. Without a word, Bea and Bonita ran out of the suddenly foul smelling place and into the fresh air of the courtyard, marveling that they had escaped getting sprayed with excrement that even now they could see dripping from the walls of the counter. As abruptly as it had come, the truck, with the blanket covered body inside, sped out of the courtyard and careened down Hurricane Street toward the hospital, the horde of people, at least a hundred, running behind.

Only a few stragglers remained at the police station. From these, Bea and Bonita heard the story as people began to talk and gesture in little groups among themselves. The body on the truck had been that of a seventeen year old girl who had been killed by the handcuffed man—sixty-seven years old, they had later learned, though he didn't look a day over fifty—out on one of the barrier islands, called cays, where the man lived.

"She da cheat on he; she da he gial. He shoot she out dere, drink gasoline and jump inna sea, try for kill hesef. He sons, dey jump inna sea and ketch he, tie he up, put he inna boat wit she, and brung dey to Rivertown. De police, dey pick he up da riverside, once da boat mek it heah."

"OOOOeee! He da trabel inna boat with she and he da muddder she?"

"Fer tru! He sons tie he up; he no have one choice!"

"De police tek de body a 'ospital nuh."

And the story went on and on and on. With the police captain outside trying to catch his breath and wait for the unlucky prisoner summoned to clean up the mess to finish doing so, Bea seized upon the opportunity to complete their business—small stuff, it seemed now, in relationship to what they had just heard and witnessed. The captain was a bit more receptive to their importuning now, appeared to listen a little more closely, and when Bea suggested a peace bond, the captain finally said that he would take care of the situation.

"Go home, Miss, get outta the street. Go to your house and stay there for a while. Never worry yourself no more."

As the women left, both knew that Bea's requested "peace bond" would translate into the captain's keeping Musa—who had arrived with the curiosity seekers following the prisoner and the body—at the station long enough for Bonita to get home, and giving him a stern lecture telling him to "behave yourself." Such was Largotian justice as Bonita had experienced it. In the days following as they had heard Largotians talk about the murder on the cay, they had heard little sympathy for the victim. Instead, people, even some women, talked about how "loose" the dead girl had been, how she had finally gotten what was coming to her for thinking she could "act like mon."

As Bonita listened to Jeannie worry now, she was reminded of all of this—herself and her baby, the murdered girl, of being attacked by her ex-boyfriend after the police incident and having to escape—run home to the States because she had refused to see Musa anymore, all things which she had indeed tried to blot out while trying to get herself back together in the States.

Why do we come back here? She thought. *After all that, I am still back here in this beautiful, unspoiled looking, yet quietly violent place, barely eighteen months later for a visit. What draws us here? Here to a place where you can be cherished today and hated tomorrow?*

***

Jeannie was engrossed in her own thoughts. She had been shocked when Bea had told her what was going on with Mrs. Peay. A school teacher herself, she was part of Rivertown's middle class, and although she knew that much went on inside people's homes that never made the light of day, she had not had the least idea that Mrs. Peay's household was anything but perfect. She had been walking with Bea one morning last week as was their custom at five thirty each day. She had noticed that Bea had seemed preoccupied for the last few days but knowing that she was always thinking anyway, figured that she was just not in the mood for talking. Finally, on Thursday, after they had walked a couple of miles and were near Rivertown High School, Bea began. "You know, Jeannie, something is bothering me, something I have to confront, and I may need your help."

Jeannie had quickly replied, "Of course, Bea, you know you can depend on me."

Bea was best friend to her eleven year old daughter, and Rachel spent a lot of time on Bea's verandah talking with Bea about any and everything that came into her head. At first, Jeannie had thought that Bea was only tolerating her and would caution Rachel not to bother her, but gradually, came to realize that the two of them got along very well and neither seemed to tire of the other. Now, Jeannie wondered if it had something to do with Rachel.

She saw Bea hesitate, said: "What is it, Bea?"

At which point, Bea began to tell her the incredulous story that had led to this morning. "Mr. Peay has been having sex with his daughter, Yala, and I have been trying to convince Jaye to get her daughter away from him. He says it has only happened once, but I know better. I never trusted that man for a long time, Jeannie. He is too close to that girl, won't let her have boyfriends, or even friends. Just keeps her down there all to himself. I used to think something was wrong before I found out that he had admitted it to Jaye. Now, I just know it has been going on for a long time. The signs have always been there as far as I am concerned. Jaye just can't see it. She still seems to trust him. I don't know how she is going to get away, but she simply has to get that girl away."

Jeannie had been horrified, disbelieving at first, although she trusted Bea, knew that she wouldn't be making up such a thing.

"Did you talk to Jaye? Do you think it's still going on?"

Bea had continued almost as if Jeannie had not spoken. "That man is evil, Jeannie, thinks he is God. I can see it in him. He won't let those kids, any of them, have friends. Won't let them go to church or have anything to do with anybody. God only knows why he lets them come to my house 'cause I don't think he trusts me any more than he trusts anybody else. He probably just can't help himself because Jaye and I are friends."

Jeannie was still pondering the first part of what Bea had said. "But, Bea, you think the man has actually had sexual intercourse with his daughter? He doesn't look like that kind of person!"

Bea had sucked her teeth. "That's just the way his kind gets away with it. They are always so damn pure, so protective. Butter won't melt in his mouth. Always sitting up on his ass talking about protecting his children, making sure no harm comes to them. He won't even let Yala go to school. How long she been out of school now? Four years? First, it was that she was too young to leave home; then, she can't take care of herself, something out there is going to get her. You ask me the bastard is never planning to let the girl go, he's planning on keeping her for his own personal sex slave. And you know what else? It must have been going on a long time too, Jeannie, because he couldn't have just started with Yala after she got older. That's something he has taught. No telling how long he's been messing with that girl!" By now, Bea was walking furiously, becoming angrier it seemed, so that Jeannie had to quicken her already fast pace to keep up with her.

"Girl, what can we do?"

Bea had stopped in her tracks, turned to look at her: "What do you think? Do you think going to the police will do any good? Jaye doesn't think so. Would they help?"

Jeannie had stopped herself, and reflecting, had to agree with Jaye's assessment. She could just see the scenario: the police would maybe go and pick up Mr. Peay, take him downtown, he would talk his way out of it and say that the woman was crazy, that he was a good citizen—just ask anybody—demand proof, and the police would let him go. Who would believe Mrs. Peay over what the man had to say?

Jeannie thought of her own situation now. A few weeks earlier, when Bea had first come back to Largo and they had begun the morning walks, she had confided in Bea about a situation in her own house. The American man who lived next door to her, Mr. Black, a white man who claimed he was black who had come to Largo to live many years ago and wormed himself into Largotian and Rivertown society, had made improper overtures to her daughter, Rachel. Jeannie had always instructed her children to obey the adult neighbors and run errands for them if they asked.

Mr. Black had called Rachel one day and tried to entice her into his house with a five dollar bill. Rachel said that she had at first thought that he was asking her to go to the store for him, so she had gone closer in response to his "psst...", but when she had stopped to start toward him, he had been standing on his balcony grinning "funny" and motioning for her to come up the stairs, holding out the money to her. Rachel had run away the first time, not telling anyone about it. When Mr. Black tried the same thing a week later, Rachel was sure that he had been trying to entice her up the stairs for something bad, and had gone to Jeannie and told her. He had also tried the same thing with her playmate. Jeannie had told Bea about it, and Bea had told her to tell her husband, so that he could speak to him about it, make sure it didn't happen again.

Mr. Black was a big man about town, was always contributing to or sponsoring programs for children, helping to clean up areas for children's recreation. Indeed, he was a regular fixture around the basketball courts he built for children, standing with his hat pulled over his head and wearing his long sleeved shirts in the hot, sultry, tropical weather. Jeannie had noticed over the years that lots of young girls climbed the steps to his house, but had always thought they were running errands or using Mr. Black's phone. After Rachel's revelation, she wondered, and decided to take Bea's advice and tell her husband. When her husband had come home for the weekend from his job out of town, she had related Rachel's story to him. Rachel was her only girl, one of four children, the others being a boy older than she, and two younger boys. When she had told Fletcher, her husband, he had not opened his mouth. He never asked a question or responded in any way. It was almost as if Jeannie had not been talking.

Telling Bea about it, she had become angrier. "Bea, he didn't say anything, not, "she's lying, Mr. Black wouldn't do such a thing," or even "dog, go to hell," for that matter. He was mute."

Bea had been incredulous that this man with one tiny daughter would do nothing to try to protect her. Jeannie had smarted from this slight of her daughter by her husband, but had not decided what to do about it. Now, she was hearing this story! Rachel's story paled in comparison to this! My God, suppose something like this happened in her house. What in the world would she do? It was true that she and Fletcher had not gotten along very well since she had left the country for two years to get her degree but that still did not account for his sullen failure to respond when she told him about Mr. Black. And the thought had gone through her mind that he didn't think it was such a big deal.

Somebody touch my daughter like that, I will kill, thought Jeannie when Bea had told her about Yala. She liked Yala, knew her to be the smartest girl to have passed through Rivertown High. How in the world could something like this have happened to her? Bea told Jeannie that she would need to use her telephone because she didn't want to make too many calls from the exchange what with the lack of absolute privacy, and possibly, a nosy operator or two. Jeannie agreed, told Bea she could depend on her any time of the day or night. The very next morning, while they were walking, they had met Mrs. Peay on the road, on her way to the hospital where Mr. Peay had taken Yala minutes earlier. He had had her in the bush overnight, she had become ill and he had hitched a ride the twenty one miles to Rivertown, stopped off in Tall Palms to let Jaye know but refused to wait for her and brought Yala on to the hospital. The whole weekend had been a blur of activity, phone calls, trips to Capitol City, everything, as Mrs. Peay had finally figured out that the incest Mr. Peay had confessed to was ongoing and continuous.

All these thoughts were going through Jeannie's head as she stood in the doorway. Bonita had started to do exercises on the floor. Listening, Bonita realized that Jeannie was now talking to Casey, Bea's helper, a Sarawee boy of eighteen who looked like a stateside twelve year old. Casey was asking for Bea. It was now seven-thirty. Jeannie told him Bea was at the airstrip and that he should go and check out the situation to make sure Bea was all right. Jeannie knew she could trust Casey because Bea did, and although he didn't say anything to her, didn't have the details, he knew something was amiss. Bonita heard Casey as he quickly took Bea's bicycle from the back porch and lit out for the airstrip. Five minutes later, he was there.

4

Quickly rolling the bike to the ground, Casey flung one leg over it after pointing it in the direction of the airstrip and began pedaling furiously. *And a good thing Aunt brought this bike from the States, not like these slow bicycles in the stores here*, Casey was thinking as he kicked up dust with the lightweight blue ten speed that Bea was often seen cruising around town upon. In a few seconds, he had the ten speed going dangerously fast, and was barreling along the road hoping nothing got in his way. Chickens and the few children already outside playing in the early morning got out of his way as he rang his bell over and over again, alerting all in his path that he was coming. Both could tell that he couldn't stop easily so he had free run of the road.

Jeannie said go fuh check on Aunt. What happent? Yesterday, she tell me leekle bit bout what going on with Mr. Peay, tell me to watch out. I di come dis mawning early fuh mek sure nutten happen. She nuh home. Whar she now? Airstrip. What happent? She dah leave sheself? No. Somebody else leave mebbe? Mrs. Peay? Mr. Peay try fuh do someting? Who dere wit she? Jeannie and Bonita, the American gal, both look worried, upset, like someting bad wrong. Did someting happent to Aunt?

All these things ran through Casey's head as he rode the bike for all it was worth. He had been watching the hospital for Aunt all weekend, keeping an eye on Mr. Peay's comings and goings. He had not talked to Mrs. Peay even though he had seen her going in and out of Bea's house the last few days. Casey knew Mrs. Peay well from his having worked for Bea for two years while Bea lived in Largo and on her extended visits to Largo for two years after that. Aunt Bea had helped him a lot. She always talked to him, made him see a lot of things differently than he was used to. She was a good person, always paid Casey well, and told him about the world and what the world expected of him. After those first two years, Casey had joined the Largotian army and been quickly promoted.

"Dat's cause Aunt taught me how to work," Casey would often remark. "Taught me how to work for people, how fuh talk to people, please a boss. I get promoted over the odder fellas what nevah have such experience."

When Casey had left the army for the reserve unit, he had been asked to work at a small hotel in Rivertown where they were pleased with his work. Everything had gone well until an American man had taken over the management. The man expected Casey to spy on the other Largotians, mostly Sarawee men and women, and become a stoolie for him. When Casey refused, the man had begun to find fault with his work and Casey had quit. When Bea had arrived back in Largo for a visit last month, Casey had turned up within days, and resumed working for her as if no time had elapsed at all.

Now Casey rounded the bend to the airstrip and unencumbered by the growing bush in between the road and the strip, his eyes fell upon the goings on. There was Sister Deer's little red truck and a blue van and Mr. Elton's Cessna. Was Aunt going somewhere? Now, he saw people getting out of the van, Mrs. Peay, Amos, Yala, and Mrs. Peay's two littlest children. Casey rode up, braked to a quick stop, just in time to help Sister Deer put the two suitcases on the small plane, chatted a moment with Amos, stood and watched the Cessna take off. Aunt told him to meet her back at the house, and he had left. As the plane had taxied down the small paved road that served as a runway, Jaye Peay could see Sister Deer and Bea standing with their arms around each other's waist, both with an arm outstretched and waving. Mr. Santos was still standing at the back of his van looking as if he didn't know what was going on. When the plane was out of sight, Bea and Sister Deer stood to chat for a while. Sister Deer got into her little red truck and went to school. Bea and Mr. Santos got into the van and he drove her home. At her house, Bea asked Mr. Santos how much she owed him.

"Well, Miss, you know it usually six dollar for the ride to the airstrip, that's where I think you going when I left."

Bea reached into her shirt pocket, pulled out twenty-five U.S. dollars, handed it to Mr. Santos, looked him in his eyes, and said, "Thank you, Mr. Santos, you have been more than helpful." Mr. Santos took the money, looked at it, with a "you're welcome, Miss," got into his van, and removed himself from her door.

Family Secrets

In the little plane, Jaye Peay saw her house from the air for the first time and marveled when she was able to recognize it. She could see the new roof she had insisted on putting on and about which Amite had been incensed. Bea had questioned whether or not it made sense as she knew Jaye Peay was leaving but it had been one of two acts of defiance Jaye Peay had committed just prior to leaving, acts which had prepared her for this moment.

***

Jaye Peay had arisen at five thirty that morning. Unknown to her, a lot had already gone on for her long before she was up that day. Sister Deer usually arose at four o'clock every day. This day had been special for her. In addition to being at the Rivertown Hospital by six o'clock to visit the man with AIDS, she knew she had to visit with Yala. Yala had been a favorite of Sister Deer's, a former student who used to spend a lot of time with her. Sister Deer planned to visit Yala as usual but would say her silent goodbyes because Yala, of course, did not know she was leaving.

Throwing back the single sheet that served more for modesty than anything else in the tropical heat, Sister Deer rose quickly from her bed, awakened herself, and fell to her knees; and in the early morning privacy of her room, said an extra prayer for Yala, her family, and their safe journey. Prayers finished and morning toilet complete, Sister Deer quickly crossed the courtyard separating the convent and the church and entered the Church of the Good Shepherd. It was almost five o'clock, time for morning mass. The sun had begun to glisten on the Caribbean Sea, *similar to Christmas sparklers*, Sister Deer often thought when she looked out at this hour of the morning. Rainy season had not begun yet, so the sun was fairly predictable on the horizon. In June, a month away still, all manner of colors and shapes accompany the sun's showing itself. Sister Deer took one last appreciative glance at the rapidly rising sun and entered the church. Sometimes the priest conducts the mass; other days, the nuns gather, hold services and prayer, and depart for their various occupations spread throughout Rivertown—ministries which consist of teaching, nursing, counseling, and various other deeds of mercy performed by the sisters of the Order of the Sacred Heart.

Today, the priest is not there. In the pews, on her knees, Sister Deer prays this time beside another sister who is also a teacher and stifles the urge to confide in her since she knows that Jaye Peay would not want her to break the confidence.

Today may be rough but not insurmountable, thinks Sister Deer, as she crosses herself. *And we shall all reach,* as the local people say. And thinking of the wonderful idiom, she smiled. Promptly at five thirty, Sister Deer left the church to go in search of the police captain. She must inform him of Jaye Peay's intended departure and alert him to the possibility of trouble at the airstrip. She found the captain just as he was opening his door, quickly informed the sleepy and equally surprised man of the situation she was involved in and hurried away. Back in her little red truck, Sister Deer sped along, headed back to the church and stopped again. She must tell the Sisters to pray. With an agility that belied her fifty years, the athletic nun, who has spent most of her adult years in Largo, hit the ground running, and hurried inside the church to find the sisters about to leave. It was almost six o'clock. Rushing up to them, and without any ado, Sister Deer said: "Listen, my Sisters, I need your prayers. Please pray until I return. I cannot tell you why you are praying. Just keep praying until I get back. Ask God to be kind, loving and merciful. And don't stop praying, Sisters, just pray! Please pray!"

With that having been said and without waiting for questions or offering any further explanations, Sister Deer turned away from the inquisitive, though understanding eyes of her sisters, made her way back down the center aisle of the Church of the Good Shepherd on stockinged feet encased in good, sensible, wedge-heeled sandals, out of the unpretentious doors of the little church and to her truck. Without missing a beat and seemingly as if it were one action she opened the door, swung herself in, and headed the truck in the direction of the hospital. Inside the church, the nuns had already fallen to their knees again. It would be almost two hours before Sister Deer would return. It was now five minutes to six. Five minutes later, at Rivertown hospital, Sister Deer was walking in to see Mr. Everette, the man with AIDS, Largo's first victim. Even though Yala was uppermost on her mind, she had to see Mr. Everette as she was his only visitor, ever, the nurses had told her. And he would not be there long, as he was becoming more and more emaciated with each passing day. *Minute,* thought Sister Deer. *He is fading by the minute.*

Approaching his door, Sister Deer steeled herself for the sight of flesh stretched across bones, stopped briefly to cross herself and pray for Mr. Everette's soul, and entered the room with a smile on her face.

After chatting with him for a while, holding his hand and praying with him, Sister Deer left Mr. Everette and headed toward the women's ward.

***

Sister Deer was born Mary Elizabeth Deer in Natchitoches, Louisiana, the eldest of two girls of a devoutly religious Catholic mother and an indulgent, tolerant father. When Mary Elizabeth announced her plans to enter the convent at puberty, no one was more surprised than her father who had thought she would be a beauty queen instead. A pretty, light brown skinned girl with a head of heavy, curly hair, she could rival the prettiest of the Mardi Gras queens who sat atop the extravagant floats in New Orleans each February. At the very least, her father had figured she would marry one of the "Paisson Blanche" (near white) boys who usually attended parochial schools, and become the wife of a doctor or lawyer since the lighter-skinned ones seemed to fare better economically in the racist climate that was Louisiana in the fifties. But such was not to be.

Sister Deer entered the convent at seventeen shortly after graduating from the Catholic school she had attended all her life, took her vows a few years later, and headed off to Largo "to serve the poor." Her mother was elated. Her father never understood it but consoled himself when Mary Catherine, her younger and equally pretty sister, became a nurse, worked a year and married a doctor of the description the old man had visualized for Mary Elizabeth. Mary Catherine, in good Catholic fashion, had taken to marriage admirably, had five children over her sickly mother's objections and was now a slightly chubby matron, her family a pillar in the community.

"But I have more children than Mary Catherine," Sister Deer would protest jokingly on visits home in those early years as Mary Catherine continued to produce and she was away in the then British owned backwoods colony that was Largo. "I teach loads of children every day. I'm raising more children than Mary Catherine ever could."

And indeed she was. Sister Deer—you probably could not find a person in Largo who knew her given name or had thought of the fact that she might have one—was an excellent teacher, counselor, friend, and confidant, to scores of the thousands of children whom she had taught in over a quarter century in Largo. What made Sister Deer different was even though she wore the habit every day in those early years, she could be counted on to do something outrageous and human ever so often.

A good example was her offering to dance at the charity ball one year with the richest man in town if he donated a thousand dollars to the school. When people finished gasping to show their astonishment, gently patting the clavicle of their necks after the fashion of the British, the matter was ended and the poor, underfunded school was a thousand dollars richer. Sister Deer could also be counted on to coach the drama group or the beauty pageant contestant if the need arose or give rides to the picnic in her truck. So for all of Mary Catherine's little normal life, Sister Deer probably had more contact with humanity than Mary Catherine would ever have dreamed of or deigned to stomach.

Today, as Sister Deer made her way through the corridors of Rivertown Hospital, away from the deathlike AIDS chamber that served as Mr. Everette's home for his last days on earth, she stopped momentarily, shook herself of the ominousness, and turned her thoughts to Yala. *Go away, Death*, she thought. *This is life*. And turned to enter the ward to find Yala. It was six-thirty a.m.

5

On the Tecumseh Airlines jet soaring in the skies over the Caribbean Sea headed for Miami, I finish filling out the forms and assist the children with theirs. Idle once again, my mind moves inexorably to the past, over a year ago to the revelations that had started me on the rocky journey that led to this day.

It had been a day like any other of late—hot, sultry, tropical. Pulling up the stubborn weeds that threatened to choke my mother's rose bush in front of my house, I wished once again that our spot in beautiful Largo were nearer the sea, not six miles away from the coastal hamlet called Rivertown.

"Largo is beautiful all over," Amite had cajoled, in urging me to buy the land six miles outside of town. "We don't need to burden ourselves with town. The children may get in trouble and Rivertown is crowded. People are bound to stay in our business, Jaye. And besides, the countryside is the best place to raise children. Get away from the noise, cafes, bars, and vehicles everywhere, too many distractions."

It had all made perfectly good sense. However, when you stopped to think about it, Rivertown was hardly more than a village, albeit a bit crowded because people liked living in the small town where the river met the sea and they had equal access to both. The people of Rivertown were no noisier than Caribbean/Africans anywhere. A healthy mix of four major ethnic groups—Creoles, Sarawee, Hispanics, and Mayans—comprised the population of Largo and in this, Rivertown was not unlike the rest of the country, though the Sarawee tended to predominate. There was a smattering of several other ethnic groups in Rivertown as well—Chinese merchants and their families, Mestizos, and East Indians. Creole was the common spoken language in Largo, although English was dubbed the "official" language.

In this, Largo was not unlike my own country, Bemi, one of the first in the Caribbean to become independent in the late Sixties. We had, as young people, watched Bemi transform itself with independence and therefore, considered ourselves a bit more "cosmopolitan" than people in newly independent Largo. Still, the language, food, customs, people—in a word, the culture—of Largo was all quite familiar. On the physical side, the "noise" and "distractions" amounted to one main street that split Rivertown in half, a few "bars," usually empty watering holes for the occasional tourist during the week, bars that transformed into dance halls on the weekend; two restaurants, both run by Chinese, a market to buy fish and vegetables which also held a taco "factory," one supermarket for the "been-to's" who craved food from abroad, a few food shops and fruit and vegetable stands, and several mercantile, "dry goods" type stores. On the first of the month, on the weekend, the town swelled with Mexicans and Guatemalans who invaded it spreading their brightly colored woven blankets on the ground to display their wares: all manner of plastic bowls and aluminum cookware, cheap underwear and shoes, various whatnots, statues of the Virgin Mary, Jesus, and whomever. These establishments, if they could be so called, along with the high school where I taught, four church related elementary and infant schools, and a virtual plethora of churches of every denomination imaginable trying to compete with the safely established Roman Catholic Church, served the approximately ten thousand residents of Rivertown.

***

On the plane now, the conversation that my mind keeps returning to occurred in January, 1988. That morning, Amite revealed to me that he had sex with our daughter, Yala. I had run out of the house. Weeding the garden had been an excuse to get away, to get outside the house, which had all of a sudden become too stifling, too much for me to take. Suddenly, there was no air. My heart was bursting. Then moments later, when I could breathe again, a piercing, unbearable pain sliced its way across the left side of my breast, like someone twisting the blade of a knife. I had known for a long time that something was wrong, but had been unable to get Amite to talk to me about it. He was moody, prone to unreasonable outbursts, demanding and more domineering than usual. The children and I had been tiptoeing around his temper in order to avoid agitating him and incurring his wrath. Amite said that he had sex with Yala once but that it was only to satisfy her needs so that men would not take advantage of her.

Family Secrets

"Mek you notice di child, Jaye, then you see dat she frustrated."

Although he promised me that it would never happen again, Amite put all the blame on Yala, saying she was a precocious child and that she had, in essence, seduced him! He said it was my fault because I was cold and unavailable to him and that I should have been closer to Yala like he was so that she could have confided her needs to me. When I asked Amite how he could have done such a thing and what did he expect me to do, he responded coldly: "You and Yala are strong. You'll get over it."

I had not known what to do. Stunned beyond thinking, I had done nothing. Now, thinking about what Amite had said to me, my mind moves to the long ago past, to abuse in my own childhood:

One weekend, when I was visiting grandmother, a man came into the store to seek shelter from the rain. I was playing out front and took scant notice of him until grandmother went into the back for something, and the man called me over to him.

"C'mere, lee gal."

I stopped the game I was playing with my imaginary friends and ran over to see what he wanted. He reached down and patted my vagina.

"Is it cold?" He inquired, smiling down at me. Tearing away from the man, I ran as fast as my little legs would carry me to call my grandmother, but by the time she came out, the man had disappeared.

"Grandmother, the man touch me pinky!" When I told her what happened, my grandmother thought I made it all up and scolded *me* for lying. I was five or six then.

I shake my head to rid myself of the troublesome thoughts— the helplessness of being five or six—and look around to see about the children. The youngest two are enamored with the clouds, this being their first plane ride. Both are somewhat agog and I smile to myself as I remember New York Bemi-ites who complain of the newly arrived who walk into people on the streets while they are looking up at skyscrapers for the first time—"rubbernecking," we call it."

But the thoughts won't go away, my thinking returns to Bemi again: Grandpa took me to Bonsai for Easter one year. On the second night of the Easter celebrations and one week after my arrival on Bonsai with Grandpa, he came to my room for his regular bedtime stories. Of course, I was delighted. He started to rub my privates as part of the story he had begun to tell me.

47

"And then Papa would come home and pat her forehead and sing; and then Papa would come home and pat her lips and sing; and then Papa would come home and pat her cheeks and sing; and then, 'close your eyes, Jaye,' Papa would come home and pat her heart and sing."

He continued to sing the story patting each part of my body, to the tune of Old McDonald Had a Farm. "Then Papa would come home and pat her patsy and sing," this time putting his hands between my legs, and patting me there.

He repeated the same thing the next night and sang the same way even though his wife was in the dining room and his stepdaughter was lying next to me in bed. When he did it a third time, applied spittle to his hands, put some on my patsy and some to his penis—which he called his "coco"—I did not feel scared or worried. I fell asleep, and my only impressions, as he was messing with spit and Vaseline, and pulling on his flabby "coco," were of pigs slopping up their food in the troughs we had at home.

When I told my mother what Grandpa had done, she said I was lying and showed me "bad face" for a long time. I was, by then, eight years old.

***

Amite's confession of having had sex with our daughter, Yala, had come in the middle of another crisis concerning Yala. Instead of dealing with Amite, I had focused all my energies on the first crisis. A co-worker, Mr. Ervin, had made improper overtures towards Yala for a second time and I involved myself in alerting the school authorities and trying to make sure he was exposed. Whenever I did think about it, I would try to convince myself that Amite was lying, that he had made the whole thing up. I wanted to believe anything but the truth.

In the days following, I had confronted Yala who swore that nothing had happened, that her father was making it all up. She didn't know why he would say such a thing. I became even more confused. Was Amite really crazy? He expressed no remorse, never asked me to forgive him nor did he ever show any other signs of outward emotion. I had always prided myself on the fact that Amite and I shared a friendship beyond being husband and wife. If a friend confesses such a thing to another friend, shouldn't there be remorse, sorrow for the deed? I wanted Amite to apologize to me, say he was sorry for having defiled our daughter and our marriage bed. Why was I silent for so long? Who could I tell? I had asked myself that question over and over again in the ensuing months whenever I let myself think about what had happened.

"Nobody," came the answer. This is something that has happened in your household, something terrible, true, but it is still family business. Nobody must know. I tried to analyze the situation. It was bad, but would I leave Amite because of it? I closed my eyes and tried to imagine life without my husband, my children without their father and I could not. How could I make my children just another set of statistics, fatherless children growing wild and unprotected, like so many in the world? I could not.

So what was the next step? I knew I could not break up the family by taking the children and leaving. Besides, Yala was sixteen, out of high school for three years now. She would soon be leaving home to go abroad to school. Amite had promised. I would just have to hurry the matter along, convince him to let her go. But what of Nefertiti, my ten year old? Could he ...? No. He had said that it had happened only once with Yala, a mistake. Amite would not try that again, I was sure. Besides, what were my alternatives? I was in a foreign land, had not lived in my own country, Bemi, for many years. My homes had been Canada, Africa, and Largo.

Where would I go? The economy of the Caribbean was in chaos and my home, Bemi, was no exception so I dismissed it without serious consideration. My sisters were in Canada. Could I return to them in shame, me, the one with so much promise, the smart one, with the perfect husband and family? No. I would have to stay here and face the music. Besides, although we had come to Largo with sizeable savings, the two year experimental return to Bemi and travel around the world looking for our black paradise on earth, had gradually eaten up every bit of the surplus. Though we had bought property, we now lived pretty much from paycheck to paycheck—mine—supplemented by the tiny income the farm had begun to produce.

Leaving Amite was out of the question, I reasoned. When I married Amite at seventeen over the strenuous objections of my parents, it had been for better or worse. Twenty-three years later, this was the "worse." That's what marriage was all about. I remembered the immigration officer who interviewed me as a young bride ages ago, it seemed, when I was about to immigrate to Canada from Bemi for the first time. He had given me a lecture: "As a young woman, you should know that Canadian women are spoiled. They want all sorts of rights that are impossible for a woman to have. I want you to know that a woman can make or break a man! You have a choice."

Amite would remind me in later years that it was my duty to "make" him. And was this what I had made? This man who had snored in my face for twenty-three years who had disrespected me, my daughter, our hearth and home? Was this my fault? Who would understand what had happened?

I thought of the few women I knew in Rivertown, indeed in Largo. Sister Deer? Too much of a shock, I reasoned. After all, she is a nun, likely to condemn Amite, even though she is a patient and understanding friend, one whom I trusted. But could I trust her with my shame? Mrs. Orlando? Ex-nun, now married to a politician. What if she told her husband whom Amite neither liked nor trusted? It could have grave consequences. Bea? She wasn't here anymore. Should I call her in the States and tell her? I had called her earlier to say that Amite seemed to be having a nervous breakdown, and she had advised me to urge him to seek help. But there was only one psychiatrist in Largo and he worked for the prison system, an East Indian man, whom I seriously doubted was a psychiatrist anyway. Besides, Amite was not about to admit to any problems in his head. He would simply tell me that something was wrong with my head for thinking such a thing: What would Bea say now?

I could hear her: "Get away from that Nigger, Jaye. Take your children and leave," or "Go to the police."

She would have definite ideas about what to do in the situation. I knew, but could I do it? Would I be willing to take her advice? Besides, how could I form the horrible words out loud to tell her? I could barely think them in my head. I was too ashamed. So, this is a family crisis, better borne within. I would just have to be strong and carry this one alone. Yet, inside, I was in total disarray. I needed to talk to someone, anyone. But what do you say? How do you say it?

"Amite has been having an affair with Yala."

"Amite screwed our daughter."

"Amite says Yala seduced him."

No matter how you phrased it, it flowed out as filth, pure filth. Better let it lie.

I need not have wondered what Bea would think. She let me know in no uncertain terms. Over a year later when I finally broke down and told Therese at a women's health workshop, she told Bea and Bea confronted me. It was just ten days ago. Ten days ago? It seems like an age.

"Let it lie! Let it lie! Jaye, what do you mean, you decided to let it lie? How could you? What in the name of God do you mean?"

"But, Bea, don't you see? He promised me. He said it would never happen again."

"It doesn't matter what he said. It will happen again. It HAS happened again."

"I don't think so. I have been keeping watch, and I talked to Yala and told her to tell me if he tries anything, anything at all, she is to come to me."

"But, Jaye, you just said she denied it! Is she going to come and tell you something happened again that she has already denied happened in the first place? Be for real! You're hiding your head in the sand, girl. Wake up and smell the coffee. And anyway, how can you be sure it hasn't happened again?"

"He promised me; he gave me his word."

"His word! And what good is the word of a child molester? Listen, Jaye, be reasonable. You say he is taking her to the bush every week, three nights away from home in a thatch roofed house. Are you sitting there telling me you honestly believe it's not happening? Come on. And he's taking her over your objections? You can't stop her from going. And I don't care if Amos and Hannibal are there. They can't protect Yala from their daddy. You can't watch him there, Jaye. You teach every day. You can't even watch him when he's at home with her."

"I—I try. What else can I do? If I'm going to stay with the man, I have to reestablish trust in him. I have to believe he wouldn't continue, Bea. What else can I do."

"Jaye, Jaye: Don't you see? It doesn't stop just because somebody says it will. The evidence is all on the other side. Look, nobody talks about this in Largo, but we know it happens here—everywhere. And we talk about it in the States now. The black community is beginning to finally talk about it even. It's always existed, Jaye, people were just too ashamed to voice it. And it's on all the talk shows now. When I got back home, it was all over the television, because it's out in the open now. Oprah Winfrey, Sally Jessie Raphael, Phil Donahue. Even rich people, important, famous people are beginning to speak up and tell what happened to them as children. It's out there and you have to face it. Incest is a terrible problem, hard for people to talk about, but that doesn't mean that it's not happening. Sometimes they put the abusers on the talk shows, too, and they talk about repeating their behavior, how they wish they could stop. But they never do, not without therapy, sometimes not even then. God, I wish I could make you understand. Jaye, Jaye, don't you see? You've got to get your daughter away from that evil man!"

"But he is my husband. He is the father of my children. How can I get away from him? Besides, he won't let us go. Bea, I can't get Yala away from here. I've tried everything. I tried to get her passport, so that I can send her to my sister in Canada, and I didn't want him to know I was trying to do it just yet. I thought about forging her signature, but I knew I would have to face that when the passport came, so I thought better of it and asked her to sign the application. You know, she showed the papers to her father before she would sign it. She won't do anything without him. So I can't do anything in secret. The children are always going to tell their father, especially Yala. She doesn't trust me. Amite had all sorts of questions about why I was applying for a passport for Yala. I told him that when Yala is ready to go abroad to school, her papers will be ready. I'm not sure he believed me, but he did let her sign the papers. I don't have any way to get away from here myself, but I've been plotting and planning as best I could to get her out of here as quickly as I can. I don't want Amite to think I'm trying to betray him, to do something without his knowledge."

"What the hell do you care about what he thinks, Jaye? You are not the one who has committed the crime. It is a crime, you know? Incest is against the law in all civilized nations. Largo is no different, no matter what they think about women. It is wrong, Jaye, in the sight of God, *and* legally, incest is forbidden."

"But Amite says it is my fault, that I'm not a good mother, that if I were, this would not have happened. He never apologized to me, Bea. He never—ever—said he was sorry. He just kept saying how it was my fault."

"Your fault! You didn't fuck your daughter, he did! Jaye, Jaye, I'm sorry. But I get so damn mad. I'm sick of stories like this. The nerve of that asshole to try to blame you for his despicable shit, trying to keep you on the defensive for something he needs stringing up about!"

"But, Bea, you believe in God. Don't you think someone can be forgiven for something like this? Don't you think he could repent?"

"If he had a God, maybe. Forgive him? Forgive him if you wish, but don't be stupid and sit around and wait for something to blow up in your face, Jaye, cause that's what you're doing, you know. And it ain't gonna get no better. It's going to get worse. Bank on it."

"But these shows you talk about. Don't people ever stop? Can't there be one person who stops, checks himself and it never happens again?"

"Hell, I don't know! How should I know? What I do know is that the odds are against you, Jaye. Why? Because I've been watching that husband of yours for a long time. Why do you think I kept on telling you those stories about people in the States for the past two years, before I left here, even? Every time you came to me worrying about Amite refusing to let Yala go away to school, I thought about it. That guitar he's been teaching her to play for so long, and all the time they spent together because of it. Admit it, Jaye, it even made you jealous. It was you who told me that she looked just like you when he was teaching you to play the guitar as a child. I thought it was an unnatural fixation, and I told you what happened to Annie Carol, but I never dreamed the bastard would go that far, not at first. And then, just before I left here in 1987, you remember Calypso Rose came to town, and I went with you, Amite and Yala. I watched him dance with you, Jaye. I remember that he danced with you first. Damn! He danced with you like you were his daughter. Then, I checked out his dancing with Yala. It was like a young boy with his gal. I thought it strange. It went way beyond a man enjoying a dance with his daughter, made me feel uneasy, embarrassed for you. All that torso movement—it's common here, I know—but somehow it didn't seem quite right with his daughter. Wild abandon, it was. I wanted to say something then, but how the hell could I suggest such a thing, even to a friend? So, I didn't say anything. And you know last fall, when I came here and you were going through that birthday thing with their wanting to celebrate their birthdays alone, away from the rest of the family, I told you then what I thought. Damn, Jaye, that was 1988. This is April, 1989. When did he admit it to you?"

"January, 1988."

"So when you were complaining about their wanting to exclude you and the family from the birthday celebration, you already knew?"

"Yes, he had told me that it happened once."

"Damn! So I was right! God, why was I right? Jaye, have you any idea how I agonized over what I said to you that day right here in this room in '88? Do you remember what I said? I remember it so vividly because it took so much out of me to watch you wither when I said it, and I went back to the States and worried about it for a month thinking that it was the worst offense I could have done you if it were not true. I remember the words exactly, Jaye, because they echoed in my head, the miserable refrain: 'And if he is not already fucking her, he soon will be.' God! Do you know how awful I felt after you left, after I went back to the States? But I couldn't help myself, Jaye. Listening to you, it sounded like a love triangle, it was acting like a love triangle, so I knew it had to be a love triangle. But, my God, I was praying that I wasn't right. That pious, pompous, sonofabitch! Who the hell does he think he is?"

"Bea, I know it sounds bad, but ...."

"Jaye, get your daughter away from that evil man. He is never going to stop using her. You've got to think about Yala now, not yourself. Yala. Think of her. Don't you know, Jaye that the chances are that it's been going on for a long time? Do you seriously think he could have succeeded with a sixteen year old Yala for the first time? You know how smart Yala is. No, this is some low down shit this man has taught her. It's been going on, Jaye. If she hadn't been taught by her father over a period of time, he could never have gotten to her at this age. Think about it. And while you're thinking about it, Jaye, think about this: Yala is waiting for you to rescue her. Do you seriously think she wants to be her father's woman? She knows you know, Jaye. You say you confronted her with it, remember? So she knows you know. Oh, it doesn't matter that she denied it. What could she say: 'Yes, mother, I fucked daddy!' Stop flinching, Jaye! That's the reality. And if you don't rescue your daughter, you are going to have to live with it on your conscience for the rest of your life. And when, and if, she manages to escape, she is going to hate you. Because you did nothing to rescue her, Jaye, and you are not going to be able to say you didn't know. And, even if it's not continuing, can you take the risk? Can you risk losing your daughter because you want to trust this man? Face it."

"But, Bea, I am trying to face it. But how? What can I do?"

"Jaye, you decide what you want to do. I'll figure out how to do it. If you want to take her and run, I'll help ...."

"No. All my kids have to go with me. I can't trust him with my kids if I'm not there."

"OK, Jaye. Then what?"

"Bea, today is just three weeks till school is out. I know what you're saying is right. Maybe I can plan to go as soon as school is out and then we could just tell Amite that we are going on holiday to visit you in the States. That way, he won't become suspicious, and then ...."

"Jaye, Jaye, you're in crisis, for God's sake! Stop trying to plan your way out of a crisis. Who do you think you're talking to? Do you think Amite is going to be any more willing to let you go in three weeks than he is today? You know, Jaye, if this were somebody else's problem, you would pounce on it in about a minute, jump on it with both feet, and have it solved. Why can't you do that for yourself? Because you're in crisis, Jaye. You're in the middle of your own crisis, now, and you've got to let somebody else help you. You can't see your way out, but I do. You have to make a move, Jaye. And, yet, I hear you insisting on trying to keep on acting like everything is normal. It's not normal, Jaye! Accept that, accept help. Why can't somebody who understands all the social ills of Rivertown and Largo understand that she is in trouble herself? Let you go? Amite is never going to let you go, Jaye. You have to go."

"But, Bea, I'm afraid. I don't want confrontation with Amite. I have to get away, and I have to figure out how to do it without confronting Amite. He would stop me, you know. If he so much as thought that I was trying to leave him, he would go to the police and tell them I am trying to take his children out of the country and who do you think they would listen to? Me? You know who would win. They would stop me. You know they would. All he would have to do is accuse me of trying to break up his family. Oh, he could stop me with hardly any trouble at all."

"OK. Then you have to slip out. Slip away. Is that what you need to do? Then how? Let's plan it."

"My God, there's so much to overcome. The kids need passports. Where will we go? We can't get visas to the States."

"Where do you want to go? Canada? Bemi?"

"I don't want to go home—there's nothing there. What would I do? Both my parents are dead. Bring my family back to my sister? She can't take care of us in Bemi. Besides, it's too embarrassing."

"What about Canada? Don't you have sisters there?"

"That's exactly why I don't want to go there. What would I tell them? They don't know anything about any of this and they would be hard on Amite. They don't care for him anyway. It's too embarrassing to face them."

"Jaye, you might be surprised about just how much they know or might have guessed. But no matter. Do you want to come to the States with me, just until you can get settled?"

"But how? How can we get passports, visas, in a rush. We might be able to get passports quickly, but visas to the States? Impossible."

"But I thought you already had a multiple entry visa to the States?"

"Yes, but do you think they will give me visas for my children?"

"They might. We can try."

"No, Bea, the Americans will never give me visas to take all my children to the States. They would be sure that I wouldn't return."

"But, if you told them you were going on holiday, they might. After all, you already have free access to the States yourself, so why shouldn't they let you take your children there on holiday? You're a working woman here in Largo. You have a job, land, and property to come back to. Why shouldn't they trust you to come back? You are not like the average person who goes there looking for a visa."

"Bea, you're an American from over there. You don't know. You just don't know."

"Jaye, I refuse to believe that we're stuck here in this place with nowhere to go. This is an emergency. Nobody can be that heartless. Won't they believe you if they know that you are married and have a husband back here?"

"Bea...?"

"What about the truth? They have to be moved by the truth, Jaye. What if we told them the truth? Maybe they would listen then."

"I don't know. Besides, I don't have any money. Bea, it will cost a small fortune. We're dreaming."

"Jaye, where there's a will, there's a way. Don't you worry about the money. I'll figure that out. You just need to make up your mind when you are going to get out of here, and do it. We'll get the money for the tickets, I know we will. Don't worry about the money."

"Bea, I'm so scared, I don't...."

"Well, my dear, while you're being scared, be scared of this: Suppose someone who is looking on the outside reports Amite to the police, and social services. Somebody else knows, you know. They just haven't said anything. If the police get involved in this without your telling them, you could be arrested as an accessory because you know what is going on. Be scared of the trouble you could get into, child."

"Bea, let me think. I need time to think. My head is hurting, it's too much."

"OK, and while you're thinking and making up your mind what to do, stop that man from taking that girl to the bush and raping her every week!"

"How can I stop him from taking her to the bush?"

"Just tell him he can't take her anymore! Put your foot down. Tell her she can't go this week."

"Bea, how can I stop him?"

"What are you scared of? He knows what he is doing, knows why you don't want her to go! Tell him he can't take her and tell her she can't go!"

"But what if he doesn't listen? Suppose he tries to take her anyway? What do I do?"

"Hell, I don't know! But, try, Jaye. For God's sake, try to stop him. Say it to him. And she will know. She already knows why you don't want her to go. You can't just keep sitting there doing nothing. Do something! Try, girl, try!"

"Just let me think, Bea. I've got to go!"

"Then go, my dear. But think. And Jaye, while you're thinking, think about this: You have known about this for a year. God has been good to you. You are being offered help. If you don't accept help now that it is being offered, God may lift his protective arms from around you. You are trying to wait almost a month, and that's a menstrual cycle. If God abandons you now, you may find yourself a grandmother to your husband's child."

"Bea!"

"Just go, my dear, and think about it. And, Jaye: Peace be with you and Godspeed."

***

We have made it this far!

On the Tecumseh Airlines jet now, my mind has begun to accept the objective and reasonable. Can Amite stop us now? Amite cannot stop us now! He cannot catch up with this airplane. Amite cannot stop us now! I keep repeating the words until I believe them strongly enough to let my mind go back; I close my eyes, but not to go to sleep. I let my mind go back, way back again to the long ago past, trying to figure out how I got to this place.

6

I grew up on the island of Bemi in the eastern Caribbean, an especially beautiful place, rivaled only by its sister island, Bonsai, which chose to become a part of Bemi in the 1960's when Bemi gained its independence from Great Britain. My mother was the only child for her mother although my maternal grandfather, a musician, is said to have fathered at least forty children during his lifetime. My grandmother did not fraternize with any of these people, however, so my mother knew very little about any of her siblings and grew up as an only child. Unlike her mother, my mother had a gaggle of children—eight in all—the oldest two, a boy and a girl, having been born before she married my father at age eighteen. I was the first child resulting from the union of my mother and father and when I was born in 1949, they had been married for eight years. My oldest sister, Elsie, was then eight years old, and in fairly rapid succession, my mother bore five more children for my father, with the final tally for her being six girls and two boys. We were a fairly typical middle class family which meant that all of our needs were met as well as some of our wants. My father doted on me as his firstborn and as I grew older, I always took particular joy in pleasing him. This was especially important to me since he worked away from home and we children didn't get to see him very much. His homecomings were occasions for much preparation, general house cleaning and being on our best behavior. My father was a strict disciplinarian without having to use the rod very much. An open and loving person who always wanted the best for his children, he set very strict standards for us all. My mother was different, a bit aloof, and prone to display favoritism among her children. Even though my dad hired help for my mother around the house, the bulk of the work of caring for the younger ones fell to my oldest sister, Elsie, and with six girls in the family, the task of combing and grooming all that hair was upon her shoulders. My mother had little energy for either Elsie or me when it came to dishing out affection but we had each other and both of us had my father as he made no distinction between his biological children and the two stepchildren. I suppose it was only natural that Elsie was my favorite from the start since she was the official "handmaiden" of the household and I "the ugly duckling." My mother was a pretentious, selfish woman who loved pretty, was wont to dress herself up—even donning white gloves—and go alone to the cinema twice every week. We children instinctively knew not to trouble her too much but would instead go to Elsie with our needs. I never thought, and I don't think any of us did, to question any of this as a child; it was just the way things were. I was not pretty. A tiny, dark brown child, I earned the nicknames, uglita (for ugly), praying mantis, horseface, four eyes (after I got glasses), and bones. In contrast, the sister next to me, Lena, was pretty and held the enviable position, along with another younger sister, Vera, and my oldest brother, Josh, of being one of my mother's favorites. In fact, all of my sisters were considered prettier than I. Although I don't recall worrying then about my position on the totem pole of beauty, I know that I was aware of it even then as there was nothing subtle about the messages.

As I grew older, my mother would laughingly remark: "That little uglita is smart; if you don't want her to know something, you'd better not let her see it!"

I learned early on that although brains were not comparable to beauty in females, they could go a long way towards making up for lack of comeliness. And even when I felt neglected or ugly, it was never for long because I had Elsie, my father when he was home on furlough from work, and my grandmother, with whom I spent most of my weekends from age five to about eleven years old.

By the time I was eight years old, my sister Elsie, at sixteen, had begun to keep company with boys. Elsie was pretty, talkative, and had a figure like an hour glass so neighborhood boys were always hanging around our house trying to catch her attention. I hung around her, too, and when she displayed interest in a particular boy, I hastened to try to become part of the duo because I never wanted to be too far away from Elsie. One such boy was Amite Peay, a rather lonely looking, thick-skinned fellow who shrugged off Elsie's insults and indifference in order to remain in her presence. As the Cinderella of the family, Elsie always had work to do and Amite never seemed to mind. As she did her daily chores, they would speak Pig Latin together to keep me out of the conversation, and after I learned it, and they would shoo me away, I would still peek through the knotholes in the wall to try to keep up with what they were doing. I didn't discover much: just a lot of chatter, and a few kisses here and there. I loved to dance, so sometimes when Amite brought other boys to the house to show off my sister, he would play music and "allow" the boys to take turns dancing with Elsie while I watched. He would look at me and wink conspiratorially while the fellows had their dances with Elsie as if to say, "Just wait until we show them!" Then, when they were finished, Amite would dance with me, all the while teasing his friends and telling them that they had not been dancing at all, that he and I were the experts. I felt included and a part of the action, superior to any of the others with their two left feet! And even though Elsie never took Amite seriously, he became my pal.

Although Amite was a taciturn fellow who generally kept to himself, he was always ready to pass out advice at the drop of a hat. Around this time, Amite began to escort us to five o'clock mass on Sunday mornings. We, all little girls, would walk down the road together to his house, which was no more than a quarter of a mile away, and call out to him. Sometimes there would be as many as a dozen of us, sometimes fewer, and we would all meet up along the way to his house which was on the road to the church. Amite, then a devout Catholic, would walk us back home, always giving us advice about life. He was otherwise quiet, had few friends his own age and unlike most adults, seemed not to mind spending time around kids. When he and Elsie drifted apart sometime later, I barely noticed because, living so close to us, he was still a part of the community, someone I saw often, even if just in passing now. I was still spending most weekends with my grandmother in another community called Edna, a few miles from Georgetown where we lived. My grandmother was a pretty woman, a great dancer, and in her youth, she had been the belle of the balls, countrywide. She had also been wild, a fancy dresser, a gypsy of sorts, and had lots of men in her life even when I knew her. Although she usually stuck with one boyfriend at a time, I recall a succession of "uncles" when I was around. Indeed, it was the brother of one of these "uncles" who lived with my grandmother, who first impregnated my mother at age fifteen or sixteen, first with Elsie, then with my older brother, Joshua. Even so, grandmother was a devoutly religious woman, and one of my most vivid recollections is of her crossing herself, face serene and upturned, and praying for everybody. Grandmother would say the three mysteries of the rosary every night, then pray for the sick, her children, the government, and the poor, and follow it up with the litany of the saints. Grandmother backed up her religiosity with good works as well. At least once a month, we would go on a religious pilgrimage to a monastery in Bemi, and visit the "poor" houses along the way to offer food and prayers. I looked forward to these excursions because grandmother always bought a new dress for both of us, and the new clothes, coupled with the excitement of being in new places outside of my rather small world, always made me tingle with restless anticipation once I knew we were going. Grandmother was very kind to me, never called me by any of my homebound nicknames and seemed to relish my company. To all we met, she would find some way to comment on my intelligence and say how proud she was of me. I read a lot, lived in a world of fantasy much of the time, and tried to live up to her image of me. Indeed, as I continued to grow, most people would remark about how smart I was. I grew to seek for and savor those observations. When I received a scholarship to convent school for tuition and books at age eleven, the whole family was proud, but nobody was prouder than Elsie and my grandmother. By then, Elsie had married at age seventeen and was living with her husband. There had been a big ruckus because mother didn't want Elsie to marry, although she refused to let my father send her to high school even though he was willing. Elsie would come to the school to see me, bring any kind of treat she could sneak out of the house under the watchful eyes of her abusive husband, and take me for an outing sometimes. On one such outing, we were riding in a taxi with a man Elsie knew. "David, I want you to meet my little sister, Jaye. She is a convent girl, you know. Very smart."

The man, famous for his jokes, had turned around to look at me, then looked back at Elsie. He peered at me again, looked closely at Elsie, then straight ahead. He repeated this action exaggeratedly for at least four times, finally whistled low, looked at me, and said: "Girl, you are like hog food compared to your sister!" Elsie gently chided him, tried not to make much of the incident in order to spare my feelings, and changed the conversation. Of course, his joke hurt and even today, I can still see his face as he contorted it to make fun of me. By that time, I had learned that brains could offset anything, though, and whenever I received slights, I consoled myself that I was probably smarter than the person doing the slighting.

Family Secrets

At eight, I became interested in the piano, loved music and was already a good dancer, a skill which had been reinforced by Elsie's boyfriend, Amite Peay, years earlier. I was not allowed to play many games except "house" because my mother seemed to genuinely feel that I would break in two with roughhousing, as my nickname "Bones" suggested. But when grandmother acknowledged my love of music by paying for piano lessons for three years, my mother allowed me to play the piano. I was a gypsy of a child, alone a lot, as my mother thought I was far too precocious and seemed to want to have little to do with me. When she did take notice of me, my mother spent time instilling in me the importance of being smart, and would whip me for letting anyone "outsmart" me. She would look at me, sadly it seemed, and say, "Jaye, you have no looks, but you have brains, so use them!"

Sometimes, on the infrequent occasions when she took me with her, she would play games designed to test my mental agility. After a few seconds in a strange room in somebody's house or in the marketplace, she would have me close my eyes and name as many of the things in the room as I could. Most times I would come up with at least eighty percent.

But being with grandmother was a different story. I never had to prove myself to gain favor with her and the subject of beauty never arose. With grandmother, I was freer, more inquisitive and left largely to my own devices.

Although grandmother was an independent woman who owned her own grocery store and cafe, we moved around a lot.

When next my grandmother moved, my piano lessons abruptly stopped, and although I missed the piano, I had already discovered dancing again, so I had something new to think about. At home, my father insisted that dancers were nobodies, and had little tolerance for my new ambition, but my grandmother's next move provided a perfect opportunity for me to explore dancing. This time, grandmother moved to an apartment that was owned by relatives from my father's side of the family. Their adopted son was a fantastic dancer and contralto singer, and belonged to a dance troupe. This adopted boy, who I think was about eighteen at the time, was given all of the hard work to do and since I admired his singing and dancing, I spent a lot of time around him watching him work. The house had wooden shuttered windows so I would sometimes open the window to the breeze and sit in it, listening to him sing as he worked or watched him cutting a jig on one of his breaks. Sometimes he would teach me the steps to the dances as well. One day, while I sat in the window watching him scrub the floor, I leaned over and out of the window to allow him to get to the floor underneath my feet, so that I was balanced on my stomach on the window sill, holding my feet in the air. As I did so, he stuck his finger into my panties, inside my vagina, and jabbed me with his finger.

"Ouch! Femi, dat hurt! Stop it, buoy! I tell me granny on you!"

"I sorry, Jaye. I di mek it bettah, I promise. Nuh tell you granny, heah? Auntie beat me if yuh tell. Promise me yuh nuh tell she. I mek it bettah if yuh promise not to tell. I mek you feel good. OK?"

Mollified somewhat at his quick repentance and profound apology to a small gal like me, I allowed Femi to lead me over to another area of the room, where he set me on his lap and patted my vagina for a while before putting me down on the bed. Then he crawled on the floor, pulled one leg of my panties aside and peered upwards to gaze at me. He said that if he looked at it, he would know what to do for the pain. When he was through examining me, he put me back on his lap and began to poke at my vagina with what felt like a dull object, not his sharp fingernails this time. Ever so often, he would stop and feel me with his fingers, and ask if it felt better. I said yes, because it did not hurt as bad as his fingernails had, but I complained to him that I was still hurting down there. Then he showed me his penis, his "loli," he called it. It was stiff, shiny, and slimy on the end. "Dis da medicine, mek yuh feel bettah. Mek I give it to yuh," he said, and proceeded to try to enter me with the huge black thing he called a loli.

When I cried, he stopped, and began instead to pull the thing back and forth against his stomach until something white came out of it.

"Dis da medicine, Jaye, heah, tek it inna yuh mouth and swallow it so yuh wounds will heal up."

I reluctantly opened my mouth and swallowed the "medicine," as sticky and foul smelling as it was and when it was over, he cautioned me again not to tell because then we would both get into trouble and he would no longer be able to teach me to dance. When I came to my grandmother's the next weekend, Femi was all smiles, showed me a new dance step, and thrilled me by dancing for me longer than he ever had before. Later, he put his finger inside and hurt me again and when I cried, he gave me the medicine again to make it better. He became my pal, dancing with and for me and showing me off by dancing with me at family functions. On these occasions, I would be happy, thrilled and awed by him so much that I would forget what he had done. Then later, he would take me underneath the house saying he needed to check to see if I had healed, look at my vagina, jab me with his fingers, and follow it with the medicine from his loli. One weekend, I arrived at my grandmother's and was disappointed to find that Femi had gone to perform with the dance troupe and was not there to sing and dance for me. To amuse myself, I began to play with the family's pet cat and noticing that its tail looked a lot like Femi's loli, I cut it off, down to the stub. Sometime after that, on another visit, I became enthralled with a cockroach and fed its white innards to a neighbor's child, telling him it was "medicine." Of course, I was beaten for both incidents, as I did nothing to hide any of this, but would simply lie later and say I didn't do it. I started to get more and more beatings for lying so that I developed a reputation for it within the family. And my lies were usually preposterous and ill conceived. For instance, I peeled the label off my grandmother's medicine bottle and when she confronted me about it, swore that I knew nothing, even though my fingernails were still clogged with the strips from the label. My grandmother was very upset, more about my lying than about the bottle, reached for the switch she had begun to keep for me to "break up my lying ways," and began to beat me.

"Granny, I didn't do it; don't beat me, granny."

"Stop yuh lying, wretch. I looking at the evidence. You tink ah one fool? Why yuh tell so many lies? I break yuh neck if I hafta. Where yuh learn ta lie so? Why yuh do it, gial?"

"Granny, I didn't do it! I didn't do it! Don't beat me, granny!"

"Shet up! Shet up! Stop yuh lying, gial. Yuh got demon inside yuh, huh? Why yuh lie so?"

"Granny, I didn't do it!"

Exhausted and defeated, grandmother finally dropped the switch, letting her arms fall to her sides, for fear she would kill me, I guess. But I would not admit to tearing the label off the bottle. After that, I lied at will. Granny moved again and I missed Femi and the chance to dance with him, but I was growing up and though I continued to lie, I suppose I became a bit more circumspect so that I was never again caught quite so red-handed—though I still got caught a lot—as I had been with the medicine label strips underneath my nails.

At age eight, too, a big change occurred in our lives. Grandmother took Lena and me and registered us at a Catholic elementary school that was close to her store. We had been attending a private preparatory school that gave instruction to children from ages three to fifteen, all in one room. When the fifteen year olds "graduated," many of them would become teachers for the others. Though we learned a lot, not too much advanced teaching beyond the basics went on there. The denominational schools operated by various religious groups—Catholics, Protestants, and the like—were much better. Most of the people in the school Granny wanted us to attend were of "high color," that is, very light skinned, or were the children of people who had good, usually professional jobs. Granny was quite political and knew that since more locals were being elected and occupying more and more seats in government, there was pressure on the denominational schools to admit a greater cross section of the community if they wanted to continue being supported by the government. Granny seized the moment, decided that Lena and I would receive instruction at the school nearest her store—Saint Therese's— and set about getting us admitted. Although Saint Therese's was out of our district, Granny told the people we were her children and took us to the gates every day for two weeks straight only to be told every day by the head nun that the school was full. Since Granny said light skinned and big shot children seemed to get in anyway, she persisted, replying each day, to the nun's answer: "Today it full, but mebbe not tomorrow." Granny had set her sights on Saint Therese's, not simply because of its proximity, but because of their excellent reputation for turning out good students, most of them going on to win island scholarships to its sister high school—Our Lady of Fatima convent. Whether or not the school was playing games, or if it was simply a matter of Granny's perseverance and tenacity, we never knew, but after two weeks, they finally relented and let us in. Granny was elated.

"Nuh mess around dere; study yuh books, study haad. Yuh got good head on yuh."

Lena and I were shunted around from class to class for several weeks until it was finally determined that I belonged in standard three, well above my age group, and Lena was placed one grade below me. Granny said that meant we were tops!

Not satisfied with simply being deemed a good student, I set about trying to find my niche at the new school. Of course, Granny gave us extra money for snacks and I always managed to carry a few goodies to school with me. After displaying those a few times, the class bully and dunce, a sugar head, green eyed girl, who, Granny said, was probably the child of a U.S. soldier and a "low life", appointed herself my big sister and took charge of me and my money. She was well developed for her age and came from a far away village. She was worldly wise and for once, I had met my match, because she "knew things." She would be removed from class often for bad marks, tardiness, or misconduct, but it did not seem to faze her. She would, on return from the office, flounce her uniform skirt to show us that she didn't care what Mother Mary Magdalene had to say about her behavior. I would offer her my stuff to comfort her upon her return from the office where she had done penance—often a strapping that resounded throughout the eight hundred student populated school building, sometimes the fifteen mysteries of the rosary—and this seemed to endear me to her. Little by little, she began to confide in me some of her "business," relating to me some very high classed sexual activity that she had engaged in with her boyfriend, Carl, who was her taxi driver. Not to be outdone, I went into graphic detail about my own sexual encounters with my boyfriend, Harvey. Although my story was a complete fabrication, there was indeed a boy whom I knew named Harvey, who lived far away near some relatives of ours whom we had once visited. I suppose I built the rest of the story around my incidents with Femi. About this time, too, there was an outbreak of polio in Bemi and the nuns took health precautions by trying to isolate and send home until they could be tested, those who had been in contact with polio victims. Not to be outdone, I again built up a story. This time, the story was based upon some vague knowledge I had gained in passing about a family with polio whom my neighbor had mentioned. Of course, both stories eventually got to the nuns, and I was called into the office. In the office with Mother Mary Magdalene, I tried my best to explain that I had been lying even though lying was a bad enough infraction of the rules, and I hated the thought of doing penance for it. Try as I might, however, I could not convince the Mother Superior that I had been lying then and was now telling the truth. She sent me home for a week. I didn't tell my mother. I was suspended on a Friday, and the next week, there was a holiday, so I bore the burden of the secret several days before my mother found out. Only when she questioned me after realizing that I was not getting ready for school, did she discover that I was suspended and went to the school to talk to Mother Mary Magdalene. She was able to refute both stories. My vivid descriptions of the places where my sexual activity was supposed to have taken place and the very existence of the boy in Georgetown were all fictional, and my mother was able to convince the Mother Superior that neither formed a part of my environment. Of course, I had not come in contact with any persons with polio, either. My mother, however, was terribly embarrassed by the whole thing, refused to speak to me for the rest of the week that I was home on suspension, and told me that she would never, ever, attend anything on my behalf at the school—ever.

Lying would form a part of my life right through high school where I assumed the role of the prime minister's niece. I would read the papers religiously and listen to the news broadcasts following the prime minister's activities, then go to school and announce, "Uncle Will (His name was Wilfred Townsend) is going to Grenada tomorrow. He says he is going to bring home samples of the spices and sweets for me and my mother," or some such. I would present this information as if I had spoken to the prime minister by phone or received correspondence from him. What amazes me today is that nobody ever challenged me. Perhaps they pitied me instead.

The Catholic School years passed rapidly but not without my undergoing a number of significant changes, although outwardly things remained pretty much the same. I seldom saw Elsie except for holidays now, and I spent a lot of time going to political meetings with Granny at night, reading Enid Blyton mysteries while I was doing dishes, continuing with a flashlight after my mother turned off the lights, and writing my own stories about the people around us.

Around this time, my oldest brother was the catalyst for much turmoil in our household. Josh was refusing to continue going to high school despite the bribes of bicycles, money, clothes, and exemption from chores which mother offered. I remember it as one continuing conflict, but mostly between my mother and father, centered around my brother. My father had wanted to send Elsie to high school, too, but my mother felt that she was too stupid to waste money on. They would quarrel and fight, and I would live in fear of my dad coming home now because it always seemed to mean a quarrel. When they did, I would beg my dad not to, telling him how much I hated it. He would listen to me and try to calm me by promising that he wouldn't quarrel. Soon, however, they would be at it again, and I would cry all over again and beg him to stop. No sooner than he had taken me to his bedroom and calmed me, my mother would come in and taunt him. He would look at me and keep quiet but she would make some derogatory reference to me that would annoy him, and the quarrel would flare up again. When his visits would be over during this period, my mother would seem happy again and would laugh with my older brother about how she had gotten on my father's nerves. She would seem happy to have him gone, and when he was expected again, she always seemed to put on a sullen face in time for his arrival. During this time, my father drilled oil at sea, and a messenger would come every three days to pick up food for him. If no messenger returned after three or four days, we would know that my dad was coming home in a day or two. If my dad spent five minutes in the house and had not handed over his pay to my mother, she would refuse to take it from him. My father would then call me in to take the money from him and hand it to her. That was always a good sign that they would quarrel all weekend. Lena and my other sisters saw it as an opportunity to go unnoticed to their friends' houses to play, and would seize upon it. I, however, would pose with a book in front of me, not reading but pretending to, and listening intently for any sign of violence. Sometimes, to my surprise, they would be hugging and kissing at the end of the weekend; but most times, the weekends ended in an uneasy truce with my father trying to smile as he petted me and told me "that's what grown-ups do."

Despite all this, I was a happy, gypsy like child. I used to write very funny descriptions of the fights my parents had and would delight my sisters when I would imitate them and the other couples around us who always seemed to be undergoing the same thing. Whenever fights would break out among the neighbors, my mother would locate all of us and shoo us upstairs so we wouldn't hear or see the violence. We would obediently go to our bedrooms and tiptoe to the windows and have a balcony view of the whole thing. My mother never came to see why we were so quiet upstairs; I suppose she herself must have been listening intently downstairs and welcomed our silence. One day, there was an unusually violent, loud fight with our neighbors next door. They lived in a fourplex apartment, and listening, it seemed that the wife refused to pay the bills because her husband was carrying on with a woman. The bailiff seized their furniture in a few days and they moved. Soon, another family moved in: six ugly boys and the homeliest baby girl I had ever seen, with a matching mother and father. The wife was extremely dour, hog faced, we called it, and would refuse to speak to children when they would bid her the time of day. The father was a lanky man who played music in a band, and sometimes the entire band would practice at their house. In those days, the entire neighborhood would congregate in front of our house and try out their dance steps. They would alternate with marble games in the road or play a game called "kick the pan." Although I was not allowed to play with them, I had my ringside seat on my verandah. More often than not, Mr. Jack, the husband, would practice his chords without the amplifier, and I would sit and strain my ears to hear him play jazz, calypso, meringues, and sambas. I spent all my free time with book in my lap pretending to be reading. Many strangers traipsed up to Mr. Jack's house with their black and brown cases with instruments inside, and it was not long before an old familiar face appeared — Amite Peay. He would wave to me whenever he passed by or he would make "sweet eyes" for me. I would giggle with pleasure because when I used to follow him around when he came to see Elsie, he had done that, and he had never been able to teach me how to wink back. As time went by, I would venture out on the road and say hello to Amite and answer questions about my family, and get a chance to touch his guitar. I confided in him how much I liked Mr. Jack's music, told him what tunes I liked and would subtly hint that they should play them again. While he was there, the next hour or so would be simply heavenly. It would seem that he had turned up the amplifier just for me. Soon, I began to plague my father about asking Mr. Jack to give me guitar lessons. Josh had a guitar he had never touched and my mother paid him $20.00 for it. Mr. Jack consented and I became his first female student, though I was not to find that out until much later. The first tune I learned was one called "I Just Can't Help Falling in Love with You," a song made popular by Elvis Presley. Although Josh's guitar was warped from non use, and soon caused calluses to develop on my fingers, I loved that guitar and labored over it night and day. Amite Peay heard that I had started to take lessons from Mr. Jack and when he came, I would run out to boast to him what I had learned. We would chat a bit and Amite would tune my guitar, and perhaps make a comment on its condition, how hard it was to play. The lessons continued, and I was learning fast. One day, after about six months, I was sitting on the bench outside waiting for Mr.

Jack to come out so I could have my guitar lesson, when his hogface of a wife came out. She walked directly to me, said: "Jaye, yuh can't come heah for lessons no more 'cause yuh forever di mek monkey face ah mi child; and di look up inna mi husband face when yuh di play yuh guitar."

She didn't ask me anything, nor did she give me a chance to say anything, but turned and went back inside. I sat on that bench a long time before getting up and walking what seemed like an infinite fifty yard walk back to our house. Of course, I didn't tell anybody for a while that I had been "fired," as I thought of it, but would instead respond to questions with, "I just don't feel to go, that's all," telling the lie with a straight face. Now, I stayed away from the front verandah because I was too ashamed to face Mr. Jack. He had never shown up that day or even later, to defend me. I thought old hog face was crazy. *Smiling at Mr. Jake? Why, his mouth smelled!*

He smoked and nobody I had ever known at that point did. Grandfather smoked, but it was not until after the incident with hog face that grandpa walked into our lives.

And Gramps was another story! One day, just after Lena and I had come from school, a white-shirted, locked hat man, wearing black woolen pants, came to our door with two black suitcases in hand. My mom was ecstatic. It was our grandfather! Until that day, I had heard very little about him. There was Granny, and uncle after uncle there and my uncle Timothy, who was my godfather, but a grandfather was something else! I knew he was a photographer who lived on Bonsai, somebody who had lots of children, but he was never mentioned at our house except sometimes when Mom and Dad quarreled and my father would say: "Yuh crazy, like yuh fadda."

After evening tea—supper—my Grandpa sat in my dad's big chair and thrilled us with his stories. The next night our sitting room was filled to capacity with neighborhood children. Grandpa was at his best:

"A riddle, a riddle, a ree."

"Crick, crack, monkey on yuh back."

"Once 'pon a time, monkey drank de wine."

"And if yuh see when yuh walk down the street, a man with one leg and a hoof, yuh must say 'whoo-ee!' or yuh skin will fall off at midnight."

"And when the man got tired of running around the tree with the tiger behind him, he nailed the tiger tail to the tree and it fall off at midnight."

There was no end to Grandpa's tales and we children, unused to storytelling on so grand a scale, and with no television in our lives at that time—only radios—were absolutely enthralled. Although Grandpa had only come to spend a few days, we all begged him to stay longer. He would flash a gold toothed smile and say, "It all left to yuh mudda." Lena, Mercedes and I operated on my mother, and although he did not extend that visit, Grandpa was soon back with more tales and riddles and jokes and more and more children flocked to our house. We became immensely popular about the neighborhood, and bargains were made with "If you don't give me your marbles, I won't let you hear my Grandpa tonight." On the second visit, my grandfather brought pictures he had made. He boasted of his trick photography and showed us subjects playing cards with themselves, double exposed portraits framed by hibiscus or sunflowers. To cap it all off, Grandpa also played the violin. He would play the saddest tunes and even played the classics I had learned to play on the piano. When it was time for him to leave, I did everything possible to keep him—getting his slippers, emptying his pipe, addressing his letters, ironing his clothes—waiting on him hand and foot, and for a change, my mother seemed happy to have me around.

This time when he left, he took my mother with him to Bonsai for a short visit, where he showed her his property and she said that he even hinted that he might leave it for her. When next he visited, sometime around the Easter holidays, Grandpa took me back to Bonsai with him. At that time, people flocked to the beaches on holidays, and Grandpa and I went to one where a lot of races were held. The people held goat races, chicken races, crab races, and any outrageous thing that could be raced. Grandpa had invested in a Polaroid camera, a novelty then, and took pictures of the tourists. I was made his assistant. I would collect the money and give change and apply the gloss to the developed prints. I was never so important in my life!

Grandpa lived on Bonsai with a woman twenty years his junior who had teenage girls. They all seemed to welcome my visit and during his after-tea story telling times, would leave the house to visit friends and relatives. The girls confided to me that Grandpa was very strict with them when I wasn't there. They also showed me a girl of about fifteen who had just had a baby for Grandpa. They said she was one of his women. When I asked him if what they said was true, he smiled, his gold tooth glistening, and said, "If they say so." Grandpa came to my bed each night to play patsy-cake games long after others had gone to bed. Soon, however, the visit was over and I went home.

Within a year and a half, Grandpa came to live with us, my mother vowing to take care of him for the rest of his life, in exchange, I suppose, for the property he had on Bonsai. My father did not seem too pleased with the idea but he didn't stand in the way of my mom's decision. My Granny openly expressed her displeasure but my mom said she was just jealous of Grandpa. For a while, Grandpa's patsy-cake games ceased but every now and then, he would turn up in my bedroom early in the morning with some phony excuse, hold my mouth, and pat me, breathing hard. This holding my mouth had an element of force, so I threatened to tell my mother and for a while, he would stop. But my mother seemed so happy to have him with us that I couldn't bear to ask her if what Grandpa was doing was all right. Besides, Grandpa and I played beautiful duets together and that seemed to be adequate compensation for what I had decided was the "craziness" in Grandpa that my father used to talk about.

My grandfather's arrival with his violin, photography, and jokes, created quite a stir in the neighborhood. Soon, Amite Peay, who pretty much stuck to himself, heard about it, and turned up at the house one day with his guitar and played with my grandfather all day, talking to him about photography. Finally, when he got up to leave, he noticed me, and perhaps having heard about my dismissal from Mr. Jack's, asked me about my guitar and inquired as to whether or not I wanted it tuned. I explained that my Grandpa had been tuning it for me but that it had become too difficult to play. When I brought it, Amite noticed that it was cracked at the board, winked at me, smiled, and told me he would see what he could do. Amite's seeing what he could do turned out to be offering to sell me his beautiful guitar for $60.00. He had another and was expecting an electric one from the Hofner Company in Germany. My dad agreed to pay in installments of $20.00 each week. I still had the problem of no lessons, however, and when I told Amite, he offered to come to my house once a week free of charge and give me a half hour lesson. Now, I didn't have to tell my father about leaving Mr. Jack! Amite's once a week turned out to be about once a month because he worked swing shifts on his job so my first lessons with him were sporadic at best. In August of that year, my name appeared in the paper as a scholarship winner. I was eleven years old. Amite met me on the street on one of his evening rounds and rubbed my head, stooped down so his eyes could be level with mine, and said how proud of me he was. He wanted me to study my books and "don't let no boy take advantage of yuh." It was the first time that anybody besides Granny and my parents ever used that expression—and certainly nobody who was so young, like Amite, who had girlfriends himself. I puzzled over it for a while, this business of a boy "taking advantage of yuh," but dismissed it finally because I had no boyfriend anyway.

Granny was still afflicted with her gypsy ways and was now a regular "house sitter" for some of the expatriates living in Bemi whenever they would leave for extended periods to go abroad. Some of them would go away from Bemi to the States or Europe for a month while others would be gone for as long as six months or more. Granny would live in the house and keep it up while they were away. In 1960, shortly after I received the scholarship to convent school, Granny invited me to share one of these houses with her and I happily received the news, remembering the good old days of spending weekends with her which had suddenly ceased when I had started to menstruate earlier that year. Granny had cried then, and said, "Gial, yuh turn big woman now, it only have trouble in that."

Now, as I packed my bags to go, it was if I were getting away from Bemi itself, so elated was I at the thought of having a holiday in a neighborhood removed from my own, even though it was only about two miles away. The house belonged to "rich people" and was in an upper class neighborhood away from Georgetown and nearer to the sea, a real adventure for me. My next sister, Lena, who spent all her spare time making herself prettier and who was wont to display bouts of jealousy now and again, teased me unmercifully.

"Oh, you gwine broad, hey, gial? I do declare, if only I coulda tek dem prayers, prayers, prayers, ah woulda go wid yuh. (Lena found Granny far too religious for her taste, and never wanted to stay with her.) Mind yuh fix yousef up over there, don't be running 'round looking like Bones. Ask Granny to buy you some new clothes. You might catch something!"

Lena was totally preoccupied with herself, a trait which mother fostered by always buying new clothes for her. Later, my mother would even take my scholarship award for uniforms and use it to buy clothes for Lena sometimes since I had little interest in clothes or how I looked. I saw myself as hopelessly ugly still, a perception that was reinforced by my mother, so I didn't even try to make myself look better. I was always clean and neat, did not straighten my hair, but instead wore it in "picky" plaits, wore no makeup or any of the other embellishments that females indulged in, and I never, ever dwelled on my own looks. Now, Lena's remarks made me look at what I was packing to take with me when I joined Granny. In truth, my "wardrobe" was, in a word, tacky. A couple of rather faded summer shifts, shorts and pedal pushers, and a few blouses. No frills, just the basics, were about all I could lay claim to. I hastened to finish packing, slammed the little cardboard suitcase shut, and ran out of the house to remove myself from Lena's knowing taunts. The house we were to stay in belonged to one Mr. Timothy Perkins, an engineer who had worked in Bemi before independence and who was now supervising the construction on the new Pan Am building that was scheduled for completion soon. The house was a modest, six room white cottage which sat back off the main street with a nice cobblestone lane leading up to it. Hibiscus hedges grew along both sides of the lane and in the smallish yard, all manner of flowers grew and bloomed with abandon so that the place was running over with color—red, yellow, pink, orange, purple, and every hue imaginable in between. It seemed as if someone had tried to include samples of all the flowers in Bemi and a few from elsewhere as well! From Johnson Square at the roundabout where the bus had let us off, Granny and I had walked two blocks down Grover Lane, turned left on Hyacinth Avenue, and walked three blocks to Oceanview Road. "Dere," said Granny, stopping momentarily to point as we reached the corner. My eyes followed her finger and there, standing at the corner of Hyacinth and Oceanview, I first saw the little house. Tears popped into the corners of my eyes because it had looked so perfect, like a picture on a postcard. It was not that I had never seen such a house, nor even that it was the prettiest I had seen that morning on the short walk from the bus. My sudden emotionalism came from the fact that I was going to live in it.

Inside, the house was much more unpretentious than one would suspect from its outside demeanor. There were two bedrooms, a kitchen, a bathroom, living and dining area. The floors were wooden and polished to a shine without the obligatory linoleum or other material covering it the way I was used to, except in the kitchen where the floor was tiled to facilitate cleaning. There were nice built-in teak cupboards and lots of storage space. My two favorite spots were the front verandah and the back yard. The screened in verandah had twin swings facing each other and from there, I would sit and read or simply observe all the goings on of Oceanview Road, not that there was too much. Unlike in Georgetown, the people in Scottsdale seemed to stay inside their own houses, not visiting, and only coming outside occasionally to get in their vehicles to go somewhere. Since they had other people to do their laundry, there was no hallooing back and forth as people were always doing in Georgetown while they washed their clothes, prepared vegetables for cooking, or cleaned fish underneath their houses. Occasionally, I would see a gardener about the well kept yards, tending flowers and shrubs and Julie Mango trees, but by and large, Scottsdale was quiet. I would see a few Bemijians passing by sometimes, walking along, pushing the expatriates' children in prams, but here in Scottsdale, they too, were quiet, uncharacteristically different from the countrymen I was used to. Sometimes Granny would join me on the verandah in the other swing and it was then that we would chat, her telling me to continue my studies and not spend time worrying about boys. Living in the little house on Oceanview those weeks before my first year in high school gave me the opportunity to read to my heart's content without worry of being disturbed; and I had few chores as it was easy for Granny and me to keep up the place without any stress at all. We would go to the marketplace for food, or over to Georgetown to see my folk, or to Edna to check on Granny's things in her own house. Sometimes I would sit on the back steps and daydream. A few months shy of twelve, I was still small, spindly legged, and weighed only about seventy five or eighty pounds. There was a nice grove of mango trees in the backyard which cut off the view of people in both houses abutting the lot on which we lived. So the place was cool and private. Unlike being on the front verandah, in the back yard, I felt totally isolated. Compared to the pace I had been keeping in Georgetown, what with my daily chores, I felt like the idle rich, and marveled over my good fortune for a couple of weeks until I began to get bored. Mr. Timothy Perkins was a reader, however, so pretty soon, when my own limited reading matter ran out, I invaded his bookstand, and began to "spend" my days in the States, France, Amsterdam, Germany, wherever the books—mostly adventure stories and romance novels— took me. Mr. Perkins must have had children because I had never seen so many Mary Enid Blyton mysteries before, not even in the library. About three weeks after we arrived, Granny and I made our usual trip to the market up near the roundabout for vegetables only to discover that the man had no tomatoes.

Granny was peeved, grumbled, "What?" So how comes yuh no habe tomatoes? People need dey, yuh know. How yuh run out?"

The store owner explained to Granny that there was a catamaran boat race going on over at the marina and with visitors in town, people were buying more food for their guests. He then told Granny about a vegetable stand ten blocks away, almost out of Scottsdale, where they were likely to have fresh tomatoes. We finished shopping and set out to find the stand. The stand was indeed a long way from Oceanview Road and was operated by a Creole man. Although it was in a crude looking little shed, the vegetables were fresh, varied, and yes, they had tomatoes. Granny liked the vegetables, struck up a conversation with the man and promised to come back. The man gave Granny a little bucket full of plums when she said that, and we started the trip back over to Scottsdale proper ten blocks to the market to pick up our bags, and another five or six to Oceanview Road. Granny grumbled about the distance. She didn't like green plums, but I did and since she liked the man's tomatoes—they came from his own farm—we decided that we would buy our vegetables from him whenever we could. A few days later, when it was time to buy more fresh vegetables, Granny sent me alone to the little shed, early in the day so she would not have to worry about me. I found the man— Mr. Bert was his name—and purchased enough to last a few days since Granny didn't like keeping vegetables in the fridge too long. There was a boy there whom I had seen hanging around the shed with Mr. Bert when I first went with Granny. I knew him but only from a distance. He was from an elite black family, was already attending high school. I later found out that he was interested in economics and was visiting with Mr. Bert to gain firsthand information on small business development. He had not said much today, but when I finished talking to Mr. Bert, picking out everything that Granny had sent me for, he spoke up.

"Well, hey! Seems like I know you. Aren't you Jaye Bartholomew from over in Georgetown? I'm Allan, I live close to here, over in Citronella."

I replied yes, that's who I was.

"Didn't you just pass common entrance?"

I was a little taken aback by his question although it was a point of community pride in Georgetown that Lena and I both had passed the exams—a victory for the community. But over in Citronella with the big shots? I never expected this boy to know about it, even though it had been the first common entrance exam that had allowed black people, Catholic or not, to go to high school. And to top it off, I had won a scholarship for free books and clothing besides, as I had placed among the first four thousand students out of twenty thousand who had taken the exam. From that point on, I had become a teacher. Everybody came to ask my mother to have me tutor their child. Before I could start at the convent school, I had begun to tutor and had eleven students.

I answered Allan now: "Yes, I will be entering the convent school in the fall," this a bit more shyly as I was not accustomed to interest from boys at all. "Well, I'm waiting for results myself. I've been pestering Mr. Bert because I want some practical information about economics before I settle on studying it."

Silence. I didn't know how to keep up a conversation with a boy so it was left to Allan to continue.

"I don't remember seeing you in this neighborhood before. You new around here?"

Now, I readily answered, "Yes, me and Granny live over on Oceanview."

I listened to the way I said that, not bothering to point out to the boy that we were house sitting. As I packaged up the vegetables including some couscous and root vegetables, Mr. Bert asked me about the plums and I responded that Granny liked them and had sent word to thank him. *Two lies in one*, I thought. Granny had neither liked the plums nor had she mentioned them again after her initial complaint about receiving a gift for which she had no taste. Now, upon my telling the lie, Mr. Bert poured out another bucket of the green plums for Granny into my already loaded sack, making it quite cumbersome for me to carry. I looked on with some dismay, thinking: *That's what you get for lying; now you got this additional burden to carry almost two miles.* Allan grasped the situation and immediately offered to help me carry my bags home, happily putting some of the plums into a smaller bag and handing it to me. He then hoisted my large satchel onto his shoulder and we set off. He was an even bigger talker once we were away from Mr. Bert. He talked about his love of economics, how he admired Mr. Bert for being in business and for his obvious good judgment in locating the vegetable stand on the outskirts of Scottsdale and Citronella, a community inhabited mostly by

Creoles with a smattering of East Indian blacks. The site was ideal, he said, because Mr. Bert could pick up trade both from the native Creole population in Citronella and from the people, mainly foreigners, who lived on that side of Scottsdale. As I listened to Allan talk on the walk home, I realized that I was enjoying being with him. I had never liked boys too much mainly because they never showed too much interest in me, but Allan was easy to talk to, like being around a girl, but without the nosiness and competition. Allan talked about getting ready to go back to school, and eventually college, how he wanted to major in economics so that the people could begin to recognize benefits from our country, and not allow outsiders to take over as the country continued to develop its tourist industry. Walking along, I began to eat some of the plums from the sack I was carrying, which caused me to think of Granny. I didn't think she would mind the boy helping me with the bags but I was afraid he might mention the plums and Granny would catch me in a lie, so I decided to confide in him.

"You know," I said with a grin, "Granny doesn't like plums, but it's OK because I do."

He looked at me, "Good, then they won't go to waste. No matter."

I guessed he was older than me, and serious, I thought, to worry about food going to waste, almost like the adults. By now, we were approaching Oceanview Road and I looked up to see Granny peering at us from the verandah.

"Your Granny won't mind my helping you, will she?" He'd asked on spotting Granny sitting in the swing.

"Course not," I replied. "She can see the packages are too heavy for me." This I had said with uncharacteristic aplomb, though I was not at all sure what Granny would think, as I had never tested her or my parents with boys. They didn't even know I was friends with Amite; and I had never brought a boy home before. But I need not have worried. Granny was all graciousness in the face of a guest, even a young boy, thanked Allan, and after he had chatted her up a bit, he announced that he had to hurry back to Mr. Bert's. He said good-bye and departed. Granny carried the vegetables in the house and I moved to help her at the sink, where she began to wash them in preparation for storing in the fridge. After a few minutes, during which I could tell she was thinking mightily, she ventured: "That's one nice talking buoy. What you tink he want here?"

I imagine I must have looked shocked and frightened at her mention of Allan because she laughed, continued: "Nevah yuh mind. Yuh goin' ta high school now. Lotta boys gon like yuh. Yuh like the ones yuh want, and take no truk from no boys or mens 'cause they come dime a dozen."

Recovering, I hastened to reply: "But he just help me with the load, Granny. He never mean anything."

Granny laughed. "Course not. Him hep all hepless old ladies tote dey bags home, too. Cain't do his work fuh tekking vegetables home fuh ole ladies. I sure a dat!"

This last she said with derision, though not meanly, leaving me totally nonplussed and at a loss for words, not even a quick lie. I didn't know what to say, whether the boy was interested in me or not, or whether Granny was saying I shouldn't be interested in boys. Seeing my confusion, Granny let the matter rest, though she seemed to be chuckling under her breath as she walked back and forth in the kitchen. I went back out on the verandah and stayed there for most of the rest of the day, alternately reading and daydreaming. That evening, Granny joined me in the backyard where I was watching the sun go down, and I was apprehensive about her being there considering our conversation of the morning. However, I realized she was not angry as soon as she began to speak. She gave me a lecture about boys, reiterated the importance of my studies, school and eventually college, and told me how proud she was of me. I assured her I was not interested in boys. Granny listened to me, but did not mention the boy again nor did she say he couldn't come back. I was glad because I secretly hoped Allan would be there the next time I went to the vegetable stand. I did not have to wait that long. On Friday, two days later, Allan showed up with plums "for Granny." He had told me on the walk home that his family had an orchard, that his plums were sweeter than Mr. Bert's and that he would bring some for me. He brought plums already marinated in a jar. Allan stayed to visit for a while and we talked some more about school, what subjects I would be taking in high school, and finally, getting around to my love of books, photography and music, we talked about carnival. I loved carnival because of the music and when I said I planned to attend, he said he would be sure to see me there.

The time in Scottsdale went on just so with Allan regularly visiting Granny to bring her plums and stopping for a few minutes to chat me up. I looked forward to his brief visits which sometimes consisted of his riding by on his bicycle, whistling, so that I would run out and get the plums, and riding on off. Except for Allan, I had met no one in Scottsdale who was my age. I only stayed with Granny at Mr. Perkins house for about six weeks, since I was plunged into numerous activities as a result of winning the scholarship. As an instant tutor, I did not have much time to pine away about the missing guitar lessons with Mr. Jack although I still waited patiently for the day to come when hog face Mrs. Jack would come to me on her knees to beg my forgiveness for having wrongfully accused me, but she never did. At least, not then. Besides, Allan now knew where I lived in Georgetown, and would sometimes ride by my house.

In January, school started and I entered the world of Our Lady of Fatima High School as a scholarship student. There were plenty of adjustments to make and some I refused to make. First, although a number of students had gained entry to the convent school by passing the common entrance exams, the majority at the school was still white and the few blacks there were mostly very fair skinned or well off. The next year, my entire class took a trip to the Woolworth's store to see the first black employee. She had to be pointed out to us because she was very light skinned and didn't look black at all. At the school, the lifestyle was different from what I had known at home. One did not take local foods to school for lunch, for example. One had to take hot dogs and hamburgers. Also, you had to wear a different colored uniform for each day of the week, and the cost was so prohibitive that the newly arrived started off with suspensions, low marks, and absenteeism because one could not attend any class without the correct uniform. Although I was fortunate enough to have won a scholarship and have my needs taken care of, I felt empathy with those who didn't and for the first time, I actually valued a relationship with God. Allan had started to write me notes and send them with his sister who was my appointed Big Sister and a school prefect at Our Lady of Fatima. His notes were in Spanish, and since I had just begun studying the language, it used to take me two weeks to translate them and write back, a confused jumble of words which I am sure bore only slight resemblance to the Spanish language. At the school, too, I realized my need for a hobby and some cultural activity in my life. Everyone at the school was either in a choir, had to go to pee-ah-no lessons or violin or ballet or something, so I needed something to add to my conversations. I remembered that Amite had said that he taught himself to play the classical guitar and it had been a good new one that he was awaiting. All the songs we had learned in school earlier were classics since calypsos were considered low class there and one just did not sing them. Before long, I decided to seek out Amite and see if his promise still held. When he responded to my message and turned up one evening in January with his new classical guitar and the beautiful lectrum guitar he used to play, no one in the world was happier. He used all his fingers to play the classical guitar and he would play some of the songs that gave me chill bumps when the choir sang them at school. He would come every other day and sit and play for Grandpa who would whistle a harmony or accompany him with his own arrangements on the violin. If I could finish my homework and get rid of my students on time, I would play duets with him, marveling all the time at how much I remembered about reading music from my piano lessons years earlier.

Depending on his shift, Amite would come on Saturday mornings to sit with me as I practiced the guitar. One Saturday morning, I whispered to him that I had to leave him for a while because I had to go call out to Allan at the back of the house. Allan had continued after I came home from Scottsdale to bring his plums and when plum season was over, he would bring me sapodillas and golden plums and balattas and star apples and every conceivable fruit that Adam must have tempted Eve with—anything a tropical paradise had to offer. Sometimes I would not see him but would find the gifts left for me outside. When he had discovered where I lived, Allan found that we were separated by only a valley through which the main highway ran; and our view was blocked by several huge concrete buildings in the affluent community of Citronella where he lived. We both lived on hills, however, and when we explored his discovery, we made another amazing one: If I were to stand at the back of my house and he climbed on the balcony of his, we could see each other. Once we had tested it by waving red cloth, and when I shouted out his name, it echoed across the valley, and he heard it. All self respecting adults had business in town on Saturdays and children were left at home to do chores. Saturday was our day to talk. Our conversations, across the two mile span, were just great:

"Al-lannnnn."
"Jaye-eeeeeee"
"How are you-oooooo?"
"Great-ate-ate-ate."

"How about you-oooo?"

"Great, too-oooo."

"Whatcha doing-innnnnn?"

"Cleaning the house-ouse-ouse-ouse."

"You-ooooo?"

"Cleaning the yard-ard-ard-ard."

"Good-ood-ood-ood."

"What did you say-ayyyyyy?"

"Good-ood-ood-ood."

"Good, what-ut-ut-ut?"

"About the work-urk-urk-urk."

"You have no work-urk-urk-urk?"

"What-ut-ut-ut?"

We would have a fine time misunderstanding each other and enjoying it. Now and then, he would ride by and thrill me no end with the shrill ring of his bicycle bell. I dared not get up from the table where I tutored the ten and eleven year olds who were aspiring to be like me, and who looked like my elder brothers and sisters. I dared not respond to the bell, but it never failed to make me glow and feel warm inside. I didn't want to miss my Saturday morning once weekly "call" to Allan so I felt I had to tell Amite. Amite promptly inquired into the matter and it was with great pride and ado that I allowed him into the conspiracy of my puppy love relationship. He smiled a lot about it and gave me the impression that he was someone whom I could trust, a real pal. After all, I had kept his secrets about Michelle and Jane, his girlfriends. I felt really close to him then, each of us keeping each other's secrets.

Amite, too, seemed to need some time on Saturdays to run home just for a second. At first, I did not know the cause but one day it was so obvious that he confided the whole thing to me. It seems that from time to time during our guitar lessons, some sticky stuff, lots of it, used to run down his pants leg. He explained that whenever he got excited by his music, it happened. That explained to me why my big brother didn't do it because he didn't play any kind of instrument. This confirmed to me that I was grown up, where menstruation had only made me vaguely aware of it. Imagine, Amite being my true friend! So our relationship as each other's confidants continued to grow and develop. I told him about Allan and how I felt about his notes and his bell and I asked him if he felt the same about his girlfriend when he received her notes. I was a regular chatterbox. My mother would come home and ask him if he had a chance to teach me anything at all, knowing how much I talked when I got started, that there was no end to it. And there was no end to what I told Amite, about my love for nature, open spaces, music, books, and Allan, Allan, Allan. Now and then, Amite would interrupt me with a question, and some chastisement.

"Did he kiss yuh?"

I quickly responded, "Shucks, no. Allan wouldn't do that."

"Well, don't let any boy take advantage of yuh."

There was that phrase again. My mother had said the same thing when I started to menstruate, saying that if I did, I would get pregnant. I was really meaning to ask somebody about that. Was Elsie allowing her husband to take advantage of her? When she came to see me in school last time, she said she had come from a visit to the clinic because she was pregnant. It all seemed very complicated. I guessed that was why Granny had cried when I told her I was having my menses. Anyway, Amite asked me if Allan had told me he loved me.

I told him of the time that Allan had said: "Gial, I really like yuh fuh tru," and he had touched my hand ever so lightly.

"And how did yuh answer?" Amite wanted to know.

Well, that took a long time coming and Amite had to promise, promise, promise, cross his heart and hope to die before I told him what I had told Allan.

"I don't like people to like me because I does feel like not to like them."

This made Amite laugh and I laughed when I remembered how Allan had laughed and said, "Well, I like you and I hope you feel like you could like me."

Not long after that, I lessened my stories about Allan because Amite always warned me about rich boys or this taking advantage thing.

7

Soon Carnival was in the air and there was much big preparation. People were sewing clothes, costumes, and saving up their money to have a good time. Granny had bought a new outfit for me, and I was all set for my date with Allan. It was not a real date in the sense that we made plans to have him come for me or anything but I planned to meet him at Carnival and spend the balance of the day with him. Besides, to have him come for me would have been pushing it a bit since my mother always made sure that we were properly chaperoned at Carnival by someone older, usually my sister, Elsie. Grandmother would spend a lot of money on us for Carnival as it was around Carnival time that she would get royalties from the oil on her land. I pressed the new outfit— white shorts and a lavender blouse trimmed in white piping—and spent an unusual amount of time getting dressed, provoking comments from Lena.

"Oh, how we primp up, fix weself this year for Carnival. I better tell Elsie to watch you, gial, mek you be careful somebody don't run off wid you."

Lena said all this mockingly as the thought of my having a date was the furthest thing from her mind. I shooed her away and when Elsie came for us, I had long been ready and waiting, though we had to linger a few minutes more for Lena who was still inside prettying herself. As we waited, Elsie talked to me about boys. She worried about me a lot since she had allowed herself to be enticed into marriage by an older man at a young age mainly to get away from my mother, and she didn't want me to fall into the same trap she had, with babies to feed and a husband who beat her whenever "she wouldn't listen." I assured Elsie that I wasn't about to ever let boys and men take advantage of me. I was going to make something of myself. She beamed at me and gave me a big hug, telling me how much she loved me, and how she only wanted the best for me. Soon, Lena emerged, looking for all the world like a black china doll, preened until Elsie told her she was pretty, and we headed off to Carnival. I was excited but tried to contain it as I thought about seeing Allan again and enjoying Carnival with him. Amite played with a band but we couldn't go to the adult dances he played for, so I would not be able to listen to his music. I could visualize Allan and me walking together through the crowds, he chatting with me about high school, stopping along the way to describe one of his teachers, or asking me how I was getting along with my studies. I visualized our standing before one of the bands, listening, with Allan commenting on the music, before we moved on to the concession area. There, he would buy treats for both of us—perhaps snow cones to cool us off in the heat. No, too messy, I thought, Coca-Cola would be better—and perhaps even one of the fried corn dogs if we were hungry. Oh, what a day Carnival was going to be this year! The crowds at Carnival were always large but I had faith that I would spot Allan right away even though, on thinking about it, I wished that we had made plans about where to meet. No matter, I thought, I will be looking for him and he for me, so we ought to find each other pretty soon.

At the Carnival, no sooner than we had arrived, Lena quickly ran into friends and gaily waved good-bye to me and Elsie. Elsie was chatting with me and occasionally with people we met though I heard little of the conversations as I was busy searching every which way for Allan. I finally spotted him near one of the bandstands listening to music. I knew it was him immediately without having to take a second look, though we were a good distance away. I was excited but contained myself as I did not want Elsie to know I had planned to meet him. I steered Elsie in that direction anyway, mentally framing greetings and expressions of surprise as we approached the area. *He looks older in dress clothes*, I thought, more sophisticated, and it looked like he had gotten a little taller. He was wearing a nice light blue shirt, with matching dark blue trousers and just as we approached, he turned to leave the area, which made him face us directly. Holding onto his arm, fairly tripping along to keep up with his long legs, was a pretty black girl, with almond eyes, curls in her hair, wearing a blue shorts set that looked like it came from the States. I looked from the girl to Allan who had by now, spotted me and was saying hello as we had been scant feet away in our approach. I managed a few words, introduced him to Elsie, mumbling something about Scottsdale. He introduced the laughing eyed girl as Trixie Halton and moved on away, headed in the direction of the concession stands we had just passed. Elsie and I found a place to listen to the band, a friend of hers walked up, began to chat, and I was, mercifully, left alone in my embarrassment. How could he? What did he mean making a date with me, then showing up with some rich girl? Everybody who was anybody knew the Haltons. Their father was the local manager of Shell refinery over in Portsmouth. Was she his girlfriend or had they just met at the Carnival? Why didn't he tell me if he was bringing her to Carnival? Then I remembered Amite's warnings about "dem rich boys tink they bettah dan you. Doing things in the dark wit you, but bringing they real gals out in public."

Was that what Allan had done? Was he ashamed of me? I thought back through our friendship in Scottsdale. Had Allan just been seeing me to pass the time? Maybe Amite was right. I had forgotten who I was in Scottsdale. I had never had a boyfriend before so I didn't know how boys acted. Maybe what Amite had said was true. Had Allan seen in my eyes how shocked I was? Of course, he had—he was very sensitive when it came to such matters. Was he laughing at me? I wanted to believe he wasn't; but he had broken our date, made months earlier, brought another girl to Carnival, forgotten all about me. It was a miserable, miserable Carnival for me, made the more so because I had to keep up a front with Elsie, pray not to run into Allan and the laughing eyed girl called Trixie, and wait for Lena to finish having fun before I could escape home.

I was still smarting from Allan's slight when we went back to school after Carnival and I confided in Imelda how I had felt. Of course, she told her brother, whereupon Allan came the very next day, meeting me upon the road as I walked home from school, to try to explain himself. Imelda had told me at school that day that she thought he might come. I was still hurt, angry with him. *He looks so good*, I thought, as I watched him approach me. *How could he have been so mean?* Allan was brown of color and had beautiful skin, unmarked from squeezing the zits which seemed to be plaguing the boys at school. And he walked with confidence. Before, after I had started to school at Our Lady of Fatima, Allan would walk with me sometimes and flatter me by allowing me to carry his blue blazer while he pushed his bicycle in one hand and carried my books in the other. That was the sign that someone really loved you. At five feet, six inches, he towered over me, not quite five feet tall. Watching him approach me, I thought of his "Trixie" and immediately felt ugly. "So,

hey, Jaye. How's school treating you? You still making good grades?"
He'd said by way of openers.

How dare he try to make small talk about what he had done! A
sullen hello was about all I could manage in response, and sensing my
anger, Allan launched into his explanation about Carnival. In Scottsdale,
when he had said he would see me at Carnival, he had not really meant
to make a date with me. Trixie was his regular girlfriend, and had
returned from her holiday with an aunt in the States, and he had, of
course, brought her to Carnival.

"Of course," I mumbled.

He hoped we could still be pals like in the past, did I understand?

Again, I mumbled, "Of course."

After a few more attempts to chat me up the way he used to do in
Scottsdale, poor Allan finally gave up, said good-bye, and wished me
luck with the semester. *Shucks!* I thought to myself as I watched him
depart hurriedly, and kicked a stone hurting my toe. Lena chose just that
moment to catch up with me.

"Who's that handsome boy you keeping company with, talking
'pon the road, Jaye?"

At least, she hadn't called me Bones in public as she still did
sometimes around the house. I struggled for calm. "Just somebody I
know from Scottsdale," I said noncommittally, trying to shut her up.

"But, isn't that Imelda's brother? Rich boy? I saw him at Carnival
wid he gal. He trying to chat you now?"

God, Lena didn't know just how close she was coming to the truth.
She was everywhere at once, much more socially outgoing than me, and
knew far more about who was dating whom because she was interested
in such goings on. Now, I couldn't hide my exasperation.

"No, Lena, he was not trying to chat me. He just gave me a message
to give Imelda because he isn't going to Scottsdale right away."

It was a lie with holes in it but Lena didn't pick up on it, as her
antennae was elsewhere already picking up on one of her many friends
who had caught up to us as we talked. She happily forgot about me and
walked on ahead with him and away from me.

As I walked home alone, I tried to figure out what had happened.
Allan had, indeed, had a girlfriend already. That was obvious. Why
hadn't he said so? In truth, he had never mentioned my being his
girlfriend, but hadn't he spent all that time with me, pretending not to

know Granny hated the plums and continuing to bring them to me even after I came back to Georgetown? And what of his, "Gial, I like you for tru" business? Why was life so complicated anyway, especially where boys were concerned? Why did people hurt you so much if you liked them? I hated everybody right then. I hated Allan, not only for already having a girlfriend and acting like he didn't, but also for coming to me now to rub salt on an open wound, embarrassing me further. I hated Lena for her prettiness and always guessing what I was doing and thinking. I hated Imelda for telling Allan I was hurt, and I hated Amite for always being right. But most of all, I hated me.

After the disastrous affair with Allan, I plunged into my studies with a vengeance and continued to take guitar lessons from Amite. I had begun to talk to him more and more now since he had so accurately predicted the end of the Allan relationship, but I carefully eschewed any talk of Allan. One day, instead of asking to be excused, Amite stopped lessons and took my hand and asked me to go along to the study with him. We always had our classes in the living room, an open space that was connected on each side to different rooms in the house. At first, we used the study for my lessons, but when my students increased, my classes with them were held in the dining room. But from the beginning, my mother had me take guitar lessons in the living room. So I was quite puzzled by Amite's request that I go to the study with him. As soon as the curtain separating the living room from the study fell into place, he turned me around to face him and kissed me. I was startled. He asked me again if I had ever been kissed and when I said no again, he said he would teach me. It seemed quite boring to me but he encouraged me by trying again and advised me to concentrate. I don't know if I improved or not but after another two times, he hastily peeked out of the study, asked an excuse to go home, and took off. After that, Amite began to complain about the constant interruptions of our lessons by Lena and her friends and my other sisters, Miriam and Mercedes, who insisted on playing records and dancing; and Vera, chasing our younger brother. His complaints about Allan increased too, nothing really sound, but they made me uncomfortable, and since the carnival incident seemed to confirm Amite's prediction, I found myself avoiding the backyard on a Saturday. I don't know if Allan did the same. His sister, Imelda, was graduated that year, but most of our conversations centered on someone she had met from a Protestant college, and this person replaced Allan as a threesome on our walks home. I had to walk with her to 'claim' her guy as mine in cases of emergency—like her father spotting us on the way home or something—but their conversations were boring, full of "uh huh's" and "umm's." The last straw came when after days of anticipating a gift he had promised, after I had smacked my lips imagining the taste of a piece of hazelnut chocolate bar, this boyfriend, with pomp and ceremony, gave Imelda a pen knife. After that, I started to take my taxi home again and meet Amite on the path to home, talk my head off about real and imaginary things, listen to his newly acquired knowledge of photography, suffer through one of his kisses so I would be allowed to go home, and that was it. That was life. Amite succeeded in convincing my mom that the full concentration necessary to play the classical guitar could not be achieved at home what with all the distracting noise, and since that was true, our lessons moved from my house to his band room. From my mother's little knowledge of the structure, she felt that it was safe enough, since it was in the open, fenced on three sides by chicken wire, and that no harm could come to me there. It was in the band room that Amite declared that he was my boyfriend and would protect me forever.

***

My baby boy, Hannibal, seated beside me on the Tecumseh Airlines jet, begins to stir, looks up at me inquiringly, smiling a sleepy smile. Can I protect him? Amite has always made such a big to-do about protecting his children just as he had told me when I was a child and dependent on him as my only true friend. Had it all been a mere sham? Could I protect my own children without Amite? I force myself, as uncertain as I am, to smile back at Hannibal with what I hope is a parent like *everything-will-be-just-fine*-smile. In point of fact, I feel like a fish out of water myself, a regular babe in arms. Seemingly satisfied, after stirring from what had been a nice long nap, Hannibal turns his head back inwards near my right shoulder and drops promptly back off to sleep. Thankful and relieved that I don't have to answer any questions from the children just yet, I escape the reality of my present runaway state once again, and return to the relative safety of the distant past.

8

By the fall of 1960, I had, been taking guitar lessons at Amite's house for several months. Amite had many more rules about promptness, and not missing classes than he had been able to enforce at my house. I arrived for guitar lessons one day and because I was four minutes late, Amite refused to teach me. He said he had begun to work on something else and did not want to interfere with it. I began to argue, even beg a little, until I noticed that he was putting the finishing touches on a little bird cage he had built. I was so intrigued by the cage that I soon forgot all my excuses, arguments, and the missed guitar lesson and became caught up in the drama Amite was putting into motion. I watched Amite trap little birds in the cages, silver backed, singing bullfinches that gathered in the sunlight on the breadfruit tree next to the verandah of his mother's house. He wanted to hear the birds sing to him, he explained, and the only way to do that was to catch them.

"But how comes you think you're going to catch birds? They can always fly away; they are free," I ventured, in my wisdom, with just a hint of scorn. The thought of this plodding man thinking he would be able to trap something as free as a bird with wings without killing it was, to me preposterous.

Amite had responded: "Just you wait and see! I gonna trap dey! I got something they like. Watch!" And so saying, he led the way from the band room to the house and up to the verandah to gain an access to the tree whose branches spilled out over it.

First, Amite situated the cage in the breadfruit tree, perched just so on a very nice limb. Then he began to scrape the sticky resin from the branches of the breadfruit tree, spreading it all over a little twig. Next, he put the twig inside of the bird cage, not all the way in, but with part of the twig sticking out on the same tree limb where the bullfinches loved to sit and sing. He explained that we would have to sit back and watch the tree and wait. This part had to be done the next day because the birds usually gathered to sing around six o'clock in the morning, lots of them. The next morning, a Saturday, I scrambled out of bed early and made my way to Amite's, arriving a few minutes after six. I found him already watching, looking at me disapprovingly as I approached because I had allowed him to beat me to the post on the verandah, but giving me a "shh-shhh" with his finger to his lips as the birds were already out and he didn't want to scare them away. I quickly mounted the steps and eased onto one below him and close enough to the top to allow me a good view of the tree and the birds. I did not have to wait long. The little silver birds, their coats glistening in the morning sun, were singing away. As I listened, I tried to fashion a song from their singing, but the melody was theirs alone so I soon gave up, put my hands underneath my chin and settled down to listen. The bullfinches seemed to sing without reason or motive, I thought, just because they were alive. Looking at them, I saw that others had stopped singing to look for the resin they were accustomed to finding on the tree limbs. Of course, the aroma from the newly disturbed resin on Amite's little traps was strongest, and soon, the birds sensed it, and curiously, hungrily, stopped to peck. Drawn by the smell, the innocent birds followed the twig into the cage, and before they knew it, they were not only inside of Amite's little cell-like cage, but they were stuck fast on the resin as he had spread more of the sticky stuff on the part of the twig inside the cage. No matter how hard they struggled, frantically lifting their tiny wings, fluttering helplessly, they were unable to get out of his cage. "See! I tell you, Jaye," Amite exclaimed triumphantly, "anything is possible if you put your mind to it. Now they can't get away unless I let them!"

I thought it was pretty smart myself, and looking at the birds that had been free only moments before, now caged and in a futile exercise to regain their freedom, I was at one and the same time sorry for the birds, but awed by Amite's ability to effect their imprisonment.

Pretty soon, Amite had built several cages and in that way, caught scores of the beautiful little singing bullfinches. With the birds stuck fast in the cages, he would quickly slam the door shut and wait for them to sing for him. But they would not. At first, he thought they simply missed their mates, so he would open the little prison of a cage and wait for their mates to come looking for them. Eventually, the mates would come, following the same twig of entrapment, searching for the lost love, and following the same lure, they, too, would be trapped by the sticky gum of the breadfruit tree. Happily, triumphantly, Amite would slam the door shut again, smile and sit back to wait for the trembling birds to sing for him. But even together, mated, the birds would not sing for him once they were inside the cages. He would wait and wait, hiding himself from them sometimes, hoping they were simply shy to sing in his presence, but they would not. He examined them to make sure they were the singing bullfinches who used to carol so beautifully when they were free. Disappointed with each group's refusal to sing, he finally let the birds go.

Amite had begun now to walk me home from school, some days taking me by Allan's area on the way home, insisting on kissing me in my uniform within view of the big shot blacks. I asked Amite to explain to me what he meant by boys taking advantage of you. It was the end of my second year of high school, and about the same time we had moved to the band room. He explained that adults have sex and I think he explained it fairly accurately, but not without instilling some fear in me about it, as he emphasized the pregnancy aspect. Somehow, a lot of things clicked and I became worried that I might be pregnant by Grandpa because he was the most recent molester since Femi, and though I would fall asleep with his still insisting on trying to get his floppy penis inside of me. I couldn't be sure that nothing had happened. Amite did say that you couldn't get pregnant by just kissing, and although Grandpa had not tried anything for about four months or so, I still thought I might be pregnant. Fear made me ask him in a roundabout way about my chances of being pregnant. He was amazed at the story and advised me to tell my mother. When I did, my mother did not believe me, said I was lying, and showed me "bad face" for a long time. But Grandpa let me alone then, and I learned much later, went on to cousins and other little visitors trapped by his storytelling. When I related this to Amite, he showed me how much my mom disliked me and offered me his protection if I would listen to him. Together, we decided that I would go to see a doctor. Amite made the arrangements and agreed to pay for it. When I arrived, however, the doctor refused to see me without a parent, so I foolishly went home and told my mother. She went with me to the doctor, probably thinking that I was pregnant, the doctor examined me, and then talked to my mother. He told my mother that Amite had already paid him for the visit. My mother took me home, told me that I had embarrassed and shamed her again, and that she would have nothing to do with me. A year earlier, my mother had finally relented and gone to a program I was in at school. Lena was at another school and had a badminton game, so my mother agreed to go to both, and bought Lena a new outfit. However, I had to dance in a skirt that needed some repairs about the waist since it was torn and jagged from my having pinned it up too many times. My mother, a seamstress, did not take time to repair the skirt, though, so while I was dancing an Irish dance the nuns had taught us, the pin holding my skirt together popped, and the skirt partially fell down. The dance required holding both hands in the air at once, but I had to hold the skirt up with one hand in order to finish the dance. My mother—I was watching her from the stage—got up with a straight back, strode out of the auditorium in the middle of the program and went home leaving me to come home by myself. When I went home she told me how much I had again shamed her and that she would never attend a function for me again. Of course, I told Amite—he was my best friend—and he used this example to show me that I shouldn't trust my mother at all, and he began to discipline me himself, both verbally and physically. If I had not prepared my lessons, he might box my ears to show his disapproval, all the while reminding me that I had to learn obedience and discipline. Boxing my ears—using his open palms to simultaneously slap my ears—caused my whole head to ring, so I strenuously tried to avoid breaking Amite's rules.

Amite had few compliments for me. He would look at me and say: "Jaye, you are certainly the ugliest girlfriend I have ever had but you are the most understanding." Later on, he would tell me whenever I disagreed with him, "You are most smart for your age, but you have a long way to go." I trusted Amite, felt he was the one person who really cared about me and my growth and development, and I continued to spend as much time with him as I could.

It was my custom to see Amite on my way to school and on my way back home again. His house was no more than an eighth of a mile from ours and was separated from view by some ten houses and several twists in the trail, but it was at the corner of the Main Street where everyone waited for taxis. Since I was not allowed to have guitar lessons more than once a week during the time school was in session, and I was allowed to participate only in my "Children of Mary" and "Legion of Mary" activities during the week, it was only at that time that our meeting was convenient or could be arranged. Once I got home I could not get out again. Besides, my homework load had increased so much that the time I had promised to spend with Amite had to be lessened, despite his protestations, to just a few minutes while I waited for my taxi to school or when I got off on my way home. (My father had hired a special taxi to take us to school. He was free to pick us up on any of his rounds.) I used to leave home early, talk to Amite, and take my taxi on the last round that would get me to school on time. After school, I would do the same thing—leave early, take the taxi, get off at Amite's house, remain talking to him on the trail near his house (later, the band room) and then I would go home, walk the distance between his house and mine before six o'clock or at a time that sounded reasonable if I had walked home because I had lost my taxi money. My father later counteracted that by paying the taxi driver biweekly for us to travel. My last sister, Mercedes, who was eight years younger than I, used to travel with me mornings. Sometimes I would put her in the early round and pretend that the taxi was too full for me to go. Evenings, the taxi driver made a special trip for children from her school, which was the sister elementary school for Our Lady of Fatima, situated next to it, and separated only by a driveway. By the time I was thirteen, my sister Elsie, had been married for four or five years to a man much older than she, and who beat her unmercifully. By now, she had four children for him and probably thought that he would eventually stop. I suppose she may have felt that she had to stay there since she was estranged from her own mother and really didn't have anywhere to go or any way to support herself and the children without him. Throughout all of this, Elsie would still manage to come to the school to find me, always bringing treats and giving me counsel about men, admonishing me not to let boys take advantage of me. During holidays, I would spend time with her because I loved her so, and it was a chance to help her out around the house. We would have much fun, laughing and talking, with my telling her about the nuns at the convent school and what I was learning. She teased me about becoming just like Granny and the nuns.

"Jaye, every time I come to the school, I find you in church praying. You not tinking 'bout becoming a nun on me, are you, gial?" I assured her I was not but what I couldn't explain was that the church gave me a lot of peace. Being around the nuns, and Granny too, had made me quite religious, and though I was far from saintly, I found solace in being able to toss all my faults—my ugliness, lying, everything—upon God, Mary, and the saints, and emerge feeling whole and complete. I don't think I really analyzed it myself then; I just knew it felt good. Too, my penchant for lying had changed dramatically as I grew tired of confessing the same sins each week. But being with Elsie, I had no need of crutches like religion. It was simply wonderful just to be with her, and my presence, she said, stopped some of the beatings that she would otherwise have gotten from her drinking, abusive husband. There was one drawback to being at Elsie's, however. Elsie did not have indoor plumbing and I had an ungodly fear of outhouses. One night, during mango season, after a leisurely afternoon of gorging ourselves, I had to use the bathroom, unusual for me since I consciously watched my intake of fruits in order to avoid any night trips to the outhouse. Always afraid of outhouses, I preferred constipation rather than use one at night. But this night, the mangos were speaking to me, growling in their insistence. My brother-in-law, Saul, agreed to hold the flashlight for me so that I could at least see. Although he beat my sister, he was eighteen years my senior, old in my mind at age thirteen, so I still respected him as an adult, and would talk to him at times. A week earlier, I had confided to him that Amite, from whom I was taking guitar lessons, was courting me.

He had been very direct, blunt: "He sticking yuh?"

"Course not Saul. You think I'm a bad girl?"

"Nuh. Yuh just mek sure he no stick yuh, yuh heah? Keep yuh dress down."

And that had been the end of the conversation. I had been so taken aback by his frankness in asking me about sex, I couldn't even bring myself to admit to him that Amite had kissed me.

On the way to the outhouse, Saul told me not to be scared, that he would hold the light so I could see all around inside the outhouse.

"Yuh have nutting' to fear, yuh heah?"

We reached the outhouse and he shone the flashlight all over it to make sure it was clear. Then as I pulled my clothes down, he held it on me, watching me as I used the toilet. When I finished and made ready to leave, he began to question me about Amite. I was uneasy, in a hurry to leave the smelly outhouse, and furthermore, had no interest in discussing Amite after the disastrous conversation of a week ago. He grabbed me as I started to walk out and put his hands on me, all over me, and began to kiss me. My first impulse was to scream, call Elsie, as I knew it was useless to struggle, put my seventy pounds up against his two hundred. Then I became fearful Elsie would see the situation and blame me for it. All the time, Saul was telling me that he wouldn't hurt me, that he just had to prepare me so that Amite would not take advantage of me. He made me hold the flashlight while he raped me. When it happened a second time while Elsie was away and I was left at home with him, I quit visiting my sister. Even today, I am still constipated when I travel because I find it nearly impossible to relieve myself away from home.

After failing to tell Elsie about her husband's raping me, I decided not to tell anyone. I simply did not think people could be trusted anymore. The more you tried to tell them about what was going on with you, the more they seemed to want to punish you for it, especially if some adult were involved. At his insistence, I continued to spend more and more time with Amite.

One evening I had planned to go on a nature walk with Amite because he had begun to complain that I spent too much time studying, and warned me that I could go crazy from keeping my head in books all the time. He supported this by pointing out a family that it had happened to. Anyway, my date with Amite that day was set for four o'clock since school was dismissed at three. I arrived at his house about three forty. Amite was sitting on his veranda ready and waiting for me. I had to take a book to a friend of ours who had asked me to check it out from the school library for him. I left my school bag with Amite and ran down the hill to Frank's house intending to be back by four. I was detained by Frank's younger brother, Mervyn, who wanted to show me his paintings. Long before Amite had made himself my boyfriend, I had told him about Frank's liking me and he used to tease me about him. I had told him I didn't like Frank, though, because his hands were always dirty. Well, stopping to admire Mervyn's work made me two minutes late getting back to Amite, and I found him extremely annoyed. He complained that I had shared his time with Frank. Frank and Mervyn were both members of our youth group and their sister, Joellen, was vice president, so I made the excuse that Joellen had held me back and Mervyn had wanted to show me his paintings. Amite was Mervyn's mentor so I figured the story would satisfy him. I was panting when I arrived at two minutes after four.

"What keep you? It's after four o'clock." I responded quickly, reminding him:

"But I told you I had to take the book to Frank, remember? I came as fast as I could. Lots of things to do, mon."

I said this last with finality, thinking that would be the end of it, but Amite was not to be placated.

"So you took Frank a book and kept me waiting? We had a date at four o'clock. It's already two minutes after four. I'm not going now. You have to learn to be here on time!"

Stung by his unreasonableness, I responded, "But, Amite, you knew I might be late. I told you I had to give Frank the book when I came earlier and...."

Seizing upon this last, he cut me off. "And I have a nature walk to take! Be reasonable, Jaye. How you expect somebody to wait on you all the time? I warned you since the last time that you can't waste my time. You have to learn that time is important."

By now, I had followed him into the band room, thinking that if I kept reasoning with him, he would be appeased and take me with him on the nature walk anyway. In the band room, he looked at me, narrowed his eyes.

"You owe me an apology for wasting my time. You know how much I dislike waiting on you."

Somehow his request for an apology rubbed me the wrong way. If he had not asked for it, I probably would have eventually said I was sorry in the course of the conversation. Now, I whirled around, stepped back:

"Apologize? Apologize for what?"

Amite had moved away from me, seated himself upon the amplifier box, and was looking at me exasperatedly.

"You need to apologize to me for being late and wasting my time." I heaved an exasperated sigh myself this time, responded: "But Amite, there is nothing to apologize for. You saw me coming up the hill. You saw I left on time. You know it was my intention to be early."

This time, only one word came out of his mouth: "Apologize."

He was becoming angry now, but so was I: "No."

I moved to go and as I did so, Amite rose, blocked my path.

"I am not letting you leave here until you apologize!"

Momentarily defeated, since I knew that there was no way I could physically wrest my way past him if he didn't permit it, I sat down in the chair in the room, a slatted cane bottom deal that Amite had made.

"No."

There was instant silence filling the room so that there was no space left to say anything else. Finally, Amite spoke again.

"Kneel, Jaye."

I didn't quite get the message so I looked at him questioningly.

"Get down on your knees and apologize to me."

I didn't move, whereupon he repeated it.

"I said get down on your knees and stay there until you apologize."

With fire in my eyes, I did as he asked, kneeling down on the hard concrete slab floor, but I could not get an apology out of my throat. I was quiet and so was he. Seven o'clock came and went. I reminded Amite that I needed to go home, as six o'clock was the usual time of our return from the nature walks. Besides one of my sisters could have seen that I had reached Georgetown when I was walking from Frank's house to his. That didn't scare Amite.

"Not until you apologize," was his only response.

I refused, got up to go again, and he blocked the door.

"Stay on your knees."

Eight o'clock came: "You know my daddy is home. He will begin to worry about me. I must go home now, Amite," I said with just a hint of deference, thinking that this reminder of my father and the wrath I would face, even now, when I was only one hour late, would make him relent and let me go home.

"Not until you apologize."

By the time nine o'clock rolled around, I knew my father and my brothers would be scouting the neighborhood for me, and I could imagine Joshua's annoyance at having to go from door to door asking if anyone had seen me. I repeated my request to go home and Amite repeated his for an apology. I refused again. Ten o'clock came, and I could visualize the whole family headed out in differing directions to look for me. I looked at Amite and he gave no indication that he was relenting. I began to play for time because Amite had to work the eleven to seven o'clock shift that night, so I felt that he wouldn't keep me past 10:30. My heart sank the closer the luminous hands on my watch crept towards ten. Amite had us in the dark because he didn't want his mother to see that I was still there that late. Since my family had not the slightest inkling that I would be with him, no one came by the band room to ask for me. This time, I did not ask again, and there was only silence as the clock ticked past ten. Finally, at eleven o'clock, Amite once again asked me to apologize, and when I continued my stubborn refusal, he finally let me go home. I dashed out of the house, angrier with Amite than I had ever been before, and quickly cut through the footpath to our front door, to find my worried father standing in it. Looking at his tightly drawn face, I knew that no ingenious lie would suffice for him, so I told the truth, or most of it anyway. I hurriedly explained to my father that I had been late to Amite's house for lessons because I lost my taxi money, that he had become upset and tried to make me apologize, but since I had felt that I was right, that I had been considerate and was not guilty of anything, I had refused to say I was sorry, and Amite had tried to force me to do so by refusing to let me come home. I let dad think that it was the guitar lesson that I had been late for, not once mentioning the nature walk or the book affair. Upon hearing the story, my father gave me a tanning anyway for coming home late and making him worry. Unlike I had feared, he did not forbid me to continue my guitar lessons from Amite but made the rule that guitar lessons could only be taken on weekends. After that, I refused to go to Amite's for lessons and stayed away from him for at least a month, but Georgetown was small, he was my neighbor, and it was only a matter of time before I would find myself in his company once again.

9

Bemi was two years old then, and I fifteen. All manner of new ideas were cropping up and growing along with the new country. Youth groups proliferated and since we were told that it was our job to take the leadership for the next generation, people were organizing with fervor. Soon, I became more actively involved in the Georgetown community, and shortly after that, became president. Amite was, of course, a member of our group whom everyone else considered "senior."

The Georgetown Youth Brigade as we called ourselves, was a relatively active group though we had not the least idea of what to do with ourselves. Some of the older ones were busy trying to fashion political ideology, warning of infiltration by Trotskyites and other communists, reading materials from abroad, and eyeing the burgeoning black led civil rights movement in the States. However, most of us were more concerned with the basics of life and matters that affected our immediate lives: schooling for everybody, how to get scholarships, study abroad, and access to jobs for those who wanted to work. These concerns were manifest in long rap sessions about the inequities under the former system of colonialism and all the flagrant favoritism and nepotism we had observed under the government just ousted. We had a couple of aspiring politicians among us for all our youthful inexperience, but few, if any of us, had a clue as to how to truly affect the fledgling government.

However, of one thing we were certain: things were not changing fast enough. We wanted change, were ready and impatient for it. Probably the most important aspect of the Brigade was the opportunity to voice grievances, though most of them remained unsolved and were indeed retarded by the insularity of the Senior Village Council that did not have the benefit of the newly found education of the members of the Brigade. Secondly, in the Brigade, we had a chance to bring to fruition projects and ideas of our own making, which included drama and music groups, and fundraising activities to create a treasury with which we could carry out our goals, however nebulous and unformed they were at present. Bemi was, for the first time, playing host to several African leaders. The Prime Minister made it a point after independence to bring Haille Selassie, Kwami Nkrumah, Jomo Kenyatta, and numerous others, in quick succession. As a spinoff from the Youth Brigade, the girls formed a band called "Les Filles," (the Girls, in French). I played lead guitar, the Vice President, Joellen, played second guitar, Lena played tuba, and Cynthia, the secretary, played bass guitar. Amite oversaw the band, did some composing and arranging of melodies and decided upon the melodies we would play in performance, serving as chaperone for us when we made public appearances. He was a good, staunch supporter, looked up to by us and the community as a responsible, easy-going, well disciplined person. He would come to every meeting, remain his usual taciturn self, sit and listen, while seeming to be a little above it all, and on occasion, would rise to offer his own tidbits of wisdom once a discussion had run its course. Although I was still angry with him, we gradually drifted back into what was a semblance of our old relationship. One night, when he was walking me home from the new community center, Amite began to talk about the meeting we had just left. The community center was a project that we worked on where Amite had been of invaluable assistance. As president, I had approached the minister of housing and community affairs for our area and had received authority to share the building that housed the community center. After much finagling, being put off, and shunted around, the request was acted upon in our favor, and we began the task of erecting the building. The government provided the funds, the boys in the Brigade provided labor, the girls brought food and delivered materials, water, etc. for the boys while they worked. Amite and his brothers were construction leaders for the project because their father was a building contractor and they had know-how. Soon, we had a new building. This night, Amite began to talk about the meeting, it had been an unusually spirited one, because Isa, a boy with whom I had been in grade school who was a couple of years older than I and already in college, had objected when the drama group proposed our putting on a British classic, a comedy of errors called *Miss Pitty Pat's Porch*, and suggested instead that we make up our own play about life in the villages of Bemi. Opposition was immediate. "So who you tink gon' write such a ting? Where dis play you talking 'bout come from?"

Isa had insisted that we could write the play, that we knew about our own lives, and we would be able to come up with dialogue that would have relevance to us, and through this medium, we would be able to dramatize some of our concerns. Though it had not occurred to me before, I had immediately grasped what Isa was saying, liked the idea, and had listened intently to his arguments before the skeptical gathering. As president, I had let the debate go on for quite some time, watching Isa with admiration as he took to the floor time and time again to defend his idea. Isa had been a studious looking fellow even in the fourth grade. Now, at seventeen, he wore glasses, dressed calmly, looked and sounded like a teacher, I had thought, as I enjoyed his brave comebacks to even the most vociferously scornful ones. Finally, during a pause in the debate, Amite rose to suggest that there had been enough debate and would the chair, please ma'am, put the issue to a vote. Upon hearing Amite's voice, I came out of my meanderings, recapped the situation and asked for a motion. Isa rose immediately: "Madam chairman, I move that the drama group form a writing committee to research and write we own play, about we own life, and that we present that play to the community instead of the British play, *Miss Pitty Pat's Porch*."

He was so literate, so articulate, so suave! I admired his ability to speak so directly and succinctly, and so apparently did the majority of the members as the motion was quickly seconded, passed unanimously with one "no" coming from Peter, an aspiring politician, and one abstention from Amite. Oh, we were perfect parliamentarians in those days, always kept Robert's Rules of Order nearby, and if things got out of hand, there was always Amite to lead us back to old Bob and his rules. A committee was quickly drafted, and with several people volunteering to participate in the novel idea, the matter was settled. Because the drama group had taken up so much time, after considering a couple of routine matters, the meeting had been over. Now, with Amite's mentioning the meeting on the walk home, I had a chance to voice my own opinion which I had avoided being obvious about in the meeting.

"Yes, it was a good meeting. I think we finally got something done. I believe we can make a good drama of our own. Isa had a good idea."

Even in the moonlight, I could see Amite's face change, ever so slightly, and his eyes narrowed, as he retorted:

"Yes, but some people—they just like hearing theyself talk, you know, Jaye. Lotta time what they say don't mean one ting. Just a lotta pretty words, sound good. They fool lotta people that way, 'cause people like hearing them pretty talk. Watch out you listen to what people say, not pretty talk alla time!"

He said this last in a rush, a bit angrily, it seemed. Somewhat taken aback by his sudden outburst, I managed to recover enough to say, "But don't you think it's a good idea? You always say we need to get rid of the British influence in our lives—that's what he's trying to do, don't you think...."

Amite had cut me off. "I never pass judgment on him one way or the other. I warning you about slick talking people reading books and tinking they know everyting, that's all!"

Again, he had gotten so passionate about the thing that I decided not to respond a second time at all, and he appeared to let it drop. By this time, we were approaching Amite's house and getting close to mine, so he steered me around to his house to say good night before walking me on home. In the band room, among his various projects and other junk, Amite grabbed me by the arms a little too roughly and kissed me. My silent protest, for fear his mother would hear us, was to endure the kiss but not submit. Amite bit my tongue, came up for air and whispered to me fiercely to "concentrate!" I was angry but closed my eyes and tried to do as he said so he would leave me alone. When he finished kissing me that time, he looked down at me and said, "That's better," turned and led the way along the footpath to deposit me at my door.

The Brigade was a big part of my life in those days. I was proud of it as I felt that I was doing good works as the nuns at the convent school were always emphasizing, and I looked forward to the meetings and being with so many young people in one place with our parents' consent but without adults looking over our shoulders. And for what we set out to do, we were fairly successful. I liked working with the group because it gave me a sense of direction, something on which to exercise my mostly unused talents. That first year, we had variety shows, sold fish, pops, and snowballs at Saturday afternoon soccer games and Sunday cricket matches, had a spot in the Independence Day parade, and could lay claim to having an active and stable membership. Of course, a few young people dropped in and out along the way, but there was a sizeable core that could always be depended upon to be faithful, so I was happy leading. The drama committee eventually came up with a decent play which we embellished upon as we rehearsed, and after the success of Isa's idea and the new respect he had gained, Isa was elected vice president. I was quite pleased by all of this since Isa was one of the brightest boys around and I had always admired him from afar. I was re-elected President, of course, and grew to respect his ideas even more as he was always level headed, not too pushy, and was willing to listen to others. The Brigade seemed to be flourishing. Then, in September, close to the beginning of the tourist season and about six months after Isa's election, I observed that he was beginning to miss quite a few meetings, not in succession but sporadically; and after realizing his mother was sick, I did not worry about whether or not his interest was falling off, but instead, hoped that his mother would get better so he wouldn't have to worry about her and miss so many meetings in order to care for her. Just as I had noticed Isa's absences, however, so had our resident politician, Peter, who had run against Isa for Vice President and lost. Our bylaws provided that if an officer missed three consecutive meetings, he was subject to removal from office and the naming of his successor to replace him. When Isa missed the meeting two weeks in a row, Peter pointed it out as we were about to adjourn at the end of the second missed meeting. Thankfully, Isa showed up the next week, and the matter did not have to come up for consideration. However, around Christmas time, with the end of the semester and final exams, coupled with his mother's failing health, Isa missed three meetings in a row. Amite, the self appointed parliamentarian and "advisor," took it upon himself to bring the matter to the floor for consideration. Isa was removed from office, and Peter was appointed vice president until an election could be held. All this was done in one evening. I wanted to delay the matter until Isa could be present and defend himself because I knew that the prohibition against three consecutive absences also included the phrase "without just cause," and felt that Isa's cause was just, especially his mother's illness. But in the face of the two of them, Amite and Peter, who were leading the opposition against Isa's continued service, I was immobilized and failed to speak up, and my inaction cost me a hardworking, loyal vice president. Throughout the brief discussion and voting to oust Isa, I sat stiffly, a little half-smile, half-frown on my face, not saying anything in Isa's defense; and in my position as president, carrying forward the motions that sealed his fate. When it was over, I wanted to cry. Instead, I hurriedly gathered my belongings and while Amite was milling around listening to the after-meeting chatter of people socializing, confident that I would wait for him as usual, I stepped outside, and quickly, fleet-footedly, ran the mile home, stopping only when I was fifty or so yards from our house to try to regulate my breathing to normal in preparation for entering the house. Thankfully, no one was around out front so I went to bed and fell asleep immediately, only to be awakened an hour later by my sister, Lena, preparing for bed. "So how comes you leave the meeting so fast, gial? Nobody see you go so. You come straight home?"

I responded that I had been tired, had come home and gone straight to bed.

"Indeed you did," said Lena, looking at me closely, nosily. "We stand 'round 'pon the road, talking, looking for you after the meeting. Amite say he never see you go. Finally, we walk home. You come by yourself?"

"Yes." At the mention of Amite's name, I was angry again, angry at him for getting Isa ousted, angry at my own cowardice in not trying to defend Isa. But I did not want to share all of this with Lena; I feared that she would not understand, so I turned over and forced myself to fall immediately back to sleep.

10

But things have a way of getting back to normal quickly, among the young, and I cannot honestly say that I spent a great deal of time worrying about Isa. By the time senior year rolled around, Amite and I had become free in our relationship. He regularly visited the house, not ostensibly as my boyfriend but more as a pal. We did a lot of things together now, going to community soccer games and other activities as they arose. My parents, even my father, trusted him. Amite thought the convent school was pretentious though, and "filling my head with a lot of nonsense," and he did not bother to attend any school affairs or outings with me. By this time, Bemi had switched from the old system of following the calendar year for school—i.e. beginning the term in January—and adopted the American styled academic year, starting in September. A big event during senior year was the Fete de Noel, a pre-Christmas dance, usually held in November. Most students looked forward to this event all during high school as for most of them, unless they were really rich and had a chance to attend a debutante's ball—ostentatious "coming out" parties held by the well-to-do for their teenage daughters,—Fete de Noel was their first chance to dress up in finery and act like adults. Of course, the dance was on my mind as well. People began to "date up" in October, shortly after school started, and during this time, girls held on to their boyfriends tenaciously lest they should have a spat with them and find themselves without a date for the dance. The dance was the one place no one would be caught dead alone, so a date was absolutely essential, although it was rumored that no one danced there. I had assumed that Amite would go with me without ever having asked him about it. Finally, one day in late October, the senior class advisor, Mrs. Jordan, passed out to us the formal invitations to the dance, entitling each senior and a guest to an "Evening In Paris," the theme we had chosen for the dance that year. The invitation was impressive with a silhouette of two dancers on the front and as I fingered its raised gold embossed lettering,

I finally started to become excited about the dance, and couldn't wait to rush home and show it to Amite. When school let out that day, girls were fluttering around, chattering about their gowns and how they planned to wear their hair. I had not thought about my dress although I knew that my mother would be able to whip up something nice for me. First, I had to tell Amite, though, show him the invitation.

I rushed home from school, leaving the talking groups of girls behind, shrugged out of my school uniform and into shorts and top, and ran over to Amite's house. Thankfully, it was my mother's day to go to the cinema so I did not have to create an excuse for rushing in and out of the house. Unfortunately, Amite was not at home, so I came home and barely able to contain my excitement, looked through the fashion books to pick out a pattern for my dress. I finally settled on a lime green taffeta princess style sleeveless dress which was draped over with chiffon that began at the shoulders, covered the arms, and ran the length of the dress. The princess style would take the emphasis off my slim, still boyish hips, and the draping chiffon would cover my skinny arms. There was little I could do about not having any breasts to speak of, but then, a dress could only do so much, I reasoned. I did not have to worry about my legs as the dress was formal and would cover them. I could either wear white pumps and gloves to match or have some dyed the same color as the dress. Oh, it was going to be so exciting! I hoped the material was available downtown in just the right color of green, but in case it was not, I picked out two substitute colors, pink and peach, my next favorites. The cloth at the general merchandise store where we would buy was imported and things could get scarce around this time of year what with Christmas, weddings, and Carnival coming up. If we looked early, however, the store would probably have just what I wanted. Mom was creative enough that she would fashion some kind of little head piece for me from the taffeta and maybe add a little matching netting to it. Yes, I must remember to tell Mom I needed a bit of netting. A headpiece made one look like a queen, regal and untouchable. When Mom came home, had settled herself in her room, and taken a nap, I knocked on her door. In the meantime, I had been back to Amite's house with the invitation but finding him away still, I had given up, decided his shift had changed at work, and that I would tell him the next day. Now, Mother responded to my knock by telling me to enter. I went into the room clutching the fashion book with the page turned down to the lime green dress, and with the school invitation on top. I showed her the invitation first, which mother looked at a long time. Then I told her about the dress I had picked out for her to sew for me, handing her the book. She took a cursory glance, appeared not to have much interest in the dress I'd chosen, and instead, asked me who I planned to have carry me to the dance. I was instantly shy, and not looking at her, answered hesitantly, almost inaudibly, "Amite. I guess."

Mother had lifted one eyebrow, and responded with a question, "Amite?" Now, I didn't know what to say, but plunged on, having gotten in that deep, "Yes, Mother, I think he will be willing to escort me."

Whereupon she had looked at me hard, pityingly, and with a sigh, had asked: "Can't you get a boy to take you?"

I dropped my head, "No, Mother, I don't have a boyfriend, but I think Amite will go with me."

She had sighed again, waving her arm wanly in resignation and said, "Oh, well, have it your way, Jaye."

She still didn't know that Amite was my boyfriend, and I continued not to reveal it to her, instead passing off the whole thing as if he were my pal.

When my father came in later that night, I showed him the dress and the invitation and chatted about the dance, the "Evening in Paris" theme, and the kind of decorations we planned to have. Thankfully, my father did not ask me who was taking me. I suppose he figured that my brother might. Some girls came to dances with their brothers or the boyfriend of the older sister, or horror of horrors, with their parents, who might sit on the sidelines drinking punch and waiting for them. I had heard of such cases over the years, the lore that was handed down about senior dances of years past. I knew I would never subject myself to such humiliation. My father said I could have everything I needed, including the dyed-to match shoes and the headpiece with netting. I was elated and continued to sit with him for a long time that evening, not escaping the way I had begun to do as I grew older. Soon, my father had begun to talk.

"Well, it's yuh senior year, now. Suppose to be a good time fuh yuh. Looking towards the future. Time to tink seriously 'bout what yuh want to do wit yuh life, yuh know." "Yes, Papa," I said perfunctorily, just a tiny bit apprehensive about where the conversation was leading. He looked at me.

"Yuh know, de country independent now; good time fuh growing up, coming into mahturity. We nevah have same opportunity yuh chaps have, yuh mama and me. We nevah coulda finish high school—opportunities limited for we. I membah, me mudda look at me when I twelve year old, tole me dere was no money fuh any more schooling, need fuh me ta learn trade so I know how care for me family. How I hated dat! I loved school, was always fust out de door every morning. But wit me Papa dead when I age ten, I know what me mudda speaking to me tru, see? And though I feel low and dejected, hung me head, I know how much me mudda love me, want me to do good. Next week, she tek me over to Portsmouth, to the capitol, and paid a man fuh me lodging so I could work as his apprentice. Imagine dat! I get no pay and me mammy haveta pay the man to work me! But I learn anyhow, mek it possible fuh me to get me journeyman's license in masonry so I could do someting fuh meself. Good ting she did, too. Lotta boys I come up wid, and girls, too, nevah do one ting for deyself and nobody else. But I always memba what me mudda said, and I work hard, mek mesef the best around, nevah haveta look fuh no job, job come to me. I di wash cars fuh many years, nothing bettah fuh do. But I wash dey the best! De big shots discover the oil in we rich country, I land job wid dem, heavy equipment operator fuh the same people I wash vehicles fuh in de past. Dat's what happen when yuh de best, Jaye, job come looking for you 'cause evahbody know quality when dey see it." He paused for a moment and I added an obligatory, "Yes, Papa," waited for him to go on. He did.

"And you, yuh quality. Yes, baby, quality! Yuh got a good head on yuh shoulders, good enough to lead de country. I nevah tink to see a black man come to be Prime Minister a' Bemi, but look see wha happened wit independence. Yuh part of the new generation getting education, yuh country needs yuh. Yuh could be Prime Minister one day; yuh got de head fuh it! I seen yuh work with de Brigade. Use yuh head, now, mind yuh don't get your head turned round looking backwards. Life too important for dat! Keep looking forward; be a good girl. The best will come to yuh!"

At this, he stopped, patted my head, and lowered his own, but not before I saw a glint of tears in his eyes. My big strong daddy was crying? I remained quiet, moved, and realizing that my dad thought so much of me, hearing him say it, I wanted to cry myself. It was a tender moment, probably the closest I ever had with my daddy, and when I left the room that night, I vowed to make him proud of me. I didn't know what the future held, whether or not I would get to go to college right away after high school, or any such, but I knew that I wanted to be the best that I possibly could for my wonderful father. Feeling totally precious for one of the few times in my life, I went to bed.

The next morning, a Saturday, I woke up feeling good, refreshed, quickly zipped through my chores, finished by midday, and decided to wash my hair. There was a soccer game at five o'clock so I figured I might get a chance to go to it since all my chores were done so early. I finished my hair, showered, dressed in Saturday-go-to-meeting clothes and sat around the house for a while, hoping Amite would stop by. I had to ask him to carry me to the Fete-de-Noel dance, but somehow, once I had gotten approval from my father for my dress, asking Amite did not seem nearly so urgent. At three, however, when Amite had not showed up, I walked through the footpath to his house, carrying the invitation and the fashion book. I decided to simply give the invitation to him without explanation and wait for him to respond. Amite looked at the invitation a long time, not saying anything. We were in the band room. I stood before him, still clutching the book in my hand, waiting. Finally, Amite moved over to a bench, sat down, looked at the invitation once more, then looked up at me.

"Where you get this, Jaye?"

Confused as to the reason for the question, I said, "Why, Amite, Mrs. Jordan gave them to the seniors at school. We pay for them in senior class fees."

Amite looked at the invitation again, appeared to be reading it all over again. Finally, with a hint of long suffering on his face, he looked back at me, sighed, then spoke: "You know this nothing but foolishness, don't you, Jaye?"

I felt just like he had dashed a bucket of cold water in my face, for even then, I sensed where the conversation was going, but didn't want to face up to it.

"But, Amite, it's the senior dance; everybody goes. I thought you would take me."

Amite was now looking at me like I had just taken a leave of my senses.

"So how you expect me to participate, go 'long with dis kinda foolishness!" I was crushed. If I had stopped to think about it before, I would have realized that Amite would respond that way. But I had foolishly been caught up in the euphoria and excitement of the moment, going along with the crowd, completely dismissing what I already knew about Amite. When I didn't say anything, Amite had continued talking about the people at the convent school putting on airs, filling up children's heads with everything but knowledge. He had expected more of me. I decided not to say anything else, being well aware of the futility of arguing with Amite when he had taken a position he thought was right.

All of a sudden, my dream of floating around in beautiful billowing lime green chiffon, floated right out of the room into the air, borne away on the blanket of Amite's scornful disdain. I didn't bother to show Amite the dress, or even try to reason with him further, and it never occurred to me to try to get another date. I simply went home, tore the page with the lime green dress out of the fashion book, and ripped it to shreds. As I did so, I thought of my father and our conversation of the night before. He had seemed genuinely pleased to see me excited about the Fete de Noel dance, and had happily granted all my wishes. What would I tell him now? I decided not to bring the matter up again, and simply let it slide. When I didn't ask to go shopping for material, my mother finally questioned me about it, and I told her I had decided not to go. She did not interrogate me further and actually seemed relieved. My father had gone out of town to work, so I didn't have to explain anything to him, and I guessed that he had probably left the money for my materials with my mother and forgotten about it. In all my disappointment, though, I was still moved by my father's interest in me, and whenever I thought about the senior dance, I would think of the tender moments I had shared with him the night I had asked for the dress. After the senior dance, the conversation at school for at least a week was who wore what, where people had gone afterwards, and who went home late and got a tanning. However, the semester was almost over, and we were soon involved in studying for finals, taking exams, and later, enjoying the Christmas holidays. The holidays passed without incident other than the usual goings-on and I recovered.

11

By the time we returned to school in January, preparations for the spring carnival were in the air and there was something new to talk about. Carnival is the biggest holiday in Bemi, and the country rolls out the red carpet, as it were. Carnival kings and queens were selected in December to ride the elegant theme floats and the beautiful costumes had to be built, not simply sewn. There was much glitter, beads, tassels, fringes—much had to be constructed. Merchants, who made a killing out of all this, paid for floats in the parade for the different clubs and organized groups. The Brigade had discussed a float but had decided to wait a year until we had more money in the treasury. Elsie had a baby in early February, a week before Carnival, and was not available to escort us as she usually was, so Lena, Vera, and I needed a chaperone, someone whom Mom trusted to go with us. Lena and I were talking, going through the process of elimination, discarding our suggestions as we went along if we thought of someone too strict, or who would want us to leave too early—general sticks-in-the-mud—when I thought of Amite. Knowing that he would be going anyway, I decided to ask him if he would serve as our chaperone. He readily agreed, Mom Okayed the idea, I told Lena and we were on. Carnival arrived, and Amite walked over to our house to get us. Walking the two miles to the carnival grounds, Amite began to lay down his rules for the day. I had not given thought to the fact that Amite always had rules, and just assumed that he would walk us there, watch out for us, and escort us back home after Carnival was over. I could not have been more wrong. Amite informed us that we—all three of us—had to stay with him the entire day so that he could keep an eye on us. We had to remain in his sight, always. Lena was the first to speak. "Jaye can stay with you all day if she want, mon, but I going with me friends. I big girl, you know."

Lena said this last with finality and all the conviction and bravado her fourteen years could muster. Vera, the baby, didn't say anything and neither did I. Amite reiterated what he had said. We were by now upon the Carnival grounds, could hear the music and see the frivolity going on.

"How you expect me to be responsible for you if you off somewhere I can't see you? Mek no sense, Lena."

Lena was adamant. "Elsie never make us stay with she. We always able to go wit our friends. Elsie watch out for us, not make us sit up under her like babies."

Amite had snorted, came back with, "So, if you such a big gial, how come yuh mama ask me to watch over yuh? Dat's my rule! Yuh don't like it, go home."

By now, Lena's jaw had set and she was resisting Amite head on. "I not going home, and I not staying up under you all day long, Amite. I gonna join me friends like I always do!" And so saying, she turned to walk away, leaving me standing there flabbergasted, feeling guilty, and wondering what to do. Amite immediately moved forward, grabbed Lena's arm, and began to struggle with her to keep her from leaving. Of course, she tried to get away, yelling at him to leave her alone. But Amite was hanging on to her.

"Ouch! Amite. Turn me arm loose, buoy. You hurting me."

People had begun to stop and look around to see what was going on. I was now mortified, embarrassed and immobile. Vera was quietly waiting beside me watching to see what would happen. The two continued to struggle, Lena screaming insults at Amite. He held on to her two arms and walked the two miles home with both her arms under his, Vera and I trailing a safe distance behind. At home, Lena ran to her room, and following her, I found her sobbing into her pillow, and alternately whispering epithets, cursing Amite for messing up her Carnival. I felt sorry for Lena. In truth, I probably would have spent most of the day with Amite anyway without his rules, and would have kept Vera with me. But Lena was an outgoing girl, with many friends and Elsie had long since allowed her to go off with them at Carnival making sure she checked in with Elsie periodically when they would run into each other on the grounds. On the way home, Amite had reasoned with me about the whole matter, and no amount of my pointing out that Elsie always let us be with our friends would make him see our point of view.

"Be logical, Jaye, your mother make me the chaperone. If I the chaperone, then I haveta be wit you throughout the day. It's simple, anything else is pure stupidness." Since what he said was technically true, it was hard to argue, and we had walked the balance of the way home in silence. At the house, Amite told my mother what happened and left. Lena refused to come out of the room all day long and to this day, I don't think she ever fully forgave Amite. Amite never forgave my mother either because she did not chastise Lena. He used the incident to prove to me that my mother condoned indiscipline.

That was February of my senior year. In April, I turned seventeen and began to look forward to graduation and the future, although I could not quite imagine what life would be like without school. The nuns at the convent school liked me and I them. I was particularly fond of one of them, Sister Angela, a twinkly-eyed diminutive little woman who was, behind the habit she wore, of inestimable age. She would always single me out for praise or point out some good character trait I possessed, like dependability. She was an excellent teacher, one whom I liked so much that I had briefly considered entering a nunnery. Sister Angela had not pressed me at all after I confided in her, but had told me to prayerfully consider it before I made up my mind. When I later confided to her that I wanted to be a teacher, like her, but decided against being a nun, she had hugged me and still seemed real pleased with my choice of vocation.

"You will make a good teacher; you can be whatever you want to be, Jaye, I have confidence in you." But although I felt secure in my position at school, I had no inkling what the future held once I left the cocoon of my present existence.

Soon I was graduated—May, 1966—and though I didn't have immediate plans, I was not too troubled by it. I settled down for a rest. One weekend, my father came home on furlough and Amite took the opportunity to ask for my hand in marriage. My father actually laughed, so sure was he that Amite was kidding around.

"Go on wit youself, buoy! Joking 'bout me best dahter. How you go on so!" He replied, laughing and slapping his knee.

Amite stood his ground. "But she is old enough to marry!" He had burst out, refusing to try to cajole my father or go on off until a more appropriate time. Amite and I had entered the house a few minutes earlier and found my father relaxing in the living room alone. Without any ado, and as soon as amenities were over, Amite had popped the question to my father. I could see my father starting to get angry as Amite spoke a second time and he realized he was serious. The question had been as much a surprise to me as it had obviously been to my father. He was a muscular man, my father, and age and maturity had not weakened him. Instead, being a heavy duty equipment operator had made him stronger, if anything. Now, I saw his fists clench and he appeared to be holding himself back to keep from striking Amite, as he looked first at Amite, then at me. The veins had begun to stand out on each side of his forehead and his ordinarily wide nose now flared even wider, dramatically.

"What the hell you walk up inna me house asking me such a ting? Yuh crazy? Out! Out! Get outta here!"

Amite continued to try to explain himself, but my father would hear none of it, finally saying in a menacing voice, "Get outta me house, mon. Leave me dahter alone!"

With so direct an order, Amite finally had no choice but to leave. When he left, my father sat back down into his chair, cursing under his breath, looked around, saw I was still there, started to say something, stopped, and put his open palms to his face. I used the opportunity to escape to my room.

Inside the room, Lena was sitting up in bed, wide-eyed, having heard the whole thing.

"Amite asked Pops to let him marry you?!!!"

I nodded dazedly, sat down on my bed and tried to sort things out. I had known that Amite planned to ask my father to let me marry him, but it was something I had thought would happen later, much later. Amite claimed that he had told my mother and she was trying to get him to marry Lena instead. My mother liked Amite as a person, and the fact that he had a good job made it all the better. Amite says that when he insisted that it was Jaye he wanted to marry, my mother told him that he could try asking daddy, that he might make a fuss but say yes. The impression I got from Amite's relating the story was that mother felt that my father liked Lena less than he liked me and that he would let him have Lena. When I had a conversation with her about it, she was sitting, legs crossed in her pretentious manner, filing her nails, said: "But, Jaye, why do you have to go and break your poor daddy's heart and have Amite ask him a question like that?"

After that, Amite used to laud it over Lena that he had refused my mother's offering her to him, and gave me the idea to use it as a weapon against her, too. Lena was talking, awed by it all, not being catty or derisive.

"Pops plenty mad. That Amite bettah watch heself round pops. Pops take no truck offa he!"

I knew Lena was glad Amite had finally gotten his comeuppance after spoiling her Carnival with his rules a few months earlier. Amite would receive no sympathy from her. I felt sorry for Amite. He had stood so bravely before my father, fighting back, even, after my father's outburst, even in the face of his scorn, and it had only been my father's ordering him away from the house that had caused Amite to back down and leave. Then, as I thought about the two of them, I felt torn in two. I loved my father so much, always had. He had never shown me anything but kindness, and had always wanted the very best for me. And he, obviously, did not think marriage to Amite was best for me. But I cared about Amite, too. By now, he was twenty five years old and I was seventeen. I had been especially close to Amite since I was thirteen when the guitar lessons had begun. He had always looked out for me, squired me around, shared his life with me. And although there was little between us that could be characterized as romantic, he had made me feel good by telling me how intelligent I was. He wanted to marry me. But there was no middle ground! I could not please one without hurting the other and I so wanted to please them both, make both of them happy. But what if I couldn't? What if my father continued to say no about letting me marry Amite? What could I do? Defy my dad? The idea itself was unfathomable. It was a scary situation, one which I did not want to face, so I willed myself to sleep. Forcing myself to sleep when under stress and in fear was a habit which I carried into adulthood and became a part of my coping mechanism.

I woke up the next morning with a splitting headache and a feeling of dread hanging over me. As I did chores around the house, I thought again about my father's violent opposition to Amite's marrying me. I had some sense that Amite might say something to my father, but not quite so soon. About a month after graduation in May, my father had met Amite and me taking a walk upon the road and he had instantly sensed that Amite was something more to me than a friend. He had said a few words to me and Amite about taking such "liberties," and, looking at my graduation ring, he said: "That ring on your finger is not a wedding ring!" In the days following, Amite had said that perhaps my father thought his intentions were less than honorable and maybe he should ask him about marrying me. I had not taken the matter too seriously myself because I was not interested in getting married so soon, especially since we were still awaiting CXC exam results. Based on my scores, I might qualify for a scholarship or to teach, so I was sort of in limbo about my future. However, after the failed "proposal," the fight was on; and from then on, everything between Amite and my father was a confrontation.

At one time, our families had been fairly close. There were six of the Peay boys, children of a mother who dominated them, and a father who controlled the whole family. Mrs. Peay doted on her boys and depended on the oldest, Eugene, to help maintain her. The Peay boys were always in and out of our house, my mother knew each of them, so it was not uncommon for Amite to continue to be underfoot even though my father had forbade him to marry me. He was still a neighbor, a family friend, hardly a stranger. Besides, my father was not usually home during the week so he didn't run the risk of seeing him too often. The school holidays were finally drawing to a close in August when Sister Angela told me that I had been recommended for a teaching job on Bonsai, sister island to Bemi. It was a regular school that the convent operated and they were in the process of converting it to a convent school like Our Lady of Fatima in Bemi which I had attended. Ordinarily, Sister Angela said, they would never have recommended so young inexperienced a person, but I was unusually mature in addition to having high grades, and since I had been through the convent system, the Sisters thought I would be the ideal person. It seemed like a job for such a big person! But Sister was asking me? All of a sudden, I had a future being handed to me. The nuns still believed in me! While I was thanking Sister Angela for the recommendation, I thought of my father. Bonsai was another island. Would my father let me go? I didn't think so. I had never lived away from home before except with Granny, and I didn't think my father would allow it now. I told Sister I had to check with my parents and let her know.

I walked home slowly, thinking, not rushing the way I usually did when I was excited. I had only been to Bonsai once, with grandpa as a very young child years ago. It was a pretty place that the tourists who came to more popular Bemi were always putting on their itinerary as a place to go and get away from everything after they had been in Bemi a week. Bonsai was picturesque and according to the brochures, less developed than Bemi, and the few people I knew from there seemed a little less citified than Bemijians fancied themselves to be. Some Bemijians had relatives on Bonsai and would visit occasionally on holidays, taking the boat over on Wednesday and coming back on Sunday when the boat returned. A few people who owned boats came and went whenever they wanted. I contemplated how I would broach the subject with my mother. I wanted to go. The thought of getting away from Bemi, teaching school, making some money for the first time in my life appealed to me. I could always go to college, I figured, and though I felt that I would qualify for a scholarship. I knew that competition was stiff, and one could never know for sure. Besides, even if I were awarded a scholarship this year, it was likely that one would be there for me next year, too. Oh, if only my folks thought I was mature enough to go! How could I make them understand how much the job meant to me? I didn't know. I always felt that I was being judged, and the less people knew about how I felt about anything, the less they would have upon which to judge me, I reasoned. So I never gave up much information about how I felt. By the time I got home, I had convinced myself that mother and father would be angry at my wanting to leave home, and forbid me to take the job. Instead of going straight home, I cut through the path to Amite's house to tell him first. He gave me a long lecture about how long he had waited for me and that he had never taken "advantage" of me and now, look how I was repaying him. Other boys would have had me pregnant already. He pooh-poohed the idea of my going away from home by myself to a strange place to teach. What was wrong with those nuns anyway for suggesting such a thing? No, I was better off forgetting the whole thing; there was no need to take it any further. When I went home that night, I decided not to mention the job to my mother at all since I was sure that they would not want me to leave home.

About two weeks later, while I was cleaning up in the kitchen, helping mother with preparations for food she was preparing for a visit with my father where he was camping out at work, I casually mentioned the job that the Sisters had offered me on Bonsai. To my surprise, Mother liked the idea, but she did not think my father would allow it.

"Oh, I don't think your father will consent, but when I go to see him, I will mention it anyway, just to see what he says."

And with that, she seemed to dismiss the whole thing. But I knew she was proud of the offer because I heard her tell her neighbor visiting that evening, "You know, my daughter has been offered a teaching position on Bonsai, but I don't think we will allow her to go off by herself just now."

The neighbor had been properly impressed, and as I listened in the next room, I realized that in her own way, my mother had a lot of pride in the fact that I was considered intelligent, and was, just like other parents, not above boasting about it to her friends. About two days later, she went to Portsmouth to visit father, taking with her the home-cooked bread, meats, and pastries she had baked. Occasionally, she visited my father instead of his taking a furlough to come home to see us; she was usually gone about a week on these trips. Elsie came to stay with us while Mother was gone, she and mother finally having made up after her marriage and all the controversy surrounding it. Elsie was, of course, bursting with pride about my job offer, and wondering if I would need regular clothes or teacher's uniforms at the school. She was already trying to figure out how to get material to have a couple of new frocks made for me.

"Oh, Elsie," I had confided to her. "If Pops would only let me go!"

She had hugged me, holding me tightly for a while, said, "Jaye, you're the one with so much faith, praying all the time at that convent school. You have to believe he will say yes. Don't think about anything else!" I tried, but I could not totally believe. I couldn't bring myself to talk to Elsie about Amite's proposal of marriage although I knew she had probably heard it through the family grapevine. Everybody had reacted to it so negatively that I was beginning to feel a little ashamed about it myself, almost as if I had done something wrong. Elsie didn't say anything about it, now, but it was on my mind because I saw it as a strike against me. If my father thought something was wrong with Amite wanting to marry me—even the idea of his courting me seemed to be absurdly wrong as far as my father was concerned—then he might think I was trying to be grown by wanting to leave home to go to work on Bonsai. I was embarrassed to ask Elsie what she thought of my reasoning, because Amite had been her old boyfriend and I never acknowledged to her that Amite and I were anything but pals. When Lena had figured out that Amite was sweet on me and once teased me in front of Elsie about taking up with Amite where Elsie left off, Elsie—by then married—had responded in her usual frank and honest way: "Amite never me real boyfriend, gial, jest puppy love, you know. Kissing. Besides, he thought sex was dirty and nice girls nevah do dat!"

And so saying, Elsie had tossed her head, laughingly dismissing the subject, and relieving me of having to respond to Lena's teasing one way or the other. Now, in spite of Elsie's optimism, I had no hope that my father would let me go; and, indeed, with Amite being so much against it, I was willing to give up the idea anyway at least when I was around him. The week passed uneventfully, with my not thinking too much about the job offer on Bonsai but hoping that once the exam results were back I would have a job offer closer to home or a scholarship to school. Finally, my mother came home with the unexpected news. My father would come home in two days, and he had said I could take the position on Bonsai! He had sent my mother ahead to make preparations for me to go, including booking passage on the boat that sailed the following Wednesday.

Mother arrived on Saturday morning. There was much preparation around the house after that. Mother immediately dispatched Joshua, my oldest brother, to the marina to book passage for me and my father, and I began gathering together personal items I would need living away from home. Since we girls shared many items like combs, deodorant, and such, mother bought some new toiletries especially for me. I began to pack my suitcase in preparation to go. Elsie came over; we took the fashion book, and together picked out the patterns with Elsie insisting on one two-piece so I would "look like a teacher." This one she wanted me to wear for the ride over. Elsie said I would need them at any rate whether or not teachers wore uniforms on Bonsai, since teachers always had a special meeting or something to go to. She talked to me about taking care of my hair and suggested to me a style to replace the picky plaits I continued to wear, a holdover from my high school days. Elsie was trying hard to make a young woman of me. I started to try to imagine what it would feel like to be in the place of a teacher with students to be responsible for, students who would call me Miss Bartholomew, or more likely, the British inspired "Miss." Around the house, I was getting a little bit of respect already. Mom came to tell me that Joshua was back and the passage was confirmed. Joshua doing something for me? He was still my mother's favorite, assumed no responsibilities even for himself, was spoiled, lazy, and not very ambitious, but she doted on him anyway, never insisting on routine chores for him like she did with the girls. By now, Lena was tired of the whole thing—all the attention I was getting—and soon went to her room when Elsie was gone. By nightfall, when things had begun to settle down a bit, I went outside and sat on the stoop for a long time, by myself, listening to the night sounds, before going to my room. Maybe I would teach for one or two years, save up a nest egg and try again for a scholarship to college. I still wanted to get a college degree in order to be able to teach in secondary school, and earn a higher salary. Then, maybe I would get married. By then, I was sure my father would approve. But thinking of marriage again made me think of Amite and whether or not he would be angry at me for leaving and going to Bonsai. I again tried to console myself with the thought that what I was doing was best for me and that Amite would be happy for me once he had a chance to think about it. It was all too complicated so I forced myself not to think about it, went inside, went to bed, and immediately fell asleep.

Sunday afternoon, I had to go to Elsie's on an errand for my mother, so on the way back, I stopped off at Granny's. I didn't know whether or not she knew about my plans, but in case she didn't, I wanted to be the first to tell her. Walking along the road to her house, I began to think about her response. Granny would be happy for me, as happy as Elsie, I was sure. All of a sudden, I sped up, couldn't wait to tell her. I found Granny sitting underneath her house, keeping cool.

"Granny, I goin' a Bonsai, for teach!" I had yelled, reverting to raw Creole in my excitement, abandoning the English language. Granny jumped up, hugged me, laughed.

"And we a teach we class in Creole when we mek one big teaching job on Bonsai," she had responded, reacting to my uncharacteristic use of Creole.

"No, granny, I so excited. I nevah thought such a thing would happen to me, so soon!"

Granny was still holding me about the waist, and now she gently turned me around, placed me in a seat. However, at that moment, Amite popped into my mind, and I again found myself wondering how he would take the news this time. Oh, he will be happy for me, I reasoned. Wasn't he always telling me how intelligent I was? Well, the job provided the proof, I reasoned, so Amite should be happy to know his confidence in me had not been ill placed. Now, I was quiet, less jolly, and Granny sensed my mood change immediately.

"Future hard fuh try figgah out, Jaye. Yuh tek everting so serious. Tek it slow, tek it slow. Yuh bahn lucky, yuh know. Nevah get push inta anyting yuh don't want fuh do."

Granny always said I was born lucky when my sisters teased me about not having been "born." I was a caesarean baby, uncommon at that time, so Granny said that I was born for good luck. Now, I felt as if Granny had read my thoughts about Amite, felt guilty, and looked at her to try to discern whether there had been more to what she had just said than the words. But Granny was not about to let gloom enter our celebration, even though I was pretty sure she knew about Amite's proposal to my father for my hand in marriage. She shoved imported candy into my hand, ate some herself, and began to sing a little song about a lonely star twinkling by itself. Her voice was beautiful, youthful and clear, even though she was well past middle age, and I stopped thinking long enough to enjoy it. When she finished, she curtsied in front of me, holding her skirt just so, smiled and sat back down. That was when she noticed the sun and warned me that I should go lest nightfall should come before I could make it back to Georgetown. I had been having such a good time with running to and fro, not having to do anything.

"Where you been?"

I told Lena about spending the afternoon at Granny's, the celebration we had, with Granny giving me the candy.

"Whoo-eee!" She had exclaimed, "I cain't wait 'til I finish school, become big woman, go off and do like me please."

Ignoring her continued sarcasm, I said, "Lena, I'm so excited. I can't believe Pops said I can go. I'm scared, though, seems like such a big step to be taking by myself."

Lena sucked her teeth, tossed her head, like Mom did when she was immersed in conversation with her friends.

"No bigger dan thinking bout marry. Pops know what he doing."

At her mention of marriage, my thoughts, of course, turned to Amite, and I began to worry again about what he would have to say about my leaving. And so thinking, all lightheartedness vanished, and I was plunged again into dread over the thought of facing Amite. Now, I asked: "Amite come by today?"

Lena could not miss the chance to dig a bit further: "Yes, Madam, he here dis afternoon, see big preparation going on, find out me fadda coming home to take he sweetie off to Bonsai. Him nevah look too pleased."

I was scared to ask anything else, so the matter dropped to the floor, out of my hands, like a hot potato. Knowing she had scored once more, Lena picked up a stack of linen, and moved to store it in the bureau drawer.

"We going a Bonsai for big job, mebbe we forget leekle sweetheart boy back in Bemi. Outta sight, outta mind, with all dem new boys to choose from."

She flung this last over her shoulder as she finished putting away the linen and swished exaggeratedly out of the room leaving me, as usual, at a loss for words when it came to talking about my relationship with Amite. I sat down on our bed to think. Would Amite think I was running away from him by taking the job on Bonsai? Had he been angry when he came and found out I was leaving soon and hadn't bothered to tell him? But things had gone so fast since Mom had returned! I hoped I would get a chance to see him tomorrow before my father arrived so I could at least let him know that it was more my father's idea, not mine. Amite had been so against my going. How would he feel now, even when he knew the decision had been taken out of my hands? I shouldn't have told! It was my fault for telling Mom, bragging about the offer after Amite had said it was a bad idea. But I'd been so sure my parents would veto the matter till I had thought little about telling Mom that day in the kitchen.

There was nothing I could do about it now. Pops said I was going and that was that. Joe, Jr. came in crying because Vera had refused him one of the cupcakes Mom had baked earlier in the day, telling him they were for tomorrow. He was the baby, prone to acting spoiled like Joshua, but still cute as a button anyway and sweet at times. I dug into my pocket, found the lone piece of candy I had left from my visit with Granny, gave it to him, and watched him run out to taunt Vera with it. Mercedes and Merceria, the two girls next to Lena, were busy cleaning their room and chattering about all the things that had happened with the opening of school a few days earlier. It was by then September and school was in session again. Thus, the urgency of my formally accepting the job and getting over to Bonsai twenty two miles away. The evening went on with Mother in her room for most of it, and me supervising the bevy of activity in the house as needed. Finally, around midnight, with everything seemingly in order, the house quieted and I finally went to bed. Before falling asleep, I prayed that Amite would not be troubled by the decision.

On Monday, the house was up early as the younger ones had to go to school. By seven o'clock, I alone was left at home with Mother, who was still in her room. I took the opportunity to slip over to Amite's, hoping that she would not miss me before I could return, and praying that my father wouldn't arrive in my absence. Cutting through the footpath, I was at Amite's in less than two minutes, found him in his quarters cleaning his camera lens, seemingly making ready for a photography session.

"Mawning, Amite," I said on entering the band room.

"Mawning," he had responded, barely glancing at me, before returning to the vigorous polishing he was giving the lens with a soft white cloth. I stopped just inside the door, hesitating a bit, not quite knowing what to do in the face of his silence. The sun had long since been up and burned off the morning dew and any little chill that may have lingered outside from the night, but the room was cold, so much so that I had the urge to wrap my arms around myself in the short sleeved shift I was wearing.

"Well," I had finally ventured, "My father is coming today, you know."

Amite continued to browbeat the lens, spoke again, this time without so much as a glance at me.

"Yuh leaving."

That was all he said at first, and seeing as how it was a statement, not a question, I did not respond, but sat in the one chair, and waited for Amite to continue.

He finished polishing the lens, walked over to the shelf, put the camera aside, turned around, "I know what he doing, you know, Jaye. He getting you away from heah, from me! One foolish idea you ask me, send a young gial off unprotected, jest to try fuh spite me!"

Amite was taking the whole thing personally! He saw my father's agreeing to let me go to teach on Bonsai as a maneuver of my father's to try to break us up. Lena's comment as we had folded the clothes the night before came to my mind: "Pops know what he doing." Was that what Lena had meant? Was Amite right? But I wanted to go to Bonsai to teach. For me, it was the chance of a lifetime, and when Mom had come back with Pop's blessing, I had been happy for the chance to go. Besides, Bonsai was not far away, so I didn't feel like I was really abandoning Amite. He could always come for a visit. I was a big girl now, would be teaching away from home, not under my parent's noses any more. The situation might even be an improvement for us. I had pointed out all of this to Amite, but he refused to be consoled, and appeared to be as annoyed with me as he was with my father. Knowing that I was really pushed for time and realizing that I had been gone a full half hour, I soon left Amite and rushed back along the footpath to the house. And just in time, too. I carefully, quietly, let myself into the house. Mom's bedroom door was still closed. Pops had not made it home yet. I put on a pot of water for tea, knowing that my mother would soon be up as the clock on the wall said it was close to eight o'clock. I took Creole buns from the large breadbox on the table, sliced, buttered, and warmed them, opened a tin of milk, and fixed tea for my mother. In a few minutes I heard her stirring in her room. Quickly, I grabbed a tray, neatly arranged the buns and the tea, added a banana, and knocked on her door. She had already dressed when I entered which shocked me because that meant she had already been out of the room and completed her morning toilet. Unnerved by the realization that she had already gotten up and knew of my absence from the house, I steeled myself for questions about my whereabouts so early in the morning, and, trying not to act nervous, set down the tray with a "Mawning, Mom. How's the mawning?" As was her way this time of day, Mom gave up only a monosyllabic "fine," not exactly an invitation for early morning chitchat. I quickly got out of the room. In the kitchen, I helped myself to tea, avoided the buns and ate a half banana. As I broke the banana, I again thought of Amite. He was always complaining because I could eat only half.

"But, Amite," I would object. "I can't eat a whole banana, not at once. It's too much for me."

I was small, didn't have much appetite, and half a banana was plenty for me, but it was a point of irritation with Amite that I would not force myself to eat the whole thing. Besides, he never gave a good reason why I should, just said it was plain stupidness not to. He said it was all in my head, so that during the holidays when I would attend 5:00 morning mass, he would buy bananas, three for a nickel, and try to make me eat a whole one on the way home. Amite would feed me the banana piece by piece, even if I gagged on it over and over, and everyday he gave me a little more until I was able to eat a whole one. Sometimes he coaxed me gently, sometimes he would threaten me, sometimes he would bang my two ears with his open palms, making my ears ring, whatever his mood—which seemed to change instantaneously sometimes, confusing me —happened to be. Now, as I left the half banana in its hull, I thought, *Someone in this big family will come along and eat the rest long before it spoils, so why worry?* At a quarter of nine, I heard my father's car upon the road, barreling toward the house and in a few moments, he was in the yard. My father drove like a bat out of hell and my mother used to call him Joe Mashup because he was always fixing it if it made the slightest noise. I waited, not at all sure of how to greet him as Mother had said he was annoyed with me for delaying to reveal the job offer to them. Now, he walked towards me, bag in hand, a handsome, heavy set man with a booming voice, and ready smile, who loved people, but who had a temper when he was crossed. People called him Prince. Today, he was brief in his salutations.

"Mawning, me dahter. How's de mawning?"

He spoke to me as he approached the doorway where I was standing. Once he spoke to me, I moved quickly to take the suitcase from his hands and walk with him the few remaining steps to the door.

"Mawning, Papa. I glad to see you."

He had smiled, but only momentarily so, entered the house, said hello briefly to my mother who had come in to the front room by now, listened to her report about the proposed journey, then turned to me: "Jaye, get yuh tings on; we a going to dat convent school fuh see da Mudda Superior 'bout de job offer."

I turned, "Yes, Papa, right away," ran to my room, quickly donned a dress and shoes, brushed my hair down at the sides and returned to find Papa in the front room, alone, Mother having gone back to her room.

"Ready?" He said, rising as I re-entered the room.

"Yes, Papa, I ready."

And with that, he called out to Mother that we were leaving, we climbed into the truck, and in a few minutes, had reached the school two miles away, where we went straight to the Mother Superior's office. Papa accepted the job, thanked Sister for recommending me, and in less than a half hour, we were back at home. Papa had said little to me either coming or going, and had handled most of the conversation in the Mother Superior's office. When he reached the house, Mother was still in her room, though I could hear her moving around occasionally. Papa sat down in the living room, and I went to the kitchen, made a cool drink for him and me, served him, and went to get his slippers, then sat down with my drink. Soon, Papa spoke.

"Congratulations, me dahter. I know yuh habe it in yuh to mek one success a yuh life. I happy fuh you. Tank God. Yuh done yuh Papa proud."

Papa said all this as if he had just arrived, had just met me after his absence. I suppose that he had been saving what he had to say until he had been sure I had the job by hearing it from the lips of the Mother Superior himself.

I replied demurely, "Thank you, Papa," feeling for once that I might really deserve some of the praise he was always heaping on me.

"Mek yuh worrie bout nutten. Me cousin live on Bonsai, good place for yuh to stay. She tek care a yuh. Ennyway, ah talk to me friends what come frum Bonsai on de job, dey give me one whole list a people fuh contact when we mek it dere, places to choose fum fuh yuh to stay. Nevah worrie, I pick de best place fuh yuh!"

He had by now pulled a scrap of paper from his shirt pocket on which were scrawled the names of people on Bonsai who rented to professionals, mostly teachers who came to work on Bonsai. Papa then continued.

"We a lebe heah Wednesday, get yuh set up. ah come back on Sunday 'pon de boat. Den ah go back to work, satisfied, knowing me dahter inna de best place." He concluded this last quietly and with so much feeling I felt my eyes water. Jumping up, I hugged him without invitation, the first time since I was a little girl. He accepted it graciously, lingering, patting me on the back, and saying something that sounded like, "Me baby, me baby," under his breath. When he finally released me, I was a little embarrassed, shy about my unrestraint, but glancing at my father, saw that he was well pleased, and though I couldn't swear it, I think it was a tear he brushed away when he turned his head. I continued to sit next to Papa on the settee, not saying anything, just happy to be in his presence without anyone else being around. Minutes passed in the comfortable silence that followed our embrace, and all was right in my world. There was nothing to infringe then—neither embarrassment, fear, nor Amite's anger. Nothing at all could disturb my peace. Finally, Mom came in to ask if he wanted lunch before the little ones arrived from school for theirs and the silence was broken. I went off to my room to do more packing and think about my future. That afternoon, one of the girls from the convent school stopped by our house on her way home to bring me a note from the Mother Superior.

"Miss Bartholomew," the note read, "Please come to the school tomorrow to see me. Sister Mary Paul." Now, I was struck with dread again. I had just seen Sister a few hours earlier with my father that morning. Why did she want to see me now? She had seemed so pleased when we had accepted the offer earlier in the day. Had they changed their minds about me? Surely, they hadn't. Still, I could not imagine what it was that Sister Mary Paul wanted to see me about. I spent a half worried Monday evening, but was, thankfully, distracted by all the goings on related both to my father's being home and my leaving on Wednesday. Tuesday morning, at eight o'clock, I was sitting in Sister Mary Paul's office, waiting for her to finish monitoring the halls as there were still a few students headed from homeroom devotion to their first classes. Sister Mary Paul entered the office, stern faced behind the habit—she did not like to smile as did Sister Angela—and motioned for me to take a seat after I stood to greet her. She congratulated me on being the faculty's unanimous choice for the job on Bonsai, and then launched into a lecture about just what is expected of a young convent teacher. As she talked, I had relaxed, knowing now that the job was not being snatched away just when I had gotten used to the idea. *It is the same speech Granny gave me on Sunday*, I thought, *just dressed up in Sunday church clothes*, and thinking of the analogy, I smiled. Sister Mary Paul looked at me sharply, probably thinking I was being disrespectful, and I quickly returned my face to its former somberness and listened to the balance of the lecture. When she arose, shortly thereafter and smoothed down her robes, indicating that the meeting was over, I hastened to rise myself, thanked her, almost curtsied like Granny, and turned to leave the room, almost colliding with Sister Angela in the doorway.

"Well, hello, Jaye. I knew you were here," she said, shifting a load of books she was carrying in her arms, "so I came down to bring you these teaching manuals. Keep them for a while, make sure you read them before you go to Bonsai and return them to me whenever you can. Peace be with you!" She placed the books on the counter, gave me a hug and a smile, and was gone. And that was the way of the nuns—the Sisters of the Holy Family. They never pressed, just always tried to do whatever would help.

***

Likewise, Sister Deer—from the Order of the Sacred Heart nuns—had shown up at the airstrip in Largo this morning as promised although my friend Mrs. Orlando had done no such thing. I stretched my leg out into the aisle of the plane, wondering where we were in the air. Yes, you could depend on the nuns for sure. Yala looked over at me from her place on the opposite side of the plane. I managed a half smile in spite of my reticence to feel safe, but she did not respond, looked away instead. Ok, I think. Maybe I deserve that. I glance at the rest of my brood. The two littlelest ones are sleeping soundly. Amite, Jr. (Amos) is obviously still in wonder. He seems unable to really believe we have gotten away. So he vacillates—smiles, then frowns, looks carefree, then worried.

I must look like that, too, I think, because I am relieved to be escaping, yet frightened that I may be wrong about running away with our children.

12

Just two years ago, I had begun working with community women in Tall Palms and established a local economic development group. Under our own label, we canned fruit jams and jellies from cashew, mango, and guava, and sold them to the grocery stores in town or placed them in other outlets, like the local hotel, that catered to tourists. We also made plantain chips, vending them mostly on Saturdays to downtown shoppers. Our group was called My Sister's Place, a name that was inspired by our having to work alternately at each other's houses whenever we wanted to can a batch of jams and jellies since we had no building of our own in which to operate. I had worked hard with the group, spending some time fundraising as well as teaching the women the importance of quality control and consistency in product development. We were also able to secure some equipment and supplies from a church group in the States. In addition to processing the fruits, I also made cupcakes on my own and would send my oldest boy, Amos, into town on Fridays and Saturdays to sell them. Amite always stressed the importance of self sufficiency and we tried to teach it to the children by giving them projects of their own whenever possible. My Sister's Place took up a lot of time from my already pinched schedule. I retained few profits for myself but I still had the concern for others instilled in me by the nuns as a child.

I liked doing good works. I found the school atmosphere where I worked to be stultifying, macho-led, and not a place for flexing one's mind or muscles. At school, my "good works" were largely confined to being the best teacher I could be, helping individual students with their many problems and being content when the greater portion of students scoring highest in English on the CXC exams were the ones I taught. So My Sister's Place was largely an emotional outlet for me. The women, all of them married, in long term relationships or single mothers, were of varying ages, and had little and sometimes no income. There were few jobs in Largo for anybody without a profession so most people who were not born into a prosperous family had little opportunity to rise above poverty. In Tall Palms where I had lived, six miles from Rivertown, most people had a little spot of land, usually surrounding their house, where they could grow plantains or other food. The women were unused to balancing what they were spending in relationship to income brought in as they had no experience with cost analysis. Working with the group, I initiated a bookkeeping system, keeping careful track of expenses and income for the group, and providing an example for women to follow in their personal lives. We had a few successes and some failures but had been gradually developing camaraderie from within, even though petty bickering had to be warded off constantly.

The men were no help as the culture did not place a money value on women's work. Even when women were turning a profit with My Sister's Place, bringing new money into the household, many of the men would become annoyed if the woman had to spend extra time at My Sister's Place on canning or demonstration days. If we worked longer hours than they thought necessary or a meeting went on too long, it was not unusual for a child to come running to report that the husband wanted the wife to come home to prepare his food.

Likewise, the Largo Rural Women's Group was a new concept in Largo, reaching as it did the most marginal women, and they, too, experienced much resistance to the work they were doing, often, and in various forms. Many women, for example, had never been to a meeting before the establishment of the Largo Rural Women's Group. They were timid, frightened, and embarrassed to talk about themselves. The Village council almost always consisted of men only. Indeed, most women saw it as the domain of men, and did not even bother to attend the meetings. Economics was only one aspect of the Largo Rural Women's Group. They addressed health and self-esteem issues, social concerns, and education, as well. My Sister's Place only dealt with economics, however, primarily because I did not want to try to initiate too many new ideas at once, and because I did not want to spread myself too thin. Money was scarce in everybody's household, however, so there was little need to try to convince anyone of the validity of what we were doing by trying to make money. The only threat seemed to be that we wanted to do it together.

At the urging of Bea, I had, a year earlier, recommended to My Sister's Place that we become an associate member of the Largo Rural

Women's Group, although I had some apprehensions about hooking up with so large an entity fearing that our little group might get swallowed up. But Bea had pointed out that there were benefits to be derived from affiliating with the Largo Rural Women's Group: they regularly held workshops in different parts of the country, and were able to bring in speakers and resource people who could assist with local training and development needs.

In January, 1989, Yala and I went to a health workshop at the invitation of the woman, Therese, who headed the Largo Rural Women's Group. The workshop was being held in a beachside village called Shark's Point fifteen miles away. We, Yala and I, rose early and, along with several community women, took the transport—a large, overcrowded flatbed truck with built up fenders on the side—to Shark's Point. The trip took nearly an hour because the roads in Largo were largely unpaved in rural areas, rutted and dusty, and when the rains came, were sometimes impassable. The relative isolation of rural areas made it all the more important that the Largo Rural Women's Group was bringing workshops to the women instead of holding it in town the way more conventional groups tended to do.

A black women's group from the States had been brought in to conduct a workshop called "Black and Female: I Know the Reality." Sessions were structured around the attendees participating after the leader had opened up the discussion. The issue this day was the lack of self esteem among women and their resulting inability to love, value, and care for themselves. A few women soon opened up and described their situations and the group leader patiently tried to address each one's specific problems, stressing the need for self-love before we can truly love others. She pointed out that many women suffer from hidden abuse—mental, emotional, physical, and sexual; and that women in every social strata—even professional women—suffer such abuse because they feel it is their lot in life, are ashamed to tell anyone, and assume that they are alone in their pain. The leader cited statistics from the States garnered from her work there which showed that such abuse befalls an alarming number of women. As I sat in the meeting that day listening to all that was being said, hearing women venture out on a limb to share their stories, I became more and more dismayed. I could see myself in some of the stories but knew that I would never take the floor and share mine the way some of the women were doing. Besides, I reasoned, I was a professional, unlike most of the women there, and I did not want my life to be the subject of gossip mongers. Living in Largo, I knew that everybody knew everybody else's business and talked about it in detail. A woman would look at another in wide-eyed innocence and say, 'Why did you leave your husband?' or something equally personal. I looked at Yala, who appeared to be enjoying the meeting, nodding her head here and there, seemingly agreeing with the workshop leader. I had to get permission from Amite to bring Yala to the meeting explaining and promising that it was not Stateside "women's liberation stuff." Amite did not feel that such meetings served any purpose, was suspicious of Therese and women in the Largo Rural Women's Group, and would snidely remark from time to time that they were too busy helping others and had no time left to take care of their own families. Besides, he was fond of saying, whenever he objected to the time I spent with My Sister's Place, most women were poor because they had lazy men who wouldn't work to support them. Amite had felt especially justified in thumbing his nose at the Largo Rural Women's Group because a few years earlier, the husband of one of the most active women in the Group had an affair with their adopted teenage daughter. Amite had blamed the whole thing on the wife, saying that she was away from the man too much.

"What did she expect? She asked for it," was his pronouncement on the matter. He never once blamed the husband unless I persisted in pointing out that the affair had to do with a deficit in the man's character, and that the woman's work didn't enter into it. This was only a mental exercise for Amite, however, because whenever the subject came up again, we were back at square one. Always, Amite eventually drew the same conclusion: "She asked for it!" Amite's position, unfortunately, was fairly typical of most of the good men of Largo and even the woman's father, an educated man, told her the same thing:

"You leave young gial in you house, go way to help other people. It is your fault; you asked for that! What you expect?"

I was concerned at the health workshop that the impressions Yala was getting would suit her father's taste because I knew that every detail she could remember would be extricated from her as soon as Amite had a chance to query her alone. Finally, there was a break during the afternoon session and I went outside to be alone for a while. The meeting had opened up in my head a lot of doors previously left closed and I was in a state of mental and emotional turmoil. Therese made her way over to me when she got a break to see how I liked the workshop. I told her I thought the workshop was good but wondered how we would deal with all the emotionalism and the wounds left open once the black woman from the States was gone. There was so much distrust among women in Largo, what would we say to each other without the loving intervention and guidance of the resource person? Could we keep each other's secrets or would we put them in the streets, ridicule each other for situations like our own though we might not have been able to verbalize them in the meeting? Therese had looked at me, sadly, kindly, heaved a sigh, said, "I don't know, gial. I just know that it is a chance we have to take. We have to start somewhere. People are hurting too much and they need a place to get rid of it. This is a start, this is the place."

But I had persisted in my pessimism. "But if nothing is done about it, if people don't change, what is the point in telling it to everybody?"

I was a big secrecy advocate; I never told most people how I felt about anything. Talking to Bea was as close as I had come to being honest with another woman. I felt all women were gossips just waiting to get your business. My friendship with Bea had developed over a period of several years. Still, I had not been able to tell Bea about Amite's revealing his relationship with Yala even though I had seen Bea twice since then on her biannual visits back to Largo. I had not been able to tell anybody for that matter, had been unable to voice words. There was a lull in the conversation as we both mulled over the dilemma with Therese insisting that we had to begin talking honestly to each other before we could hope for change in women's situation in Largo.

Standing outside with Therese, I thought more and more of my own situation and its relationship to much that I had heard inside during the morning session, though nobody had been bold enough to speak of incest. Turning my thoughts inward, I was quiet. Therese looked at me.

"So how is Amite? What is your situation like? Any improvement?"

It was the question I had feared she would ask me. Earlier, I had confided to her that Amite had become unreasonable, more and more insistent that I give up my teaching job, sell the farm in Tall Palms and move to a more remote location more than twenty miles away where he was clearing land, a spot off the road without a name and no town in sight. I told Therese I was resisting this, had no intention of leaving my job to go anywhere, but that I had, of course, not said this outright to Amite. I had been stalling for time, trying to string him along, hoping for a miracle. Now, Therese looked at me again out of soft brown eyes that appeared to see right through me. "Well, what is the problem? Why do you think he wants to go into the woods, get away from civilization?"

I told her I thought Amite might be having mental problems again. She knew that he had been quite upset a year ago. Now, I related to her how he was taking the children to the bush—Amos, Hannibal, and Yala—for three or four days a week in a thatch roofed shed he had built, and that it bothered me but I could not stop him from taking the children.

"Why can't you stop him?" Therese wanted to know. I had responded that he would not listen to me, that they were his children and his position was that he could do with them whatever he wanted. Practically speaking, I told her, there was no way I would sell my house and move.

"Where would we live? What would we use for money?"

Now, Therese looked at me even more closely. "When is Yala going to school? Doesn't she mind going to the bush chopping like a man?"

I again explained Amite's position with the children, and that he was still refusing to let Yala go away to college even though she had graduated three and a half years earlier. There was so much to explain that I was becoming weary of Therese's questioning. She was a progressive woman, had been educated at university like I was, and though she had suffered a great deal herself in personal relationships, she was still able to do pretty much as she pleased. We had once taught together at Rivertown High years ago, but Therese had been very political even then. When she had to take maternity leave during the summer holidays, the board of education had used the excuse to fire her. The situation had been totally unjust, and the refusal to grant the leave based on spurious reasoning. However, since our salaries were prorated over twelve months, we were technically employed during the summer holidays though we did not report to work for two months. The stipulation was included that we had to be ready, willing, and able to work, if called, though in point of fact, we were never called. Since Therese was asking for maternity leave, she would not be "available" for work. So went the spurious reasoning of the board and they used the excuse to promptly fire Therese. I had felt particular pain for Therese at the time but, I, like the rest of the teachers on staff, had done little to challenge the board or otherwise come to her aid. Therese had fought valiantly and I believe, eventually won against the board, though she never returned to Rivertown High to teach. But we women, most of us in our childbearing years, had done little beyond sign a letter of protest about the board's actions. I would console myself by saying that it was Therese's politics that had gotten her fired. She was considered radical by the principal and other pseudo politicians of Largo. However, deep inside, I knew that was a cop out and I silently carried the guilt about not fighting harder alongside Therese in the situation. Standing there under the palms by the sea, smarting from Therese's even handed gentle probing, I wondered just how much I could tell her. She had known Yala in school, and admired her abilities, and she now began to talk about how smart Yala was and how she deserved better in these modern times than chopping bush with her father and brother. Couldn't I do something? At this, I began to relate some of Amite's actions, how he and Yala had refused to spend their birthdays with the family as was our custom and had insisted on going off alone to celebrate together; how we—the other children and I—had fought them over it. Amite did not believe in holidays so our compromise was to make holidays of each family member's birthday and celebrate together at home. At mention of this, Therese's eyes narrowed, but she remained quiet. I saw her glance around, and realized that the workshop was reconvening. I began to make ready to re-enter. Therese calmly waved her hand, dismissed the need to return, "Let it go. Workshop take care of itself, gial. We need to talk."

She then steered me even further away from the center, found a place for us to sit underneath a tree, told me to start over. I did. And told her everything, what I was feeling at the meeting that morning, how I thought Amite might be having a nervous breakdown even though he seemed very sane, and finally, I was able to form the words that I had been unable to voice out loud since Amite had said them to me one year ago: Amite had had sexual intercourse with Yala, had admitted it to me, said it happened only once, and promised that it would not happen again. When I finished, I was crying. For the first time in years, I broke down and cried.

Therese was quiet, listened to the whole thing, and when I was through, she finally spoke: "Gial, looks like you got to do something, you know. Some big decisions you got to make. Something wrong, bad wrong, with Amite. You need to do something, Jaye."

Now, I didn't know what to do. I was embarrassed that I had told Therese about Amite, and immediately felt as if I had just betrayed my husband's confidence. After all, the rationale that I had given myself for staying with Amite after his admission had been that he would never do that again, that the sordid act had been a one-time aberration occasioned by stress, that we would all have to get over it. I saw no way out. Leaving Amite was unthinkable. We had four children, were a good family, so why break up the family? Besides, I didn't know where to go. It was best to try to work it out. But I could not see any improvement in the situation. As a matter of fact, I viewed Amite's insistence on our leaving civilization as a worsening of his mental state, which spelled calamity because I knew that he would never voluntarily seek help.

When I left the workshop that Saturday, I was full of conflicting emotions. On the one hand, I was glad that I had told Therese, but on the other, I worried. I felt extreme loyalty to Amite and had always felt that he was loyal to us as a family. Although I had discussed misgivings about Amite and Yala's relationship with Bea both before and after his confession a year earlier, I had never told her that I knew of the incest even though she had pointedly told me on more than one occasion that she thought they were "too close." I would simply take her observations, we would discuss them, and when I left, I would analyze what she had said in relationship to what I knew and hadn't told her.

In November, 1988, ten months after Amite's confession, Bea happened to be visiting Largo during the week leading up to Yala and Amite's birthdays, which are only one day apart. The incident had been particularly upsetting to me and I had gone to Bea's house to talk about it between breaks at school. On the day I told her, I had found her reading, catching a sea breeze, with the door open in the front room of her cottage. Appearing happy for the unexpected visit, she quickly put the book down and came to greet me as I hailed her from the front verandah.

Bea is a large woman, not fat, having a stature that some people refer to as imposing. She wore her hair natural and in the heat of the tropics, usually kept it pulled back or neatly braided in small plaits. In Largo, her standard uniform was cotton shorts and blouses, and bathing suits for the sea where she swam daily. Inside her house, she was usually barefoot, a throwback, she would laughingly say, to her cotton field, dirt road days growing up in the rural South in the States. Although Largo was a foreign land for her, she understood a lot about the people, not just because they were black, but largely because Largotian technology, development, social conditions, and attitudes—in a word, culture—was very much like the South she had known as a child some thirty years earlier.

Some days when I needed a break from the tedium of school or just to talk to somebody, I would borrow a co-worker's bicycle and speed the two miles to her house during my forty minute between-class break. Bea often commented that we always had to talk fast, because I was always rushed, and she would say the word f-a-s-t, pushing it out in a rush, laughing. That day, I was still angry from the morning argument I'd had with Amite and Yala, a three-day running dispute leading up to their birthdays. I began to tell Bea the story. "That Amite makes me so angry. He knows he is breaking the rules. If I said I was going to do something like this, he would have a fit. But he won't listen to me, thinks he is right. I am very upset; the children are upset. Birthdays are all we have. I don't think he should get away with this."

Bea was at first irreverent, trying to tease me out of my anger.

"So what do you care how he spends his birthday, Jaye? Can't y'all still have a celebration without him?"

I refused to be mollified. "That is not the point. The point is we made a pact. The children can't celebrate Easter, Christmas, New Years or any of the holidays other people celebrate. Many times, he deliberately puts them to work chopping or weeding on the holiday itself and they know that celebration is in the air for everybody but them. All they have is everybody's birthday and we make big occasions of each one as a family. Now he is saying he and Yala don't want to be a part of any family celebrations on their birthdays this year and they are planning to come to town for dinner to celebrate, just the two of them."

Bea was moving about the kitchen, offering me a cool drink, gesturing to ask if I wanted watermelon. I took the drink, shook my head on the melon. Now, she stopped with a piece of melon in her hand in midair: "Just the two of them? Why don't they want to celebrate with the family?"

I had spat out: "They want to be alone."

At this, Bea set the melon down, passed by me where I was standing in the doorway between her kitchen and dining area, pulled out two chairs at her dining table, offered me a seat. I shook my head, too angry to sit and remained in the doorway. She spoke again.

"Why does it upset you so?"

I looked at her, wondering why she asked since I had just explained about not having any other holidays to celebrate. I launched into a repeat of what I had just said, the pact we had, and Bea cut me off.

"I know. I know. I understand all that. But it is, after all, only a pact, a little family rule as you put it. Why can't they deviate this year? Why are you so upset about it?"

I had blustered, "Because it's not fair; they have no right to do that. I don't see why they have to go off and leave the kids and me without a celebration."

Bea had persisted: "But it is only a celebration, Jaye. Can't you and the kids have a little party at home? You say Yala and her father are close, so maybe they want to talk about something special, celebrate their birthdays in a different way together—I didn't know their birthdays were only a day apart; maybe that's why they're so close—be alone and talk...."

I had interrupted, "But they don't have any right to go off to be alone and leave us at home!"

Now, Bea asked: "Did you suggest he take the whole family to dinner?"

I said I had. "But he won't hear of it; he says that's the point; they want to be alone."

Now, Bea took a sip of water and looked at me again. "So, it's their wanting to be alone that bothers you, huh, Jaye?"

I was taken aback: "What do you mean?"

Bea stood up, walked around the living room as she often did when talking. "See, Jaye, if I were in the situation, I would do one of two things. Either say "hell, no" to Yala, forbid her to go or totally ignore them. Let them have all the dinners they want in that funky little Chinese restaurant where the food ain't even Chinese because those people have been here so long they've forgotten how to cook Chinese food. Ever hear of anybody using canned vegetables to cook Chinese food? And if I didn't want my children to be disappointed, I would throw a big celebration for them without Yala and Amite and forget it."

I had continued to protest, angrily: "I can't forbid her to go with him. She's his child. He can take her wherever he wants. What I am going to do is this. When my birthday comes, I won't honor the rule either. I am going off on my birthday by myself to celebrate and do the same thing to them."

Bea had turned back to me. "Jaye, do you know what you sound like? You sound like a jealous lover. Like you have to pay your lover back for hurting you with another woman. Why?"

"But they have no right to go off alone!"

At this Bea looked at me again, said evenly: "Why are you making such a big issue of it? If you acted like you didn't care, they would probably abandon the whole idea. But look at you. They have you totally upset about something slightly trivial. I'll bet old Amite is enjoying this." I jumped back in. "He is! But he refuses to budge. No matter what I say, he says that is what they are going to do. They want to be alone."

Bea spoke again: "But they are alone everyday at the house, aren't they? They have plenty of time to talk. He is just antagonizing you, Jaye, forget it."

But the matter was plenty serious to me, so I continued. "They spend too much time together anyway. I think he fantasizes about her, you know, trying to relive his youth. She looks like I used to look, you know, when she is sitting there playing that guitar. And they take walks together in the mornings after I leave for school. Sister told me she sees them walking together. I just think it's unhealthy."

Bea asked, "The walking?" Bea had a way of dragging stuff out of you.

"No, the relationship. I think they spend entirely too much time together. Everything that comes out of Yala's mouth is vintage Amite, something he has said at one time or another."

Bea finally spoke again: "You know, it is possible that he has an unnatural fixation on her, and is trying to recapture his youth, as you say. My friend had a classmate in college whose father got custody of her in a divorce when she was small. She couldn't get away from her father. And when she finally came to college, her father felt he had begun to lose control—which he had—and so he panicked. When she was about to graduate from college and her daddy found out that she would not be returning home to live with him, he lured her home on some pretext, had an argument with her and killed her. Shot her to death."

"Killed her? Her father!"

Bea nodded: "And got away with it, too. He was a businessman. She had told her friends that he 'bothered' her but never went into details. He was very strict, kept tabs on her even when she was away in school. He would track her down on any pretext. Amite could be in a similar situation, trying to relive something he thinks he's lost, through Yala. That's dangerous, crazy."

Now that Bea was giving some credibility to my thoughts, I continued: "And she is becoming more and more stubborn and opinionated just like him. It is difficult to reason with her anymore. She used to talk to me. Now, all that I hear out of her mouth is what Amite thinks. I can just hear him coming through her. She is like a parrot. He is turning my child against me, Bea. I can't do anything with her anymore."

Now, Bea turned to look at me questioningly: "What do you mean?"

"Everything, nothing big, just little things. Like, he hates Therese. Yala used to like and admire Therese, always stopped to talk to her whenever she saw her. Now, she has nothing good to say about Therese or the work she does with the Largo Rural Women's Group. She didn't always feel that way. Amite is changing her slowly but surely. Turning her against me and people I like. Every time I try to tell her something, he intervenes. Last week, after supper, she took a bath, put on a thin nightgown and came back out to the dining-living area where the rest of the family was sitting around, including her father and Amos. I looked at the thing she was wearing. There she was, pretty rosebud breasts, nipples sticking up, pointed out against nylon and lace, nothing underneath. 'Yala,' I said, 'go and put on some clothes if you plan to be in here.' She stuck out her lip, didn't move, Amite piped up: 'Leave the child alone, Jaye. If she can't be comfortable at home, where can she relax?' While we were talking, Yala jumped up and went into her bedroom, and Amite followed her and stood in the doorway, continuing the conversation he'd been having with her prior to the incident. We have rules about that also. If one of us chastises the children, the other doesn't interfere in front of them with something in opposition, even when we disagree. It seems like a little thing but...."

Bea cut me off: "And she didn't put on a robe?"

"No, she does what her father tells her, and she's worn the same nightie in the sitting room since then. I'm worried. I told you about that lady at the store where they sometimes stop to pick up food and supplies in the truck. I don't know what she saw, but she said to me: 'Mrs. Peay, Ah know it none a me bizness, but ah me tink you husband and you dahter—well, someting wrong bout dey relationship. Me nevah like it. I tink to tell yuh.' She is not a gossiping lady. What did she see, Bea?"

At mention of the woman, Bea seemed a little alarmed.

"Damn! She said that to you? What did she see? Well, you know Largotians don't have too close relationships with their children, holding big conversations with 'em and all like Amite and Yala do. They're like folk when I was a child—children are to be seen and not heard—so maybe it was just that. But why would she have the nerve to comment on it to you? You know, Jaye, folk don't talk to people about their husbands or wives too fast, even in Largo, especially when it comes to something that might stir up trouble. That could be serious. And you know Amite doesn't let Yala go anywhere or see any boys. Did you question the lady. No? Girl, you better watch out, you're treading on dangerous ground. He could be like that man back home, you know. It didn't come out until she died, but he'd been having sex with his daughter since she was in her early teens. And he didn't serve any time for killing her either. How old is Yala now, sixteen? And you know it took a lot for that old lady to say that much to you so *it just ain't no telling WHAT she saw.* Don't you want to know what she meant?"

I had begun to worry a little as I listened to Bea: "Well, I took it to mean what you just said, that people aren't used to seeing parents really relate to their children the way Amite does with Yala, and I didn't ask her what she meant because I didn't want to feed it, whatever it was she was thinking. So I let it alone, chalked it up to that."

Now, Bea was being the inquisitor: "How well do you know her? Is she somebody you chit chat with?"

At this I shook my head no.

"Then, why in the world do you think she would get up enough nerve to say something to you about your husband and daughter? I think you ought to want to know!"

"But, Bea, I decided...."

Bea cut me off: "And you know what else, Jaye, the more I think about it, the more it bothers me, when you put all those things together that you just got through talking about. If he's not already fucking her, then he soon will be!" This last bit was too much for me, so I didn't comment, just let it fall, with a thud, and lie there on the floor between us. Bea, realizing what she had said, hastened to try to soften it.

"You know, Jaye, sometimes people have to be protected from themselves, especially when they're going through an emotional thing."

I couldn't talk anymore, mumbled, "Yes, maybe. Well, Bea, I got a class to get to. See you later, and hey, thanks for listening." I jumped on the bicycle and pedaled back to school, arriving just as the tardy bell sounded for students to go to my fourth period English class.

Why had Bea reached that conclusion? Should I have reached it? Bea only knew what I told her, what she saw. She did not know what I knew about Amite admitting he'd had sex once with Yala. Was it that obvious? I must have sounded like I was jealous of Yala's being with Amite because Bea had drawn the conclusion. Should I have told Bea of the incident? No. It would only have confirmed what she already thought. How could I do that? What would she think of me? Of Amite? God, it is my family! If only I could get Yala away to school! Then I could be sure it wouldn't happen again. But Amite was refusing to talk about schooling for Yala, had begun to insist that she could study at home. He had become even more adamant about her not going away to school after Yala's chemistry teacher had made improper advances to her a second time last year. I had finally related both incidents to Bea but had been careful to leave out the fact that on both occasions when the chemistry teacher had been confronted, he had insisted that Yala had told him her father was molesting her. What would Bea think if she knew that?

When Yala was a senior in high school, she, at her father's insistence, had begun to undergo special tutoring in chemistry from a teacher at Rivertown High, Mr. Ervin, my co-worker. She was more drawn to the arts but Amite wanted her to study science. He contended that blacks were being deliberately pushed away from the sciences, into the arts because whites felt we were only good for singing and dancing naturally. His reasoning was if that were the case, then why study that? No, Yala needed to become a scientist or perhaps a doctor. Since she was a bright student anyway, she took to the chemistry classes with the zeal that she gave to any academic challenge, and seemed to like the instruction she was receiving.

I had no inkling that trouble was afoot until Christmas of 1984. That was the first time. We had been on Christmas holidays from school for at least a week and Yala and her father were chopping in back when Mr. Ervin rode up on his bicycle. We were all, of course, surprised to see him and wondering why he was there since it was a six mile trip from Rivertown. I knew him better than Amite since I worked with him and as we had no phone I thought at first that his visit might have something to do with school. I was, by then, in the doorway, so I invited him inside, and Yala and Amite came in from outside as well. We made small talk as I moved about the kitchen getting a cool drink for Mr. Ervin, as it was of course, hot, and the six mile trip he had biked was over unpaved road. Mr. Ervin and Amite talked about some black books he noticed in the sitting room in Yala's library and he spoke of his daughter, Electra, who was a friend of Yala's. I was wondering again why Mr. Ervin had come. Tall Palms is on the way to nowhere fast except a few scattered villages miles away down the road, and Capitol City almost a hundred miles away. So I knew he had come to see us for a purpose, was not casually stopping by, and in spite of the conversation, the air was pregnant with our waiting. Finally, when there was no more small talk to be made, Mr. Ervin pulled from his pocket a small box wrapped in Christmas paper, presented it to Yala and said it was her Christmas present. At first, I thought the present was from Electra since she and Yala were good friends but Mr. Ervin made it clear that the present was from him. Yala appeared a little shy but pleased, thanked Mr. Ervin and he left shortly after that, his whole visit taking up about three quarters of an hour. Yala walked Mr. Ervin to the roadside down the lane away from the house and I stood in the doorway watching him depart. I noticed that Yala shooed Hannibal and Nefertiti away, back to the house, when the children attempted to accompany them on the walk. Yala spent about five minutes chatting with Mr. Ervin at the end of the lane before he mounted his bicycle and rode away. I returned to my household chores, Yala and Amite went back to chopping out back and I didn't think too much about the matter after that.

Two days later, I was in the kitchen cooking, Amite and Yala were outside chopping, when Amite stopped and came into the house, saying he needed to talk to me. He looked agitated, asked for water, and upon my giving it to him, said: "Sit down."

I did as he directed, looked at him expectantly, and he began. "I have bad news. Mr. Ervin has been fooling with Yala." I immediately grasped what he was talking about, responded, "You have to be crazy!"

Amite said, "No, she says he has. I questioned her about that present, why a grown man, a teacher, would come all the way out here just to give her, a student, a present, and she admitted that he has been fondling her."

I was enraged. The nerve of that man! "I am going to that school. I am going to kill Mr. Ervin! Something has to be done. I will kill him myself. I am not waiting around for that Mr. Posey. I will kill Ervin!"

Amite tried to calm me. "No, Jaye. School is like that. It doesn't make sense to stir up one whole lotta trouble. That's just the way school is."

I refused to listen to Amite. I taught at the school. I knew what went on there. I was determined to have justice, make Mr. Ervin pay. The principal did not have a good track record with me when it came to such matters, but always before, I had never been personally involved. Now I was, and something had to be done about Mr. Ervin's thinking he could molest my child and get away with it. The nerve, the gall!

A few years earlier, Sister Deer and I had gone to the principal, Mr. Posey, to obtain permission to conduct sex education classes at school. Posey had made a joke out of it, in an attempt, I suppose, to shame Sister into backing off. "Sister Deer. You are obsessed with sex!"

Undaunted, since he did not forbid us, we had gone ahead with our plans. Part of the program involved bringing in speakers to talk with the children about their bodies, their right not to be molested either by others their own age or adults. The first speaker was excellent. She talked about how some adults will try to take advantage of children, and said that it happens in the home as well as with strangers. She was a bit elitist, however, and said that poor people's homes are small and sleeping arrangements are many times tight and this allowed some adults to take advantage of the forced intimacy to molest children or other family members. I intervened to point out that molestation is not confined to the poor who have little privacy in their households, but that it happens in the spacious homes of the rich as well. Nonetheless, the speaker was effective and invited the children to write to her about anything they chose. Within a week or so, the speaker contacted me to say that she had received many letters from the students and that two letters in particular had upset her. One letter spoke about the past—the student asserted that teachers at Rivertown High had been having sex with students, that the principal knew about it and condoned it, that nothing was ever done about it. The second letter she referred to contained an allegation of a teacher currently abusing a student sexually and that nothing was being done about it. I went to Mr. Posey and related the information to him. Mr. Posey said that he was appalled that our students had made such accusations and that if someone would only come forward he would address the situation immediately. Of course, no one did, so the matter died. Amite was aware of the incident mentioned by name in the letter as

I had related the story to him when it happened. Amite had not liked the idea of the sex education classes himself. Yala, who was then about nine and in the ninth grade, had been in the sex education classes, and when her father questioned her, had related the part about parents abusing their children. Amite had been angry, said Sister Deer was a nun, didn't know anything about sexuality, was not qualified to teach sex education because of that, and that her teachings would cause children to be afraid of their parents. Now, Amite brought up the incident and used it as an example that the school, namely, Mr. Posey, would not do anything to help us in the situation with Mr. Ervin. I refused to listen to his reasoning. "This is my daughter, and Yala has to go to that school. She deserves to be protected. I will not stand by and do nothing about this."

Amite asked if I had a plan. I said no, but that I would get Mrs. Orlando to help. Mrs. Orlando was a coworker who was very much liked and respected at school, a person who had befriended me and Yala. Mrs. Orlando was shocked and agreed to help. I went into town before school started up again. Mrs. Orlando phoned Mr. Ervin and got him to the school on some pretext, and we—Amite, Mrs. Orlando, Yala, and I— had a chance to confront Mr. Ervin. "Mr. Ervin, I hear that you have been molesting my daughter."

Mr. Ervin began his response by expounding on what a respectable man he was. "Mrs. Peay, I would never do such a thing. I am a father, a teacher, a respectable man. I would never engage in such conduct. No way! It is her father."

I looked at Amite, shocked myself, to find him calmly shaking his head, seemingly in disbelief that Mr. Ervin would stoop so low, "Mr. Ervin, Oh Mr. Ervin," he said.

Mr. Ervin continued to accuse Amite, saying: "Yala says you're the one who is messing with her, but that you don't feel that she is sexually mature, though." I was so angry that I began screaming at the top of my voice, and the others had to keep me away from Mr. Ervin. "If you so much as breathe on my daughter again, I will kill you. You are going to get a chance this time because no sexual intercourse appears to be involved. I had better not hear one word about you, nothing about you, you hear? I am going to be watching every step you take, and I will get you. Don't you ever forget it! I am going to the principal."

"Fine, if you've already told him, then he won't be surprised when I go to him."

Throughout this time, Yala had been crying, kept repeating to Mr. Ervin, "But you told me you loved me! You lied to me! You said you loved me!"

Finally, with the meeting over, Amite went home, and Mrs. Orlando and I had a chance to talk in the teacher's room. She seemed to share my disbelief about Mr. Ervin's accusations, feeling as I did that it was a desperate attempt on his part to exonerate himself by having us look elsewhere for the culprit. Nonetheless, we decided it was better to be safe than sorry so we took Yala to Mrs. Orlando's house nearby to talk to her. Yala liked Mrs. Orlando a lot, seemed comfortable with her, and spent time around her at school, Mrs. Orlando began first:

"Yala, you heard the accusation Mr. Ervin made against your father. Is any of that true?"

"What?"

"Is any of that true?"

"No! No! Miss! That's a lie. He is lying on my dad!"

"Are you sure? You can tell us the truth, you know."

"No, Miss. That is not true. How could he say such a thing about my dad?"

I intervened:

"Yala, you don't have to be afraid of anything or anybody. Did you tell Mr. Ervin that your father has been bothering you sexually, trying to fondle you?"

"No, Mom. No. That is not true."

"Yala, this is important. You are my daughter. You are the one I want to protect. Why did Mr. Ervin say those things about your father?"

"I don't know, Mom. It just isn't true!"

"Did you tell him anything, anything at all about your father?"

"No, Mom. I never said any such thing because it's not true. Mr. Ervin is making it up."

"But why, Yala? Why did he say it?"

"I don't know, Mom. I just don't know."

"What did you say to Mr. Ervin about Amite?"

"I never said anything to him about Dad. Nothing, Mom, Honest!"

"But what happened? Tell me again what happened."

"Well, I was in the classroom alone with Mr. Ervin after school. First, he kissed me, then he felt my breasts. That's all that happened."

"What else? What did he say?"

"He told me I was not sexually mature."

"What else?"

"That's all, Mom. Honest."

"Did you tell him Amite bothered you?"

"No, Mom, of course not!"

"Has Amite ever touched your breasts, touched you anywhere sexually?"

"No, Mom, I tell you. NO."

Mrs. Orlando began again:

"Has anybody else other than Mr. Ervin ever tried anything? No? Yala, you've spent time here, and I've already told you when we have our little talks to always tell me if anybody tries anything with you and you know I've even included my husband in that. It is you we are concerned about, Yala, and if anybody has tried to do anything to you, your mother and I need to know so we can protect you. Nobody will do anything to you if you tell. We will see to that. We need to know the truth."

Yala continued to shake her head, no. "Mr. Ervin is just upset because I told on him. He is being mean and spiteful to say those ugly things about dad. That's all."

"So Mr. Peay never tried to fondle you or bother you in any sexual way?"

"No, Mrs. Orlando. He never did."

This conversation, and variations upon it, went on for hours. We would stop, have something to drink or eat, and resume our queries. Yala adamantly maintained that Mr. Ervin was lying. At the end of an exhausting and debilitating session, we finally gave up and decided that Yala was telling the truth. Yala and I went home and on the way, I continued to talk to her about the incident—cajoling, questioning—and praying that I had her trust. She remained steadfast: Mr. Ervin was lying to protect himself. The story about her father had no basis. When we got home, Amite was in the yard working. I went ahead into the house, Yala and I prepared dinner, and the family ate. I decided to lie down for a rest, the emotionalism of the day having totally exhausted me. While lying on the bed, I glanced out the window and saw Amite and Yala near the truck. He was bending over her, talking agitatedly, seemed angry and was pointing his finger in her face. I could not hear what was being said, but could tell by his expression that he was angry. I wondered what it was all about but did not go to investigate, and, drained from the day's events, I soon fell asleep. Later that evening, after the nap, I asked Yala what her father had been saying to her at the truck. "Oh Mom, he said I had better stick to my story about Mr. Ervin. That I had better not think of backing down. Mr. Ervin has to get what he deserves." Amite came in a little later and in our bedroom later that night, we discussed the conference with Mr. Ervin, assessing together what went on there. Amite felt that Mr. Ervin's accusations against him were an effort to retaliate against Yala for having rebuffed his advances. He said he was pretty sure he was giving her lower marks in the sciences trying to mess up her average and affect her future. This, he cried about.

"How in the world can we raise a child, Jaye, with people like that man who is supposed to be a teacher and protector of children going around and trying to spoil innocent young girls and then lying on other people?"

In the days that followed, I was consumed with what had happened, determined that we should go to the principal when he returned (He had been out of town over the holidays). I wanted much more resolution of the matter than I felt from the brief encounter with Mr. Ervin. By the time the holidays were over, Amite convinced me that it would serve no purpose to take the matter up with Mr. Posey, however. He wanted to leave things as they were, keep everything hush-hush, so as not to further subject Yala to any discomfiture when she still had a semester of school left to complete, and since I distrusted Mr. Posey, having seen him operate over the years, including what he had done to get Therese fired a few years earlier, and knowing that women hardly ever won in like situations in Largo, I let Amite talk me into not pursuing the matter. For the remainder of the term, I reasoned, I could protect my daughter from having close contact with Mr. Ervin at school. I figured the least said the better.

13

That was January, 1985. Things finally settled down a bit and life became fairly normal again. In March, I met Bea on her first visit to Largo. She was in Largo for one week and after meeting her at a reception, I picked her up the next day and took her to my house where the children got to meet her, and I had a chance to show her our farm. It was a pleasant interlude and I thought I would never see her again. Yala liked Bea a lot, found her interesting as I did. Although Yala appeared to be doing fine, I still had a bitter taste in my mouth about Mr. Ervin's having molested her. I had to see him at his desk every day in the teacher's room and around the campus but I avoided him like the plague, and he me. I found him odious, and was galled because there was nothing else I could do to seek justice for my daughter. All I could do was keep Yala as far away from him as much as I possibly could considering the fact that he remained one of her teachers. Yala was a student leader then, served as a contributor to the student newspaper, and was valedictorian of her senior class. Soon, all manner of preparations were begun for graduation, and Yala, along with everybody else, was caught up in them. The Education minister was invited to our school as guest speaker for graduation and Yala took the occasion to speak to him about the need for a branch of the junior college in Rivertown. She pointed out to him that some parents were reluctant to send their children off to Capitol City at such a young age when they had previously known only village life, and that many young people did not go beyond high school because of this. Yala had written about the issue in the latest school newspaper so she gave the Education minister copies of her article. The minister was apparently quite impressed by Yala, told her to contact him when she was ready to go to college and he would help her; and furthermore, that he would also see what he could do about implementing her suggestions.

By the fall of 1986, the Minister had made good on his promise and a branch of Largo College was established in Rivertown. Yala had a personal stake in coming up with a solution as she was only thirteen when she graduated from high school, the youngest person to do so in the history of Largo, and Amite had already said that she would have to wait at least a year before going away to college. We had no relatives in Capitol City or all of Largo for that matter, so there was no family to whom we felt we could entrust her care and send her off to school there. Besides, Amite felt that Yala had plenty of time, being only thirteen, and that she should stay home, and learn some practical homemaking skills before going off to college. Amite and I discussed the matter at length and although I was anxious to see Yala get on with her education, I had to agree with him because Capitol City was a tourist haven and when compared to Rivertown and Tall Palms where Yala had grown up, was fast paced, wild, and loose. I longed for Yala to go abroad to school anyway, perhaps with my sister in Canada or with one of Amite's brothers and his wife in the States where we could be sure she was safe; but since we had not settled that question, I reluctantly agreed to Amite's insistence that Yala stay out of school for a year. I reasoned that a year was not that long, would give Yala a chance to become more socially mature, and give us a chance to make a concrete decision about whether to have her go to college in Largo or send her abroad. And because Yala was such a serious student and pushed herself extremely hard, I also thought it might be a good thing for her to have a break from academics. Yala spent that first year at home with her father and baby brother, Hannibal who was two. Nefertiti was six, had started to school and was showing signs of being bright like Yala, although the resemblance between the two pretty much ended there. She and Hannibal were born in Largo and Nefertiti is an outgoing child, lovingly referred to in the family as the "flower" child, a bit on the wild side. Outspoken even as a little girl, she made friends (and enemies) easily, loved to go to school like Yala, but took no "truck" from anyone. Where Yala aimed to please others, was considerate and decorous, Nefertiti mostly aimed to please herself.

And my daughter, Yala? What was she like? When Yala was born, she was my dream come true. She was a good child from conception, a willing, patient companion during my pregnancy as I dragged myself around the university campus fighting to complete my second year of studies during the day and working at a mental institution at night. I was twenty-two, my first born, Amos, was already two. I spent the last months of my pregnancy during summer vacation poring over anything black I could find to read and dreaming about the child I would have. I wanted it to be a girl and I wanted her to be black. I mean real black. I mean blacker than I, beautiful as I wasn't and more intelligent. I got my wish on all three counts. I decided to name her after a character in one of the books I was reading, who had been named for a lake, the most beautiful thing in the world to the people of that African village. I didn't choose any names for a boy because I was certain that God would answer my prayers. Yala was born so small that the doctor at first thought perhaps she was one of twins, but she was a survivor even then. She would spew up all her milk through her nose and I spent the first few months of her life anxious and praying that she would live every time we fought for breath together. She was my sole companion for seven months as I was neither working nor attending school, a new situation for me. It was Yala to whom I talked all the time about my dreams, aspirations, and fears. She was an old lady before she was a child. By her first birthday, she was talking nonstop in full sentences, without ever having gone through the gibberish stage. Yala was the family wonder. Everyone—family, friends, strangers—would remark on her beauty and her exceptional abilities. She was everyone's point of reference: their daughter looked just like her, or their niece was as intelligent, or soon their Jenny would be reading as well, and so on.

Yala was Amite's pet, too, and when I look back, I realize that the only chore Amite ever helped me with around the house was to bathe the kids. He stopped bathing Amos when he was four because we fought over the way he bathed the children. Amite would soap their faces first, then the rest of their bodies, and hold them under the water for unnecessarily long periods. Amos would splutter and struggle and cry, but Yala would bear it with quiet patience. Amite felt that this was an exercise in toughening up and would often tell Amos that he should pattern himself after Yala. At two, Yala was reading and loved indoor games or anything that would keep her close to me or Amite. She never watched television and would choose to mimic anything I was doing at the time. Yala talked nonstop and had an insatiable thirst for knowledge. At five, she could follow a recipe and make a cake. I spent my weekends taking her to children's shows on Saturday mornings and to the park on Sundays. She was sensitive even as an infant, trusting and trustworthy as a child, but timid among strangers, seeming to cry only when there were visitors.

At four, Yala started kindergarten, but after two weeks, we were asked to withdraw her because she was "driving the teacher crazy." It seems that Yala insisted on reading story books instead of playing in the sand pit. As the other children liked to listen to her, she spoiled the teacher's lesson plans. The last straw came in phonetics class when she was supposed to be passing her fingers over the alphabet cards to trace an "a" or "b" and Yala looked at the card and asked: "What does 'all copyrights reserved' mean?"

After that, I enrolled her in foreign language kindergarten in the hope that it would slow her pace a little. However, her speed of learning as an infant characterized her childhood, and since we moved constantly, most of her early education was given at home by me or her father and her childhood experiences were gained mostly from traveling. During those early years, we moved to more and more remote places so that we never had a chance to become too close to anyone; and eventually, we had no extended family at all. Friends were hard to make because of the constant moving, and Amite didn't approve of most people so Yala seldom had anyone who could be called a close friend. Amite and I were her friends, and since I taught school and Amite worked on the farm, Yala spent more time around him. Indeed, Amite was a good teacher, always taught the children at home before sending them off to school at age six, seven, or eight. When I would return from school in the evenings, Yala would run to me with a bunch of wild flowers and the day's news. By that time, we had left Canada, the land of her birth, and after a series of moves to other countries, had settled in Largo. By the time she was six, Amite began to dislike her newsmonger habits and told me to discourage her from telling me everything that happened, because I was turning her into a gossip. Once Yala started to school around seven, she had something to exercise her mind, and she excelled dramatically. Throughout her early schooling, her teachers marveled at her intelligence and would skip her ahead to the next grade midway through the term. Thus, the early graduation from high school. During the first year following her graduation from high school, Yala seemed content and happy to be home with her father, and took up numerous projects. She asked for material to sew, made curtains for the house, sewed clothes for herself and her sister, canned fruits and vegetables, and continued to practice her guitar. Amite had taught her to play classical guitar and she looked the picture of contentment strumming her guitar in the evenings under the vigilant tutelage of her father. The house was not wired for electricity as there was none at that time in Tall Palms so we used a generator for a couple of hours in the evenings after dark, long enough so that lessons and school preparations could be completed. Evenings were short, and we would retire fairly early anyway. The days were long, filled with work on the farm, school for the rest of us. We owned a large portable cassette player on which Yala listened to music approved by her father—mostly Caribbean classics, especially music by Bemijian artists. She was not allowed to listen to the popular music from the States as did most people her age.

A couple of months following her graduation, Yala came home one evening to say she had seen Bea on the bus and had a short conversation with her. She seemed pleased that Bea had remembered us, and excitedly told me about having seen her. Bea had sent regards to me, said she would be living in Largo for a while, and told Yala to tell me to stop by for a visit. I was pleased, but dared not hope that she really liked me or meant what she had said. *She was probably just being nice*, I thought. Besides, I considered Bea in a social class different from my own, so I did nothing about following up on the invitation to visit her although I had found the short visit with her in the spring invigorating. I didn't have many real friends in Largo, only a few acquaintances from school. There were a couple of people I talked to occasionally but nobody who could be considered a close personal friend. No one in the family did. We had always kept pretty much to ourselves, which was the way I had convinced myself that I liked it, since most people were terrible gossips, naive and unsophisticated. I did long for closeness with a female as I missed my sisters, especially Elsie, who still lived there as did Lena and Vera. We had ceased to keep in close touch with each other partly because I moved around so much after leaving Canada. Too, I had been so wrapped up in making sure my marriage worked, trying to raise good productive kids, that I had sort of neglected everyone and everything, and had made few efforts to cultivate new friends.

Now when Yala spoke about Bea, my heart skipped a beat. I thought about how nice it would be to visit with her again, because I had genuinely liked her. But just as quickly, the thought popped into my head: *Girl, know your place!* I considered Bea way out of my league in addition to being a foreigner from "over there," and I instinctively knew that Amite would probably say what he usually said when we met new people: "You're going to get hurt." I dismissed the idea out of mind. School started soon and I was busy teaching in the new semester. Amos and Nefertiti returned to school. Amos began his senior year, and Yala began her tenure at home with Amite and the baby, Hannibal.

Six weeks into the school year, a co-worker told me that Bea had volunteered to teach and conduct drama workshops at Rivertown High. I quickly took him up on the idea and went by her house to see her and plan with her what she would do. I was not good at making friends with women. Most find me bossy and interpret my willingness to help as nosiness. I would usually find myself in conflict whenever I worked closely with women. However, such was not the case with Bea. She seemed genuinely open, willing to listen. Although she was quite blunt by Caribbean standards, Bea was not one to engage in malicious gossip. She liked people, was a do-gooder, understood a lot more than she appeared to, and what I found most interesting about her was her frankness, even when it hurt sometimes. As I got to know her better over the next couple of years, she told me that her honesty was a learned characteristic, that she cultivated it in order to avoid deceiving herself and others. She found it to be best in the dealings she had with people around the world, of varying races, cultures and ethnic groups. Sometimes I would wince at a sharp rebuttal or remonstrance given to a guest—usually one of the Americans who visited her in Largo—on one of the diverse topics that were discussed at her house. She was never malicious, though, and they always seemed to come back for more. So it obviously worked. I know it did for me! I recall that when I complimented her and asked her why she was giving up part of what I knew must have been hard earned vacation time to volunteer to work, teach the drama classes, she said: "Because I am lonely, and I don't know anybody but one or two people here, and when I'm not being creative, I don't do too well." Most people would have handed you some hogwash about wanting to help the less fortunate. Ultimately, of course, that was the effect of most of what she did, and although she was probably aware of it, Bea was not one to broadcast her altruism.

In December of that first year, I stopped in to see Bea one day and found her making plans to visit the States in February. She had a speaking engagement and planned to be gone about a week. When I arrived, she began to talk about Yala, asking where we were planning to send her to school, whether or not she would go in the fall coming up. At that time, Yala had been out of school for one semester, and I had hopes that she would be able to go to school that year, although I didn't know how or where. I related this to Bea.

"Well, I've been thinking," she began. "Why don't you let me take her home with me in February, visit a school or two, and see if I can get someone to give her a scholarship? My alma mater used to have a lot of foreign students and they take good care of them. Amite wouldn't have to worry about his precious baby running wild or mixing in with a lot of fast girls. It's a church school and I believe they would give her a scholarship. I think it's worth a try. What do you think?"

Well, I was a little overwhelmed, to say the least. Here was a woman I had met less than a year earlier who was offering to take my daughter to the States to try to secure her education. Most unusual. I told Bea that I needed to talk to Amite first, see if he would consent to letting Yala go. Although I had little hope that he would, I knew that I had to give it a try, and I thought a trip to the States would do Yala a lot of good whether or not she was able to get a scholarship. Bea showed me a letter she had written to her old school by way of introducing Yala and told me that as soon as I had an answer she would send it off. I cautioned her not to mention the matter to Yala because I didn't want her to get her hopes up until I had a chance to talk to her father. I didn't tell Amite that night but instead waited until two days later on the weekend hoping to catch him in a more relaxed mood than during the week.

"Amite, Bea wants to help Yala get in school, you know. She likes Yala a lot, admires her abilities. She thinks she can get a scholarship for her."

"Well, we already know she is smart. What kind of scholarship?"

"In the States. She knows people over there she feels would be willing to give Yala a scholarship based on her academic record. An academic scholarship."

"Would she have to go to school over there?"

"Well, yes, Amite. But the school she is talking about is in the South. It's a private school for girls only. Bea thinks it would be a good place for Yala. Not too different from what she has known over here."

"I don't think we have decided to send Yala to school in the States yet, Jaye."

"I know Amite, but this is purely exploration. It would be a chance to find out how well she can compete over there. It wouldn't hurt to try,

Billie Jean Young

don't you think?"

"No, I guess it wouldn't hurt to find out. How she planning to get this scholarship?"

"Well, that's just the thing. Bea is going home for a visit in February. She wants to take Yala with her, visit the school, introduce her to the officials there, and see if they would be willing to give her a scholarship."

Amite's eyes narrowed:

"Take her to the States?"

"Yes, Amite. Bea would take care of her."

"But who is going to pay for this, Jaye? You know we can't afford to do that."

"Amite, she is willing to take care of it for us. She wants to help Yala. Bea will pay for the trip."

"Why?"

"She likes Yala, wants to help. She is my friend, Amite. She is the kind of person who helps people. It's not a big thing with her."

"But it is a big thing. How you gonna accept one big gift like that from strangers, Jaye? Besides, you hardly know this woman. We can't do that!"

"But I do know her, Amite. I know the kind of person she is. I know of her background from information I have seen on her and what she has told me. I trust her. I have met her friends from over there. She is a good person."

"Jaye, have you no shame? How you justify that? You act like we need people. Taking one big gift like that from strangers. That's not right. You been in Largo too long, gal."

"I don't see anything wrong with it, Amite. It would give Yala a chance to see what the States would be like. Bea says she could spend a night on campus, let her see for herself whether or not she would like it."

"What kind of mother are you? Here you willing to send our fourteen year old daughter off with perfect stranger talking about school and scholarship, somebody you don't know that much bout, certainly don't know about her morals or nothing. It's not that important for us to take such a chance. We don't know her well enough either to accept such a gift or to trust her with our daughter. Think about it."

"Amite, I am just concerned about Yala's schooling and it seemed like a wonderful opportunity, that's all."

"Besides, if Yala leaves now, the embassy may not let her go

158

when she gets ready to leave to go to school. We shouldn't use up her opportunity to travel later for such a frivolous trip. Let it go, Jaye."

"Well, I will tell her to check on the scholarship while she is there anyway." When I spoke to Bea again, I told her that Amite thought this was a bad time for Yala to go abroad and that we should wait until we could afford such a trip ourselves. Bea was respectful and accepting of this edict but expressed regret that Yala would not be going with her. I asked her again not to mention the offer to Yala as we did not want her to know and bear the disappointment. She agreed, and said she would bring back books for Yala.

14

In January, my mother died after having been sick for a while, and losing her sight to diabetes. Word came to me at school and I immediately went home to tell Amite. I wanted to go to Bemi to be with my family. Of course, all of my sisters were going home and although we had stopped corresponding for a while, I longed to see them. Both my parents were getting on in age and although my mother's death was not a complete shock, it came as a surprise nonetheless. I went almost immediately and had a chance to spend several days with my father as one after the other of the girls arrived from abroad. I suppose since I had not been too close to my mother, it was easier for me to handle the details. I took over, even planning the funeral program myself. I had always felt that my mother was an enigmatic character, a bit selfish and idiosyncratic at times, but a loving, caring mother, nonetheless. And even though everybody knew who her favorites were among her children, she still managed to spread around quite a bit of love to everybody; and in her old age, had actually mellowed somewhat.

I planned a beautiful funeral, not maudlin, but a funeral which celebrated my mother's life, gave a hint of her personality, and her relationship to the world. Instead of people talking about how loudly everybody cried when they spoke about her funeral, they talked instead about what was said, how we portrayed my mother, the comedic aspects of the program even. My father loved it and was complimentary of the whole thing, drawing me aside later to tell me how much he appreciated the way in which we had put my mother way. Once again, I was my father's daughter, happy to please him, hoping that he somehow felt that I had turned out all right in spite of the fact that I had married against his wishes. When I returned to Largo, I felt more connected, had renewed relationships with my sisters, and felt a part of the family of siblings again. We all vowed to write to each other, were sobered by the fact that we only had Pops left, and cognizant that eventually, we would be coming home to bury him. I returned a little older, sadder, much more appreciative of my own family, and threw myself into my work trying to catch up with the three weeks I had been away. Bea had left for the States by the time I got back, and when she returned, brought with her a small library of books which she allowed Yala to check out for reading. Bea and Yala both loved to read and would often discuss books and authors from the States. In addition to her own library of books, Bea brought back several books for Yala as gifts and during that spring, Yala discovered a new world in the many books which Bea shared with her. Yala had been exposed to the classics in school—*To Kill a Mockingbird*, *A Raisin in the Sun*, and the like—but the books Bea brought were different. They were current authors, many of them women, with new, fresh viewpoints and subject matter largely unexplored in the classroom. Authors like Alice Walker, Maya Angelou, Toni Morrison, Angela Davis, and Buchi Emechetta were new and exciting to Yala and she and Bea would discuss the books at length. Bea was a sucker for anyone who likes reading so the more Yala expressed delight, the more she piled on the books. Amite too, took an interest and began to read the books and discuss them with Yala. I was so busy with school and work that I had little time for extracurricular reading and even found myself a little jealous at times when they would have long discussions about the books and the authors. It was a good time for Yala, and even though she was not in school, I consoled myself with the knowledge that she was reading and continuing to grow, not becoming stagnant as I had feared she might, what with being away from academics at such a young age.

Pretty soon, I had to concentrate on Amos who was a senior now, planning to graduate in the spring. I had hopes that he would try to learn a trade and prepare himself to make a living. He hated the farm, so he was always at odds with his father who extolled the virtues of farming at every opportunity. Amos is a boy of average intelligence, and when he applied himself, a decent student. We did not anticipate sending him to college, however, because he simply had no love for academics and would only do whatever was necessary to get by. In this, he truly rubbed Amite the wrong way because Amite read his attitude as lack of caring. Unlike Yala, Amos sought to please no one and because of that, was constantly being upbraided by his father for having no ambition. Shortly before Amos graduated, things worsened, and he finally left home, went to Rivertown and hung out at the home of some of his friends. This upset the whole household. As far as Amite was concerned, Amos' actions were a slap in the face for us in light of all that we had done to provide him with a good home and an education. Furthermore, Amos' choice of friends only exacerbated the matter. He had gone to live in a ramshackle house with several young people whose parents were in the States, and who had not been able to finish high school themselves. He was seeing an older woman who already had a child, and Amos appeared to be living either with her or her brothers. To top it all off, Amos went to work for the richest white man in town as a waiter in a restaurant. This was another even harder blow for Amite because he wanted his children to work for no one save themselves. Amos' boss was not actually white as Bea would often point out about the very light skinned Creoles whom the local people referred to as such. But as I would just as regularly point out to Bea, they were the closest thing we had to white, looked white, and acted white, so in our view, they were! Although Amite tolerated my working for the school system, he considered my job to be a throwback to peonage but it was the only steady income we had so he had to bear it. In Amite's view, working for a white person made Amos less than a peon, especially since he had spent a lifetime warning the children that they must be self sufficient and not depend upon others for their livelihood. So when Amos took the job at the restaurant, Amite simply washed his hands of him. I wanted Amos to come home, worried about the rift between him and his father and tried to force them to make amends. Neither would budge. Finally, one day, I went by Bea's house to talk to her. I was in turmoil worrying about what could happen to Amos living in town with strangers when I knew he was only a boy at heart. Bea was sympathetic. Amos had been by the day before, she said, had a meal with her and stayed a couple of hours. "Did he say anything?" I asked.

Bea said that he had not ventured much information, but seemed happy to be away from home, a little uncertain about the future but glad to be exploring the world for himself. I explained to her that Amos didn't know how to deal with people, that he was just a boy, and asked her to look out for him, try to talk to him the next time he came by. She said she would, although she seemed to think that the experience of being on his own might do Amos a lot of good, help him to grow up. Her opinion was that if he succeeded, so much the better; if he failed, he would learn from it, and probably be a lot happier when he returned home. I explained that it was not quite that easy, that Amite was totally disenchanted with Amos, and I worried that the rift between them might widen into a gulf and my child would be adrift without anywhere to go. I did not want that to happen. I shared Amite's concern about his working for the whites knowing that he could easily become dependent on the low wages, involve himself with a family of his own too quickly, and become mired in the quicksand of poverty that kept so many young people from growing and developing themselves. I wanted more for Amos than that.

As fate would have it, Amos only worked for the restaurant a few weeks. He received an offer to interview for a clerk's position in Capitol City and wanting to try for what was a much better job, went to the owner and asked for time off. Amos did not understand the workplace, however, so instead of creating a reason for wanting to be off, he told the man that he wanted to interview for another job. The man told him he could have all the time off he wanted—permanently—and fired him on the spot. He didn't get the second job and found himself unemployed. Poor Amos, he really had no concept of how the system worked. I related this to Bea and she chuckled, said maybe it was good that Amos was getting the lessons now before he had assumed more responsibilities and would be devastated by such actions. I was secretly glad, I told her, because maybe Amos would come home now. But he didn't. The next time I visited Bea, Amos had been by a few days earlier to say that he was working for fishermen, going on a small boat to the barrier islands once a week. He had been off because the weather was inclement and the fishermen were ashore, but planned to go back soon. Bea said she talked to him about going home but he appeared to be enjoying his freedom, told her to tell me not to worry, that he would be all right. We both knew that the fishing deal was only piddling work, subject to run out at anytime even if the weather was good and that it was unstable, periodic work, at best. I also worried about Amos going out in the small craft used by the fishermen to travel forty five minutes to an hour out to the barrier islands. The weather changes dramatically sometimes within minutes in the Caribbean Sea and the fishermen were seafaring men who were used to it, but I knew that Amos wasn't so I now had his safety to worry about as well. I could not discuss my feelings with Amite as Amos was *persona non grata* where he was concerned and he did not want to hear about my anxieties. All I could do was talk to Bea and pray. Amos was away from home for at least two months. Finally, when the work ran out and I suppose his welcome with his friends did, too, he came home. I was elated, careful not to show it too much, but glad to have my boy back at home where I could look out for him. Amite was still angry, however, and sad to say, the rift between he and Amos was never truly bridged. Although Amos was contrite, appeared to humble himself, Amite never let him forget his failure at spreading his wings, and constantly drove home to him that he was a stupid ox. Gradually, Amos grew to become more and more irresponsible, showed no interest in his future, and walked around with a sullen, hang dog expression most of the time. About the only time he brightened was on holidays or festivals when he would go into Rivertown to be with friends and celebrate. I insisted that he sell the cupcakes and wines occasionally since I had to give him spending money anyway and doing so was one way to have him understand that he needed to earn his own way. He seemed aimless, lacking in get-up-and-go, and seeming to require supervision for the most menial tasks. I knew that it was largely his attitude and unexpressed anger against his father but there was little I could do to remedy the situation.

I began to concentrate on Yala again. The spring of 1987 was bringing us closer to the time when Bea would be leaving Largo for good to return to the States to live. I dreaded the thought as she and I had become very close. I felt a strong kinship to her and considered her my friend. Things were not going well at home. I had become active in My Sister's Place and spent more time working with them trying to get the group off the ground. Amite had begun to resent the time I spent with the group, and told me that I was putting my work off on him and Yala. By this time, Yala had been out of school for two years and Amite showed no signs of letting her go away to school. Hannibal was still at home and Yala had taken over most of his care. Most days I dreaded going home, especially since there was always so much to do, so many things to deal with. I was becoming depressed for no obvious reason at all, and the little joy I had consisted of the times when I could grab a few minutes to talk to Bea. I managed to keep the truck on some school days and would rush over to her house between classes or after school and talk f-a-s-t. Knowing that she would leave at the end of the summer filled me with a sense of foreboding and I would often remark to Bea about it as the summer progressed. My schedule was filled to the brim during the regular school year and we had only July and August for summer holidays. I would go to school, shop for food, ice, try to find fish at the market, buy oil for lamps, transact all business, whatever needed to be done for the household. Things moved slow in Rivertown so I might go on break to purchase food or supplies to a store that had already closed for a few hours. Then, I would, of course, have to return in the evening or the next day, only to find the store crowded, and have to wait around for my turn. It was the same with trying to purchase anything or transact any kind of business. Bea often said that Rivertown moved "slower than molasses on a window pane in New York in the wintertime." I always shopped around and tried to be as thrifty as possible. I spent a lot of money, Amite managed it, and I handled the day to day affairs for the household in addition to working. One day, I ran by Bea's house to wait for the store to open so I could buy supplies:

"Girl, I am so tired. I'm tired of running, you know. Running here, running there. I seem to never get finished. Wish I was free like you."

Bea had just returned from the sea when I arrived, looking refreshed and rested. "I'm not free, you know, Jaye. Just looks like it. We all have our crosses to bear."

"Yes, but you don't have a man telling you what to do, complaining all the time if you're gone longer than he thinks necessary, second guessing all your decisions when he could have gotten up and made some of them himself."

"How so?"

"I get home and look around, Bea. There is still work to do. Yet, Amite will be standing there frowning, looking like I did something wrong, like I've been wasting his precious time, 'What kept me so long?' You know, I get tired of that, tired of feeling guilty about nothing. I have no time for myself. Besides, what does he do?"

"Well, he farms, doesn't he?"

"How? Oh, he teaches Hannibal. May help the kids with lessons now and then, work occasionally on the farm, but it is nothing like what I do. And he complains about my job keeping me away from the family. What else can I do? I have to work to keep food on the table, send my children to school. He brings in no money from the farm. Whatever the farm makes, I see to it making it work with my jams, wines, cakes and stuff. It's still me. He doesn't contribute anything but a lot of flak! I'm sick of it."

"What about Yala? Doesn't she help?"

"Yes, wherever she can, but he doesn't want her to help, says she shouldn't have to do my job around the house. Most days, I still have to cook when I go home. He won't let her. I want her to go to school, Bea, but it doesn't look like he's going to let her go. I just don't know what to do. I'm tired of doing everything."

"What about Amos? Does he help?"

"I can't understand Amos. He is still sulking all the time. I make the money. I am trying to let them see without saying it that I make the money. No matter what their father says about me, about how frivolous and wasteful I am, the fact is that I am the one who takes care of the family. I don't just give Amos money from my pocket, I go in the kitchen, cook and slave, and let him sell, so he can see that the money is the result of hard work. They don't listen to me very much you know; they think their father knows everything."

"They'll learn."

"I hope so. I want my children to enter the world of work with their eyes open. I don't want them to be fools. I want them to know the truth, you know, Bea. You said something to me that has always stuck with me. You said, 'I am so happy that I learned to face the truth. For a long time, I didn't know how, so I did what most people do, and refused to acknowledge truth when it was staring me in the face. Thankfully, I learned better than that while I was in my late twenties. What a blessing! I feel so sorry for anybody who is unable to deal with the truth. Some people never learn how and spend a lifetime lying to themselves and other people.'

"I'm a lot like that, Bea. I have always tried to make things pleasant for everyone, to not acknowledge the badness of a thing by thinking it to be good—making it good. It isn't. It keeps you from growing, facing reality. I am learning to do that. Just the other day when I was counting out money to Amos, I was thinking: *You earned this money, Amite did not. You used your labor to make the goods that this boy sold for a profit, and it was sugar and supplies bought with your money from teaching that helped to process the product. Your check from teaching that goes for bills and into this farm is money you earned, at a place Amite hates. It is not money earned by Amite or the family. You earned it. I had never allowed myself to think that before.*"

"How does that make you feel?"

"Angry! And I get angry every time Amite chastises me now about being late or says I'm wasting time. Whose time? What am I late for?

What time was I due home with all the running around I have to do? Whose schedule am I on?"

"Well, Jaye, if you feel that way, you have to figure out a way to let him know, don't you think?"

I sucked my teeth: "How? He is always right."

One great thing about Bea was that I could talk to her, say things I would never have voiced to anyone. I knew that secrets would remain secrets with her. She understood privacy and guarded her own tenaciously, which was hard to do because so many people knew her and wanted to befriend her. She was friendly and open but kept people at a distance whenever she wanted to. This had a lot to do with her honesty. If she were busy reading, writing, or just busy being alone, she had no problem saying so although the person might not like it. Her obvious love for people came through so that when she chose to be reclusive and secretive, Largotians (and I) learned to respect that, left her alone, and probably chalked it up to her being a peculiar American.

Bea was generous to a fault and I at first worried that people were taking advantage of her, but soon learned that there was method to her madness. She knew how to take care of herself. During her stay in Largo, she had plenty of opportunity to prove it. As with any newcomer in a small community, people were curious about Bea—I know I was— and since she didn't fit the bill of what people thought was a typical American, the more people learned about her, the more curious they became. And since everything in Largo seems to get labeled political, people were more than a little curious about her politics. However, she assiduously avoided politics, making it a point not to attend political meetings, or accept invitations to speak in places that were obviously related to one political party or the other. But the small "p" of politics was another thing.

The Sarawee people predominate in Rivertown, are the result of a mixture of African and Indian tribes, and they retain a good deal of the culture of both races. The Creoles, generally of African and European descent, were the next largest group, and had a higher social standing than the Sarawee, were more westernized, and the few crumbs that the foreigners—whites, Chinese, East Indians, Salvadorans—who owned the place dished out, went to the Creoles first. Bea analogized the relationship between the Sarawee and Creoles to relations between blacks and whites in the States:

"See, Jaye, the whole thing is owned by a handful of white folk at home and many, many white folk are poor like the blacks. But the poor white folk take pleasure in knowing that the owners and rulers come from their race, they identify with them, and they can rest assured that any crumbs from the table will hit their plate first."

As an African American, she saw the Sarawee as being closest in social standing to herself, having the same experiences with racism and discrimination, even though she and most African Americans had the same genetic makeup as the Creoles. Since nobody can live in the Caribbean beyond a generation or two and remain purely Caucasian, the Creoles run the gambit of the color spectrum from quite dark to very white, and the level of prosperity and allegiance to whites usually rose in direct relationship to the lightness of their skin. The only difference, Bea would point out, was that the Creoles weren't Caucasians at all, but Africans with white blood, but like the poor whites, persisted in identifying more with that side of themselves that could lay claim to whiteness even though the whites were their oppressors as well. The Sarawee, on the other hand, laid no claim to white blood at all, gloried in their differentness, and in their context, suffered because of it. The Mayans and Latinos ranked below the Sarawee in social standing and because they were small in number and had little political clout to speak of, kept mostly to themselves. The foreigners—whites, East Indians, Salvadorans, Chinese—mostly merchants and businessmen, sat above the whole fray in a class of their own, without any need to have to fight for their place. It was secured by their money. Where did Bea fit in? Ostensibly, she could automatically be dubbed a Creole. Not only did she have the light brown coloring but the means since she could live in a nice house in Largo, spoke well, and was obviously educated. The Creoles would be happy to claim her. But Bea did not fit in with the Creoles, and resisted all efforts to pigeonhole her as such. The Sarawee were clannish, parochial, not open to strangers, and prone to speak all over you in their language even though they, and most people in Largo, were at least tri-lingual. It was the Sarawee with whom Bea most closely identified, though she related to everybody. The irony of the matter is that the Sarawee probably saw Bea as being as much Creole as anyone else did.

And Bea? How did she see herself? Well, she simply related—to people—and let the chips fall where they might. Most times that meant her principles of equality for all people put her squarely in the camp with the Sarawee, but on occasion, her ability to reach out to all people, regardless of class or ethnic origin, endeared her to the Creoles as well. Bea spent no time belaboring such issues but instead went about the business of living her life working, playing, and exploring the world. And in Largo, she saw so much poverty and deprivation among so many people, it seemed foolish to stop and examine ethnicity before acting or relating to a situation.

By the time Bea was preparing to leave in the fall of 1987, the branch of the junior college in Rivertown was one year old, and I had finally managed to convince Amite to let Yala begin school there. At fifteen, she re-entered school after a two year absence, and when she performed exceptionally well on the entrance exams, I had hopes for her future. Yala seemed happy, was caught up in the world of learning again and appeared to take to her new college studies with the same zeal which she had exhibited in high school. Bea left in September and though her absence left a void in my life, it was softened somewhat by Yala's going to school which had always been a dream of mine. I missed Bea, though, and although the occasional long phone calls and letters that we exchanged helped somewhat, I longed for a friend again. Finally, in late November, she came to Largo for a couple of weeks. Although I had been pleased when Yala started back to school, things at home were not going too well. Amos was still floundering, seemed not to care about his future, or even the present and continued to drift on the waves of his father's sarcastic disdain. He followed Amite's orders around the farm, but exhibited no initiative of his own whatsoever. It bothered me but I was tired, and feeling that I had scored a major accomplishment with Amite with Yala's return to school, did not push my luck, decided to coast for a while.

Around this time, my work with My Sister's Place escalated. I had seen for myself the potential for the group to realize better profits as we perfected our products and I hoped to be able to eventually save enough money to get Yala into a university abroad where I felt she could realize her full potential. I now corresponded with my sisters off and on and felt that they would be happy to help me with her schooling. Bea's time in Largo was all too short and before I knew it, she had returned to the States again. I was not happy, but there were no catastrophes going on in my life either, so I reasoned that things might be looking up; I decided not to mention the sexual incident to Bea. However, in December, trouble struck, in the form of Mr. Ervin again.

***

After the incident with Mr. Ervin during Yala's senior year of high school, I had persisted in my determination to see to it that he had the least amount of contact with my daughter as possible. During that last semester, I would go and stand in the doorway of his room to wait for his classes to be over. Or, if Yala had to be with him, I would go and wait and watch the interaction between him and her. If he walked into a room and I was in it alone, I would walk out of it immediately. When, upon graduation, Mr. Ervin had to introduce Yala as valedictorian of the class, he had come to me to ask what I wanted him to say. I had coldly responded that he could obtain biographical information from Yala, which he did and managed to adequately introduce her. Such had been the extent of any contact with Mr. Ervin since the incident two and a half years earlier. Yala entered the junior college and was in Mr. Ervin's classes again. I taught there as well. Mr. Ervin had been made Dean of the Rivertown branch of Largo College.

The end of the semester in December brought things to a head again. I had given Yala a break from chores to study for finals. It was a Saturday, but I noticed that she was instead outside watching me and Amite work. Finally, Amite quit work, asked me to come into the house, told me to sit down. I did.

"Mr. Ervin is messing with Yala again."

Yala had followed us inside and I now looked at her: "Is that true Yala?" She quickly responded, "Yes, Mom."

Something in the way she responded made me remember the incident a few days earlier at the junior college. I had passed by Mr. Ervin's room, looked inside and seen Yala going through his briefcase. When I had asked her what she was doing, she had said that Electra had told her there were pictures of the family in the briefcase and that she could go and get them. Now, I looked at her again.

"Yala, what is this about?"

She hesitated, drew a deep breath: "Mr. Ervin made advances to me again."

I was immediately frightened again, angry at the same time: "Have you had sexual intercourse with this man?"

She was even quicker in her response now: "No, Mom. He says he is attracted to me, but that he doesn't know what to do around me."

Relieved, I let my anger take over: "This has gotten entirely out of hand. Amite, we have to do something, now!"

Amite was back to blaming the school. "She just can't go back to that school," he said. "Nothing will be done. Mr. Ervin wouldn't have done this if he didn't get the support of the administration. I won't have her going back to that school."

After a great deal of discussion and arguing back and forth, we finally agreed that Yala would not go back to school. She didn't sit for any of her exams, and when I turned in my grades at semester's end, Mr. Ervin noticed that I, too, showed no grades for Yala. As I walked away from him, he asked if he could come to see us on the farm. I said yes and went home and told Amite about the request. The following day at 10:00, we were waiting when Mr. Ervin rode up on his bicycle. We went out into the yard, dispensed quickly with the amenities and Mr. Ervin started to talk. He is a short man, even by Caribbean standards, perhaps five feet tall, a little bit stocky, early thirties at the time. He is Sarawee, dark in complexion, dressed casually in slacks and cotton shirt, not handsome but average looking. "If I were in your position, I would not have allowed me to come to talk. I want to thank you for letting me come. I am here to tell you that I have overstepped my bounds with Yala. Two years ago, I denied the accusation. I have come today to say that it is true. I know that she has told you. I have come to beg you to send her back to school. Yala says if you knew what I was doing, you would stop her from going to college. I come on bended knee to beg you to send her back to school. Yala is smart. Society needs her. Please don't punish her by removing her from school. She is a brilliant young woman and it would be a shame to damage her future because of something like this. I promise you nothing will happen again. I would make that promise in front of the principal or anyone else."

I had begun to cry as soon as Mr. Ervin began his speech corroborating his molestation of my daughter, and continued throughout. When he finished, Amite thanked Mr. Ervin for his noble speech, told him how much he appreciated his honesty. I broke in to tell Mr. Ervin how much he had disappointed me as a teacher to know that he would repeat the same behavior after making all his promises three years earlier.

"I used to make up stories for you, Mr. Ervin, to explain to people why Yala couldn't go to school, defending you indirectly. But my responsibility is not only with Yala, it is with the rest of the children in the school. You have to be exposed. That is the only way!" At this point, Amite broke in with his own oration. "You have a degree in science, Mr. Ervin; I have a degree in life. I know about life. You can't expect to put adult men and women together and not expect to have something like this happen. You will recall that it has happened at that school before with other teachers. What you did was only natural."

I continued to cry. "Mr. Ervin, I am so disappointed in you. How could you do this to me again?" Men are just plain low down, all of you are just plain no good!"

By this time, I was moving about the yard, going a little crazy, I guess, both from what Mr. Ervin had just said, and the way Amite was responding to it, as if he didn't blame Mr. Ervin at all!

Mr. Ervin broke in with, "Not all men are no good, Mrs. Peay. There are still a few good men left."

Amite continued to talk, repeating himself, and continuing to expound on what he considered to be the natural aspects of life, male and female. He went on for over an hour, seemingly glad to get a chance to say it. Mr. Ervin himself began to appear just a bit nervous and when Amite finally finished, quickly readied himself to leave.

I moved to him: "Mr. Ervin, the last time you were here, you made an accusation about Yala's father. Are you still saying that is true?"

He looked at me: "Yes, so help me God, I did not lie about that. Yala told me that, Mrs. Peay." We agreed that I was going to go to the principal and that Mr. Ervin would say all that he had told us about his abuse of Yala. He said that he had already told his daughter, Electra, and that he was willing to bring her along as a witness. I thanked him and he left.

When Mr. Ervin left, I went into the house, into the kitchen and started to prepare lunch, doing all the normal things I would have done at that time of day. When I had finished, I went to my room, sat on the bed, and concentrated on everything that Mr. Ervin had said, angrier than I had ever been. Soon, Amite came into the room, said: "Well, do you think what Mr. Ervin said was true?"

"What?"

"That I molested Yala?"

"You tell me."

"No, do you think it is true?"

"You tell me."

"Remember the man whose wife died, and he had sex with the daughter afterwards? You said you might understand how it could happen...."

"Amite, did you?"

"Yes. Yala came to me wanting sex, and in the interest of love, I gave her what she asked for."

"You had sex with Yala?"

"Yes, just once. I didn't want anybody else to take advantage of her so I did what she asked."

My heart hurt. After the physical pain went away, I was numb. I don't think I even tried to deal with it. I pushed it aside, concentrated on Mr. Ervin, how to make Mr. Ervin pay for molesting my daughter. It became my single minded goal. When school resumed in January, Amite and I met with Mr. Posey and Mr. Ervin at my request. We began the meeting with my relating the details of the first incident with Mr. Ervin. Mr. Posey butted in, cut me off: "I tell you, I didn't know what to do, Mrs. Peay," whereupon I responded, "if it were your child, Mr. Posey, I would have found a way, even if it meant telling your wife."

Mr. Posey continued to plead that he had simply not known what to do. When I was through relating the second incident, I turned to Mr. Ervin: "Is that how it went?"

Mr. Ervin cleared his throat, began to talk slowly, deliberately: "For some of it, yes. But, you see, Yala made the advances to me. I did not seek her out in any way, never. Maybe I could have done more to stop her as I am guilty of exercising poor judgment in not having done so, but she made all the advances to me. I didn't seek her out."

By the time Mr. Ervin finished describing what happened between him and Yala, he made her out to be a whore, highly sexed, and uncontrollable, something bordering on being a nymphomaniac. Amite rushed him; I was horrified into speechlessness at Mr. Ervin's sudden about face, but rushed to stop Amite before things got totally out of control.

"Come, Amite, this makes no sense whatsoever, neither of them, the whole thing is a set up. Let's get out of here!"

All those years, Mr. Posey had known and never said a word! I was incredulous. I had been sure that Mr. Ervin had been bluffing when he said he had told Mr. Posey the first time. Now, I didn't know what to believe. I didn't trust Mr. Posey or Mr. Ervin. For all I knew, Mr. Ervin could have gotten with Mr. Posey over the holidays and told him, and they had concocted this defense together. As we left the school, I felt defeated. Amite was right about one thing: there was nobody at the school to protect my daughter. Mr. Posey told me later that he would ask for Mr. Ervin's resignation at the end of the school year. He impressed upon me the hardship to other students if Mr. Ervin were asked to leave immediately in the middle of the school year as chemistry teachers are in short supply in the Caribbean. With the situation still unresolved, I decided to leave Yala at home for the balance of the year.

15

That was January 1988. Amite began to hate the school more and more and spoke of it as something evil, a place I should be ashamed to work. He wanted me to quit my job, sell our house, and move to a more remote location almost twenty five miles from Rivertown, a place he planned to clear in the bush. Of course, I refused. I had bought a house in Canada, left it and moved back to Bemi to clear land and start a house, left it to go to Largo to start a house, moved to Africa, and returned to start another house in Largo—which was the unfinished house we lived in. By this time, the romance of moving from place to place had long since worn off and I had already left too many unfinished homes and unrealized dreams. I was not about to leave another. Besides, practically speaking, it was impossible since we needed my salary as a teacher to live on. Education was very important to me, Hannibal and Nefertiti were still in school, and I did not plan to deny them their education. Amite continued to harass me about moving again and I did my best to stave him off. Now, he was taking Hannibal, Yala, and Amos with him to clear the land on which he planned to build another house. They would rise before dawn, take the bus or hitchhike and go and chop all day long. He also built a small thatch roofed shed on a spot he had cleared and began to keep the children there two or three days before returning home. He was becoming more and more reclusive, difficult to get along with and when he did come out of his shell, would fly into a rage at the drop of a hat. I called Bea in the States, described his behavior and she asked if I thought he might be having a nervous breakdown. I said I thought so myself. Bea suggested that we try to get help, seek therapy before the matter got entirely out of hand. But there were no psychiatrists to turn to in Largo. The one reputed psychiatrist was an East Indian doctor who worked for the prison and was inaccessible to us, and I seriously doubted that he was actually a psychiatrist anyway. I didn't know what to do, where to turn to for help, so I did nothing right away. I was still in turmoil following the disastrous incident with Mr. Posey and Mr. Ervin at school, still smarting from the injustice of it all, and carrying around the horrible secret—which I couldn't even bear to think about, let alone tell anyone—that Amite had revealed to me in December. Yala was still at home, did not attend school anymore and appeared consigned to life on the farm. When I spoke to her about the sex with her father, she, of course, denied it. Although I had been stunned, disbelieving, I still loved Amite, had four children with him, and did not seriously think about leaving him. We had been together almost twenty-three years then. He had stopped having sex with me for a period of time prior to the December admission and I had believed that it was simply a phase we were going through. From time to time, in the course of our marriage, he had made requests to abstain from sex because he needed time to think. (Well, he had not actually asked, but I would notice that there was no sex, and sometimes Amite would casually mention it at some point). I had respected these time outs because I truly believed in individual freedom, felt that some people need time to themselves occasionally, whether or not they are married, and I interpreted his distance as wanting time out. When we had lived in Canada years earlier, Amite would take winter trips alone to warm countries and I was not bothered by it. I saw it as time out for me, too. Now, I was sure Amite was having a nervous breakdown and since I didn't have a psychiatrist to go to, and knowing that he would never seek help on his own, I managed to get a doctor in Rivertown to prescribe medicine for him under an assumed name. Amite took the medicine and his depression eased. Things appeared to get better again. Yala was still home, not in school, but at least Amite was calmer, less demanding than before. Whenever I tried to think through the issues in my mind, they were simply too complex and having no one to discuss them with only made matters worse, since I simply did not let myself think about what Amite had revealed to me that fateful day before Christmas. Had Mr. Ervin been telling the truth last month? What about in 1984? I did not—indeed I could not—connect Amite's confession of a one-time slip up with the accusations made by Mr. Ervin on two separate occasions three years apart. It was all too confusing.

Better let it lie.

In May, Bea returned, bringing with her a friend who stayed a week and as she was busy showing her friend the countryside, I had scant time with her. However, for three weeks, we had a chance to have our old talks again. School was still in session so I had to run by her house and talk f-a-s-t again. Bea had kept the little cottage on Mango Road and being there was comforting, familiar. I talked around my problems, however, never once giving an inkling that I knew anything was amiss between Amite and Yala. I told Bea about Amite's depression, and his illogical insistence that we abandon society and move into the bush. "What are you going to do, Jaye," Bea had finally asked after hearing me out.

"I don't know what I can do, Bea, except stay with it, try to see it through. I know I am not going to move, though."

At this, she looked at me closely. "Have you told Amite this?"

I had to admit that I had not exactly refused to go outright. "Yes and no. It might be too much for him. But I don't know how much longer I can stall him."

Then Bea inquired: "What about Yala? Is he going to let her go back to school this year?"

I said I honestly didn't think so. "He thinks the school is evil, Bea. The last incident with Mr. Ervin is when he started to talk about our leaving. He won't let her go back to school and I can't seem to interest her in going again. I don't know what I'm going to do, don't know what I can do. Yala seems to have forgotten about school, and she has become uncommunicative with me. She seems to hate me, sometimes."

We continued to talk and Bea told me what had just happened to the daughter of a friend of hers. The woman had visited Bea in Largo years earlier so I knew who she was talking about. The daughter was fourteen years old, and for a period of about six months, had become mean, hateful, and spiteful towards her mother. Always a good child, the girl had taken to disobeying her mother, talking back, being totally disrespectful. Finally, the mother had discovered her diary one day when she was cleaning the girl's room, had opened it, hoping for some clue to her daughter's behavior. The diary fell open to a page where the girl had written critically and disparagingly of her home and her mother, saying that the home was a ship with a whore for a captain. Shocked, the mother read on and discovered that the girl was having sex every day with a thirty-eight year old man from the neighborhood. This man was the father of one of her daughter's friends. The mother replaced the diary and called Bea. Bea had rushed over to find her sharpening knives in the kitchen preparing to kill the man. They had talked and talked way into the night and the woman had finally decided to prosecute rather than go after the man herself. They alerted the police. The man was picking her daughter up from the bus stop every morning, taking her to have sex, then dropping her off at junior high school. The detectives decided to try to catch him. For the next week, the mother said nothing to her daughter about her discovery; she would read and replace the diary every day in order to track the rapist's actions, until the police finally moved in and arrested him. He was still in jail as Bea told me the story. I admired this woman, knowing how much embarrassment she had to overcome in order to go to the authorities to report such a thing. I felt that she had done the right thing in moving to protect her daughter from the abuse she was receiving from a man almost three times her age.

Bea also told me about another case which was still causing her a lot of worry and misgivings about her own actions. A young student had told her a disturbing story about the child of the man the student planned to marry. The man, a widow, had a four year old daughter whom the student, his girlfriend, would babysit sometimes in the course of their relationship. The girlfriend was disturbed because while she was bathing the child, she noticed bruises underneath her clothes in and around her privates. When she questioned the father, he said the bruises same from spankings and refused to discuss it further with his girlfriend. The girlfriend also noticed that the child's favorite form of displaying affection was to straddle her lap and give her open mouthed wet kisses, and when she questioned her, the child said that she kissed her father that way. When she asked the father about it, the girl noticed that he appeared uncomfortable; but she had gone further and asked him if he had problems dealing with the child. He admitted that on occasion he had dreams of getting an erection while spanking the child and that this had frightened him. Bea had advised the student not to marry the man, or at least to reconsider since she felt that something was wrong with the man's relationship with his daughter. Since the wife had died of cancer only one year earlier, Bea further advised her student that the man was probably still grieving over his wife and could not be expected to have a normal relationship with anyone so soon. On thinking through the situation, however, Bea had begun to have misgivings because she had not herself gone to the authorities on behalf of the child. Shortly after disclosing the information to Bea, however, the student had left town with the man and Bea had not heard from her again before she left to come to Largo.

Family Secrets

The stories were horrifying to me but I never consciously connected them to myself. I could not understand how the girlfriend could even consider a relationship with the man after what she had found out about him. But I never told Bea what Amite had revealed to me about his relationship with Yala a year earlier. I had finally told her about the two incidents with Mr. Ervin, but I was careful to leave out Mr. Ervin's allegations against Amite. I simply could not bring myself to do so. Bea had been to my home and she would commend me on the seemingly strong family ties we had. I did not want to burst that bubble. Bea had her visit to Largo and returned to the States after a month. I was careful to watch Amite and Yala after that. I told Yala—even though she insisted that nothing had happened—that she was to come to me if her father or anyone else tried anything with her. I struggled to get back our old relationship, wanting more than ever to convince Yala that she could trust me to protect her. I began to scheme harder to try to put money aside for Yala to go abroad to attend college. Amite continued to insist that we sell the house and use the money to build another house at the location he and the children were continuing to clear. The summer passed in a blur of arguments with my continued refusal to sell the house, trying to stall for time.

In the middle of all of this—in September—my father died. Word came to me again at the school, right after the new semester had begun. I was shaken to the roots. Not my father! And only a scant two years after losing my mother. How could he die so soon? I had taken the bus to school that day, so hitching a ride with Mrs. Orlando, I went to the telephone company to place calls to my family. I had no money to speak of, but when I spoke to my family, my brothers-in-law agreed to send me a ticket to go home to the funeral. Mrs. Orlando took me home. Amite was not there, so I told Yala about my dad, and asked her to help me pack. Soon, Amite walked into the house and I hastened to tell him the news about my dad, my voice breaking in the process. I loved my dad so much, had always been his favorite, and save for marrying Amite, had always tried to do everything he asked of me. Amite expressed sympathy briefly, and then looked at my packing.

"So what is this, Jaye?" indicating the things on the bed.

"I am going home to the funeral, Amite. I went by the phone company and I have reservations to leave in a couple of days."

Amite was immediately upset. "But why you think you can just go

179

running off to your father's funeral, now? It is a bad time, the children need you and besides, we can't afford it."

I hurriedly told him that his brothers had offered to send me the ticket, that I knew we didn't have the money, but I wanted to go home to bury my father.

"But he is already dead. It doesn't make any sense for you to jump up and go home again. You were just over there. And besides, you promised when you went to see him when he was sick last year that if anything happened, you wouldn't press to go home again. Did you forget that?"

Of course I hadn't even thought about the silly promise. Besides, I had been in the Caribbean as a CXC examiner during the summer when my father was sick, and I had simply used money to go from one island to the other to see him. It had not been a trip undertaken from Largo. And anyway, this was a different matter. My father was not sick; he was dead.

Now, I spoke. "No, Amite, I didn't forget, but this is my father, my last chance to show my respects. He is all that is left. I have to go; I need to go." I saw Amite's eyes narrow, his jaw set. "If you go, you go against my wishes and you remember that, Jaye. It makes no sense for you to go home now; it is foolish. What's done is already done. You need to stay home with your own family. What can you do?"

I was horrified that Amite would try to hold me to such a promise especially since he knew that I was my father's favorite child, that I had always been close to my father and would want to go to see him put away.

"Amite, it won't cost us anything. I know I made the promise, but it is a promise I think I need to break. Eugene will send the ticket for me, he promised. I need to go home."

Amite refused to be moved. "You are going against my wishes if you go. I think it is foolish; you are being childish and foolish again; it is those sisters of yours. I knew something like this would happen as soon as you started to write to them again. You think about it, Jaye, let me know what you decide to do. And don't do anything foolish."

At that, Amite walked away, leaving me standing there with my packing. By now, I was crying. Not only did I have the grief over my father to deal with, but I now had to deal with Amite's anger and animosity over my going to his funeral. Was I wrong to want to go? I didn't think so. I felt that I was justified in wanting to go to my own father's funeral and since I had been enterprising enough to figure out how to go, for the life of me, I could not understand what Amite's objections were about. Except for the damn promise! Why had I been foolish enough to make such a promise anyway?

I finished packing my things, looked outside and since Amite had disappeared from the yard and the house, got in the truck and drove back to town. I needed to talk to someone. Of course, Bea was not there anymore. I drove and drove, finally turned the truck toward the Church of the Good Shepherd and went to knock on the convent door and asked for Sister Deer. She was home, having not long come from school. I had spoken to her briefly at school after finding out about my father, and she had offered to help me. I told her I needed to talk. We got in her truck and she started to drive. I told her about what had just happened between me and Amite, and the argument against my going home to my father's funeral, how I felt, and related the promise I had made last year in order to go to see my father when he was sick. Sister Deer listened to the whole thing without comment, let me get everything out. I told her I was telling her to see if my reasoning was off, if I was being unreasonable and childish to want to go home. Was Amite right? Was I crazy? When I was spent, Sister Deer parked the truck, turned to me. "Of course, you are not crazy, Jaye. Of course, you're perfectly right in wanting to go to your father's funeral. I would think it unnatural if you didn't want to go. Don't pay the man any attention, child. Just pack your things, finish making your plans, and go home. Go to your father, and bury him, and come back home. The man will come around. Don't let him stop you from doing this. You have to think of yourself, your own peace of mind. Go. And peace be with you."

At this, she smiled. I needed to hear somebody say that. With all that had gone on in my life in the past year, I was becoming confused, felt that maybe I was wrong and Amite was right. I did not know what to think anymore. I had gone to Sister Deer to try to honestly relate the facts to a disinterested observer and get an opinion. I wanted to document my thoughts with someone in case Amite succeeded later in making me think the facts had been otherwise. I had become so confused until sometimes I didn't know if I had honestly remembered something differently than it actually was when Amite and I differed. I did not feel that I could trust my own memory anymore. Sister Deer and I talked a little more, mostly about Yala, her concern that we hurry up and get Yala in school so that she could continue her education. I didn't elaborate too much, but told her that Amite was not yet ready for Yala to go to school, and that I was continuing to try to work on it. Sister didn't press, and with the urgency of the situation in front of me, I said as little as I could. Soon, Sister Deer cranked up the little truck, took me back to the convent, where I got into mine and went home. Amite was standing in the doorway. I didn't say much, only answered the children's questions about their grandfather's death and tried to stay out of the way as much as possible. Amite was quiet. I had, after leaving Sister Deer, decided conclusively that I would go home. Of course, the thing left to do was to see if somehow I could convince Amite that I was doing the right thing. No matter what, Amite was my husband, I cherished our marriage, never once considered dissolving it, and had always prided myself on the fact that somehow we always managed to compromise our differences.

As I sat in my room that night away from the rest of the family, I allowed my thoughts to turn to my father. He was so kind, slow to anger, but wrathful when finally pushed to his limit. In all my dealings with him, he had looked out for me. *Even when I went against his wishes to marry Amite, he had finally come around, tried his best to smile, and given me his blessings.* My mother, whose love I always had to toe the line for, had not been so generous. She'd had her own feud going with Amite's mother. Ironically, it was not about me or the proposed marriage. My mother and Mrs. Peay were on the outs because of Mrs. Peay's older son, Eugene. Eugene had a spat with his parents and when they had been unable to resolve it, the Peays had tossed him out of the house. Eugene provided a good deal of the maintenance for his mother and Mrs. Peay wanted him back. However, Eugene had appealed to my mother for a place to stay and my mother had allowed him to bunk at our house temporarily. Mrs. Peay felt that but for my mother's giving Eugene a place to stay, he would have been forced to come home begging and she would have had her boy and the maintenance back.

16

Now my thoughts put me back in Bemi again. Neither of our mothers had attended Amite's and my wedding. It had been a turbulent time. I had gone to the island of Bonsai to teach in September of the year before, and Amite had made the journey over in November and reiterated his determination to marry me. He took a room at a hotel, stayed two weeks, spent evenings with me after work, and convinced me to marry him. When I came home for Christmas slightly less than a month later, Amite became even more intense in his determination that I should marry him. I would go to mass at five o'clock each morning with Amite and although the mass was only an hour long, I would get home sometimes three or four hours later. On the way back, Amite would stop and lecture me. He would tell me how brilliant and innocent I was, then tell me how terrible all men were, that they were just out to get me in trouble. He said that he had been extra nice to me, that most men would have had me pregnant by now. I recall that he spoke often about how evil sex is, that if someone really loved you, they wouldn't have sex with you. One day, he stopped beside a mango tree on the way home to lecture me, and as I stood there weak from hunger, listening to him, wishing for breakfast which I skipped because I would leave so early for mass, an older man happened to walk by. He stopped to peer at me for a while, finally approached and said: "Little girl, don't you think you should go home."

In those days, adults—any adult—felt free to stop you, chastise you, or give an order whether they knew you or not.

I had replied quickly, "I am just standing here talking, Sir," whereupon the man had said, "Well, it doesn't look to me like you're talking; he's doing all the talking."

When I didn't answer, he continued: "Is he a relative?"

I said no. The man looked at me closely for a while, but decided to go on. It was a terrible Christmas holiday, and just after Christmas, things worsened. Amite decided to once again ask my father if he could marry me. My father's response was once again an adamant no, and when Amite stood his ground, began to argue back and forth with my father, my father became angry, threatened Amite if he didn't leave his house, and said he was going to get his gun, turned and left the room. While he was gone, Amite grabbed my hand and ran me away from the house. Of course, my father came after us, but because we were on foot and had a head start, we could duck and dodge from my father driving the truck. We ran upon a hill behind the church, stood and watched my father's truck going around and round looking for us. There was a roundabout just below us and my father's truck made the circle several times, obviously looking for us. The police station was underneath the hill, to the left of the church. At one point, as we watched my father search, Amite said: "Well, you can't go back home now; he will shoot you for sure."

We waited a while longer and when Amite felt that my father had given up for the night, he took me to the police station to swear out a complaint against my father for threatening to kill us.

When he said "us," the desk sergeant looked at him and said, "Us? Did he threaten to shoot you or her?"

At that point, Amite gave me a nudge, indicating I was to verify what he had said, and I lied and said, yes, my father had threatened me, too. I felt terrible. I knew that I was not included in my father's threat, but somehow, with Amite's urging, I lied. He didn't come right out and say you must lie on your father, but he simply stated it as true and told me to attest to it. I did. We were a good family, knew nothing about any dealings with the police, and I felt horrible that I was doing that to my father. As we left the police station, Amite told me that he had decided to take me to his grandmother's even though he went back home. The Peay's lived only a few doors away from our house, too close to my father for comfort. Besides that, Amite's mother never cared too much for me anyway. Amite said it was my dark complexion—she was black herself and felt that her boys could do better. Amite explained the problem to his grandmother and she let me stay. He went home. That was on Friday, and I stayed in hiding for the weekend. The police went to my father's house, took away his gun, and because my father was supposed to have threatened me, called the social welfare department as well. On Monday, Amite, his granny, his old aunt and I went to a hearing downtown. Of course, my father had been summoned and I had to face him for the first time since I had run away from the house with Amite. My father stated his case: I had just graduated from convent school, had a job teaching on Bonsai. He wanted me to have further schooling in university; and I was too young to marry. Shortly afterwards, Amite began to speak and I began to cringe with shame. He started out by saying that his intentions were honorable, that he wanted to marry me and he could not understand my father's objections.

Then he dropped the bomb. "I can't see why everybody making such a big fuss about marriage. What if she pregnant? Would everybody be making such a fuss about whether or not I am doing the right thing?"

I was horrified, embarrassed right down to my toes. Amite and I had never had sex, had not even come close to it, our relationship having consisted only of kissing occasionally. I had never had sex except for the times when it had been forced upon me when I was younger. I saw my father look around at me, incredulously, it seemed. There I sat: a tiny, tiny girl of perhaps seventy five pounds, about four feet, ten inches tall, my hair in six plaits, wearing a blue shirtwaist dress with a Peter Pan collar, gathered at the waist with a sash that tied in the back. I had been wearing slippers when we ran away, so Amite's grandmother had loaned me a pair of shoes, a brown pair with perhaps a one and a half inch heel which I had trouble walking in even though the heels were fairly wide. I was not asked anything and I did not volunteer. Things moved very fast. The court set another hearing for two weeks later, and we left the place. It was then that I decided that I would go on back to Bonsai to resume my teaching position. In all the ruckus, I was already over a week late and I had not bothered to call the school to alert them. A day or two later, I went to my house to go get my clothes. My father spoke to me: "What yuh in such big rush fuh? Slow yourself down, me dahter. Take yuh time. Let Mrs. Peay's son go on off to Canada by hesef; stay heah. The buoy fickle, yuh know? Starts all dese bands and tings, nuttin evah last. Continue yuh job, yuh have prestigious job heah. Keep it, get yuh education, den let him sen fuh yuh. Ef it love, it de keep. Nevah yuh worrie bout it. Time nevah destroy tru love. Yuh got no need fuh rush, yuh know. Yuh not ready fuh one big husband. Yuh don't eben know how fuh squeeze orange juice. Wha yuh tink yuh do with one big man?"

I made some remark about wanting to live my own life, find out for myself, finished packing and went back to Bonsai. Of course, the nuns were annoyed with me and I was still miserable from the trauma of the past weeks, so the period is a blur in my mind. It wasn't more than a few days later, however, that Amite called me on Bonsai to say that my father had given his consent for us to marry and he had set a date. Amite's grandmother and his aunt had both gone to my father to intervene on our behalf, pointing out that Amite was a good boy and I could do worse. It seems they used the same insinuation about my perhaps being pregnant. I suppose the avalanche of outsiders, friends, officials, and other concerned people may have caused my father to call into question his judgment.

I don't know, but in the end, my father finally caved in. Amite went on to tell me that the wedding would take place less than two weeks later during the carnival weekend. He had already gone to the church and he was going to put up banners—advertisements in the paper announcing the wedding and inviting anybody to object to it in case you were already married or divorced. Less than two weeks later, February 4, 1967, I married Amite Peay. I came on Friday before carnival to find that my mother herself had made a wedding dress for me—white—with a hat and jacket to match. Amite had given the money for the material and my mother had accommodated his request. Everything was all set when I got there. Amite had insisted on the phone that we needed to get married right away so that my father wouldn't have a chance to change his mind. A day after I arrived, I was married. How did I feel? I cannot lay claim to having been a happy, starry-eyed bride being swept away by a suitor facing tremendous opposition to gain my hand. The greatest emotion I recall is a feeling of relief that the struggle was finally over.

But the struggle was not over. Now, almost twenty-two years later, Amite and my father were still at loggerheads—even in death. Although I was still loyal to Amite, I felt, even in my grief, that part of his unreasonableness in trying to hold me to the promise I had made the year before, was the fact that it was my father's funeral and that he would never give in. I tried to think of a compromise in the situation. What would Amite agree to? What sort of proposal could I make that would allow me to go to my father's funeral while at the same time, respect Amite's wishes? But compromise seemed to be out of the question now because I knew I would go to Bemi and I was equally certain that Amite would never agree. On the few occasions when we had opposing viewpoints about a matter, our method of resolving it was to delay a decision, give ourselves time to rethink the matter or for the situation itself to change and present an alternative. But delay was not possible now. I had to go. Our compromises usually consisted of my coming around to Amite's point of view with his maybe giving in on a tiny, usually insignificant detail or two. Here, too, the present situation did not lend itself to the solution. I thought again of my father. What would he think? And I knew: My father would have been totally disgusted with me to even think that some man, husband or no, had enough power over me to keep me away from his funeral.

No, Amite, I thought. *You can't win this one. This is not the old Jaye Peay who has been caving in for twenty-one years. This is old man Joseph Prince Bartholomew's daughter standing before you now. This is not the quiescent Jaye you are used to. I am my father's daughter and I will go to his funeral. Come hell or high water, I will go, I will honor my father. I am who I am.* And having so thought, resigned myself to the nameless fear that crept back over me, the impending dread of having to face and cross Amite.

When I returned to Largo after burying my father, Sister Deer presented me with a book, *Men Who Hate Women and the Women Who Love Them*, and suggested to me that the book would help me to better understand my situation. When I had gone to her before going home, she had not only been supportive of my decision to go, but had parted from me with the admonition.

"And don't be no fool, Jaye. Girl, don't be no fool. I'm going to pray for you, but I don't waste time praying for no fools. So, be sensible."

It had helped to lighten the moment and I had, of course, taken her advice and proceeded to go to my father's funeral. Now, when she gave me the book in such obvious seriousness, I did not take it home right away but left it locked in my desk at school. I certainly didn't want Amite to see it. It wasn't long, however, before my curiosity got the best of me. The book, written by Susan Howorth, seemed to speak directly to me. I saw myself at every turn of a page, and while I had been surreptitiously keeping the book out of sight of everybody, I began to read voraciously, not wanting to stop until it was finished. Some days I would have to put the book aside to let myself digest what I had read. So much of it hit home. As time passed and my life with Amite continued, I began to see the application of the book in my everyday life constantly, so much so that I was beginning to feel like a fool for not having recognized it sooner. This book, given to me by Sister Deer, was instrumental in helping me to make the final decision to leave Amite.

In the fall of the second year of Yala's being out of school, Amite's and my relationship had begun to deteriorate drastically. Amite complained that I spent too much time in school and that I was against trying to make the farm work. Yala had begun to take on more of the housework and the care of Hannibal and Nefertiti. I did not like it and suggested to Amite that he needed to do his share to help out, but Amite considered most housework to be my job and would refuse to help most times. Gradually, Yala became more and more surrogate mother for the little ones, especially Hannibal. She and Amite would set up little rules for Hannibal to follow and if I unwittingly allowed him to break one, I would be told by them that the child had been forbidden to do such and such and, therefore, had to be punished. Invariably, Hannibal's punishment was not being allowed to spend time with me. I did not like Yala's method of handling the children, especially after I realized that corporal punishment was a part of her strategy. She usually did not wait for compliance with an order but would slap the children around as she was giving out commands. This was particularly surprising to me since I had never beaten her, nor, to my knowledge, had Amite. When I tried to correct her, though, Amite would become angry and say that I was encouraging disrespect by the younger ones. I told Yala that she needed to be more positive in her dealings with Hannibal and Nefertiti and suggested that it would encourage respect from them. She then insisted upon their greeting her first each morning. One evening when I came home from school, Hannibal ran to the door to greet me. Very quickly, Yala moved in front of him, barring his way. "Go back and sit down with you work, boy. Leave Mom alone, she is tired."

Hannibal was trying to move around her through her legs to get to me, "But I want to say hello to Mom!"

Yala continued to block his way. "I told you to go back and sit down. Mom needs her time."

Hannibal returned to the table and sat down, obviously upset. I set my book bag and packages down on the table near him, grabbed him up for a hug, said, "But Mom is never too tired to say hello to her best boy, huh?" Of course Hannibal loved it, nestled his three year old head against my neck and held on for dear life. Yala left the room in a huff.

Later on, she complained that it was hard to discipline the kids if I would not cooperate and insisted on letting them have their way. Amite jumped in to complain that he was tired of raising the children by himself, that Yala was trying to help out, but that I was encouraging disrespect by allowing the children liberties when they were under punishment. Contrary to what we had always agreed upon, Amite began to intervene whenever I chastised the children, saying that he spent the most time with them, and therefore, knew them better than I did. My relationship with Elsie, my older sister, who did a good portion of raising me, had been totally different and I could not understand why Yala insisted on striking her little brother and sister when it had never been done to her. Pretty soon, it was almost as if Amite and Yala were the parents and the rest of us children. Both were bossy and always seemed to be on the same side of every argument. Their arguments were always accompanied by impeccable logic, rigid and unswerving. I wanted to get Yala away from home more than ever as I sensed that she was losing her desire to go to school. My one consolation was that she was continuing to read and had started her own library of books which Bea would replenish from time to time.

***

By the fall of 1986, I had realized that Amite was again not going to allow Yala to go away to school. Disappointed once again, I settled myself down to teaching. The future was made more palatable by the fact that Bea was again going to work with me, this time to put on an American play—*A Raisin in the Sun*. It was a part of the curriculum in English so I could justify bringing Bea in to direct. I cleared it with Mr. Posey at school and we began. It was then that I began to appreciate more the wealth of Bea's talents. Bea was a foreigner working with kids who had little and in most cases, no acting experience, who had to be taught even the basics of drama before she could direct them.

Bea had auditions, cast the play, and we began. She was a stickler for perfection, demanded punctuality and reliability and strove to bring out the best the children had to offer. Her cast consisted of Creoles, Sarawee, Asian, and East Indians, and she worked with all of them, individually and collectively, to hone a finished product of which we could all be proud. In the process, not only did the students produce a wonderful interpretation of the Lorraine Hansberry classic, but through it, she taught them about African American culture and history as well. Many times, I would watch her stop an actor in the middle of rehearsals and launch a discussion about what the lines meant, get the actors to compare and contrast attitudes and situations expressed in the play with what they knew about in Largo. Bea taught the cast and crew how to build a set, assume adult-like responsibility for costumes, props, makeup and the like. Even Mr. Posey, when he spoke to the general assembly at the school about the play, commented on all the ancillary aspects of the experience above and beyond the acting itself.

We toured the play to Capitol City and to Mayonne where the students outdid themselves and were overwhelmed with plaudits, and came away feeling very good about themselves. One boy in particular— Thomas—had really shone in the lead role much to the surprise of the teachers at Rivertown High. Why? Bea knew nothing about anybody who was supposed to be whom, what their social standing was, and the like, so she cast the play based on what she saw in the auditions—simply choosing the best people. The boy, Thomas, was someone who would never have been chosen for so large a role otherwise. Thomas sparkled, glistened in the role of Walter Lee and after the play, became immensely popular with both faculty and students. A few weeks after the play, he was tapped for another honor at school and found himself thrust into the limelight of things. Of course, the girls noticed and one in particular, a white girl (very light-skinned Creole named Melanie) began to chase him. Thomas was Sarawee, a black boy, the son of a single mother who farmed and worked extremely hard to send him to school. Melanie's father owned the restaurant where Amos had briefly worked. Both were in my English class and when I saw them passing notes and eyeing each other in class, I didn't like it. I told Bea about the development and she laughed: "But, Jaye, don't you want Thomas to enjoy his new found popularity? After all, he was only the best. The gal is only trying to get next to the best."

Bea thought it was cute. I didn't.

"But she would never have paid him any attention had he not been in the play. Now, I'm afraid that if he gets mixed up with her, he will forget studying. His mother works too hard...."

Bea cut me off: "But Jaye, why do you have to be so serious about the matter? First of all, she isn't white, looks black to me even with her skin color. Secondly, so what if she didn't pay him any attention before? That's the way kids are, and grown people, too—fickle—besides it will probably all blow over soon. She's just starry eyed now because he looked and sounded like Sidney Poitier. I don't think they're in any danger of getting married."

I refused to take it lightly, however, and continued: "No, they aren't and the reason it will never lead anywhere is part of my concern, Bea. She couldn't bring him home if she wanted to. Couldn't talk to him with her folks around, wouldn't talk to him if the whole school wasn't fascinated with him since 'Raisin.' Thomas doesn't need to be wasting time with her, letting his marks go down. He is only a passing fancy for Melanie. A school fancy at that. Her daddy would have a fit!"

Bea became a bit more serious now. She really had trouble seeing the light-skinned Creoles as anything but black. Now, she said, "Kinda like the white girls at home, huh? Playing around in the streets with black boys, then taking a shower and going home alone?"

I had finally scored: "You get the point, baby. And I'm going to make sure Thomas gets it, too. If they don't stop, I'm going to pull him aside and talk to him."

"Jaye, don't you think that's a little strong?"

"No, I don't. Thomas' future is at stake. That girl can fail all she wants, her folks will just keep on forking over those school fees and sending her 'til she finishes. Thomas has no such luxury. He's got to do his work and get out of school, do something with himself now. He has no time to be playing with no white girls!"

Bea was contrite, sensed my concerns and anger. "Well, Mrs. Peay, you just got me told, huh? I can't argue with that, Jaye. But don't be too hard on Thomas. He is just having fun being popular."

"Fun is a luxury he cannot afford!"

"Jaye!"

The next week the love affair between Melanie and Thomas was in full bloom and I made good on my promise to speak to Thomas, saying essentially what I had said to Bea. He didn't like it, and almost accused me of racism, at which point I began to stress the importance of keeping his grades up. He promised that his relationship with Melanie would have no effect on his school work. Of course, it did. They were always in each other's faces and their work suffered. This went on for over two months and since Thomas was a favorite of Bea's, I continued to complain about it whenever I saw her. Bea was respectful of my concerns but didn't say much. Finally, after about two and a half months, the love birds ceased to sing to each other and things were back to normal. Thomas' grades picked back up, Melanie went on her way and I could rest easy again.

One might wonder why I had so much time to be worrying about others. I saw a lot of human waste in Largo, however, and my penchant for trying to save other people was never far away. I had seen how the young can blow their opportunities in just a short while and knew that the effects could be felt for a lifetime.

17

It was 1957. Amite was all set to go to Canada in April, having already secured a job in telecommunications there, he already had his papers to travel. Of course, he wanted me to leave with him and immediately applied for me once we were married. I returned to Bonsai to teach, however, a few days after the wedding, as I felt that I should complete the term for which I had contracted. As a matter of fact, the nuns were insisting upon it. I would come home for the weekend, once a month and stay at Amite's grandmother's house. He was very annoyed with me for my refusal to jump up and leave on the April date, but I held my ground and finished out the term in June suggesting to him that he go ahead and take the job and that I would follow. Amite refused to leave without me and lost the job. Shortly after we were married, I was home one weekend and noticed Amite acting secretive about a letter he had received. He had always stressed openness and honesty in the relationship, read all of my letters, and insisted upon the truth from me, so I finally got him to show me the letter. It was from a girl who appeared to claim him as a boyfriend and seemed to be quite upset that he had gotten married. She expressed her undying love for him. Amite said she was the former girlfriend of one of his friends, that his friend had married and asked him to spend time with the girl to help her through the trauma. Amite said the girl had somehow fallen in love with him, that she had transferred her love for his friend to him when he tried to be a do-gooder, and that he had not known what to do. I accepted the story. I was to learn later, many years later, that the woman was a minor prostitute, and that Amite had made the whole story up.

According to Amite, he had had two girlfriends before me. His first heart throb was a beauty queen, a regular belle of the ball, and as Amite was considered quite handsome, they made a striking couple. They soon broke up, however because she wouldn't listen to him when he would tell her about wearing too much makeup, how to dress and the like, and

Amite began to see a much younger girl. In fact, she was a friend of mine, and we attended convent school together. We used to laugh and giggle about the usual things girls do when she would tell me about her relationship with Amite. I remember once when my mother saw Amite with her, she pursed her lips as she came away from the door, and in passing, said to no one in particular, "That Amite should find him somebody closer to his own age." I had thought that I knew about all the girls in Amite's life prior to me—the belle and my convent school friend—so the letter came as a complete surprise. Here was another girl, no, woman, I had never heard about. Amite violently destroyed the letter and asked me to trust him. The whole episode frightened me, shook me up a bit, but I accepted the story. This happened the first weekend I came home from Bonsai after we were married.

Amite's grandmother was nice to me, tried to treat me like one might a daughter, and would advise me on occasion. For instance, Amite worked the three to eleven o'clock shift at night and would get home just prior to midnight. He insisted that I wait up to take my meal with him. I would cook his dinner and begin the long wait for him to come home. One day his grandmother looked at me, sat down and said:

"Lissen, gial, yuh stomach all yuh got, only ting yuh can tek to grave with yuh is yuh stomach. Amite don't have the same stomah yuh got. Eat yuh food. Ef yuh want fuh sit wit he while he eat he food, fine. But yuh eat wen yuh hongry. No need fuh wait 'pon he. Pshaw!" and she sucked her teeth indicating just how foolish she thought the whole idea was. I thought it was foolish and pretentious, too, but felt differently about it. I wanted to appease Amite's whim—play the role of the big, best wife, I suppose—and since it seemed to be such a little thing, I didn't take her advice.

Two weekends later when I came home, I couldn't get a flight back to Bonsai in time to meet my first class on Monday. I went to Amite's aunt's house to phone the school and let them know that I would be late. Amite was working days and happened to come home just as I made my third trip to try to place the call. Not finding me at home, Amite had become angry, marched over to his aunt's house and dragged me off the phone and back home similar to the way he had dragged Lena home from the carnival two years earlier. He was upset.

"When ah come fum work, ah expect my wife to be home, no matter what else yu tink yuh got to do. If yuh late fuh work at that school, so what? Yuh teaching on my time, now, not yours. Yuh my gift to dem nuns."

I didn't know what to say. I had been on hold waiting for someone to come to the phone so I never did get to talk to the school. But I didn't have time to worry about that. I had cooked his dinner and left it on the stove; the table was already set. I rushed home with Amite and put his meal in front of him. He only ate half of his food before pushing his plate away in disgust. I felt I was to blame. I made two promises to myself then: one, that I would never be like my mother who, regardless of whether or not my father was coming home, would keep her Thursday date with the cinema; and secondly, that I would bear everything and anything Amite dished out to me with patience. I felt that whatever I got from this man, I deserved and I would keep it all to myself because there was no way that my father would ever have cause to be ashamed of me. Since I was already married, I could not change that, but I would make the best wife ever; and I proceeded to try to do just that. Whenever I came back to Bemi during those months before we departed for Canada in July, I would go to my old home whenever my father was there. My father tried not to show me "bad face" but his eyes held a hurt and disappointment that I had never seen there before and I knew that I had caused it. He still had me to take the bones from his plate and pretended to laugh and joke with me but it was not the same. My mother would greet me briefly when I arrived, and go to her room, saying, "Prince, your chilc is home."

I put on a big act for him. I was in pain because Amite had me perpetuate the lie that he had used to sway my dad's decision to let me marry him. I had bought two tent-like dresses and would wear them whenever I visited the house. On Amite's advice, I was to answer every question about my apparent pregnancy with, "I don't know." Of course, people raised their eyebrows at my bulky dress and wondered if I were pregnant, and Amite was amused by this. He said we should just make them remember that it was possible. At first, he was satisfied with my reports, but after a while, he began to accompany me so that he could enjoy their discomfiture first hand.

Finally, July rolled around and we departed for Canada. Both Amite and I had been saving money for the move to North America, so we had a sizable nest egg, about two thousand dollars. We departed on July 7, 1957 and instead of going to Winnipeg as originally planned when he had the job offer, we went instead to Montreal, to the 1967 World's

Fair. A friend of Amite's, Benson, came with us. We knew nary a soul, spent only a few weeks in Montreal before departing for Vancouver. Amite had, at first, said, before we left Bemi, that we would go to Prince Edward Isle, an especially lovely place he had become enamored of in Bemi from reading the travel brochures. The French predominated in Montreal and Amite did not like dealing with them, and he especially did not like having to rely on me to translate for him. Just before we were set to leave, Amite announced that we would go instead to Vancouver, so the three of us packed up and took flight there after about three weeks in Montreal.

In Vancouver, we lived in a nice hotel for a while, but when Amite and Benson could not find work, we moved on to cheaper quarters. It was the era of the hippie and flower children and Vancouver was full of transients filling immigration and manpower offices; jobs were hard to come by. I had known Amite's friend, Benson back home in Bemi, and in the first year or two of our stay in Canada, he was with us fairly constantly as we moved around from place to place, and later, when we got our first basement suite, Benson lived across from us and shared our kitchen. Shortly after we arrived in Canada, I recall his telling Amite that he had had a rough last night before leaving Bemi, that he had had to have sex with four of his girlfriends that night. He was bragging to Amite about his physical stamina and explaining to him why he was tired. He and Amite laughed about it; and since I was not part of the conversation, I listened but did not comment. I think Benson was a kind of Shakespearean foil for Amite. He would hold up Benson's wild ways to me as an example of what he, Amite, was not, then remind me of how faithful he was in contrast, and tell me how privileged I was to have him.

In Vancouver, Amite and Benson looked for work, not actually going out much but poring over the want ads in the newspapers for work in their field. Both had held jobs in telecommunications in Bemi and Amite was a trained technician. It had been a job in telecommunications that had awaited Amite in Winnipeg which he lost when he refused to depart without me in April. Finally, when the job search proved futile in Vancouver, we moved to Sedgewick, in Alberta province. Sedgewick was a city of approximately 750,000, and the major industry then seemed to be a fledgling oil and wheat industry. We were among the first black immigrants of the trained technical type to settle there, so much so that Immigration used to send newly arrived Caribbean immigrants to our house to get their bearings. At one point, after we had been there awhile, we would have up to eleven men congregating in our basement on Sundays. It was not the custom then for men to bring their wives with them and Amite would often remind me of how special and unique it was that he had chosen not to immigrate without me.

On arrival in Sedgewick, the taxi driver took us to the crummiest hotel in town where I spent the night sitting on a chair, crying, and refusing to go to bed. The place smelled of urine, was so infested with bugs that I was afraid to even sit on the bed. The next morning, we found an apartment and the three of us moved in. Three months went by and although Benson found work, Amite did not. Benson took a job with an Alberta phone company, but because the job required traveling the length and breadth of Alberta province, Amite refused, saying he did not want to leave me alone.

It was by then September and the two thousand dollars we'd brought with us was beginning to run out. I enrolled in school to study accounting and began to look for work. Amite wanted me to sew, so I took a job in a sewing factory which only lasted four days. My back hurt and the machines terrified me. When the employers said I was not making production, I quit, taking the forty six dollars which I had earned. I found a job at the post office sorting mail and we could worry less about what we would eat and I could concentrate on my studies in accounting. In November, Amite finally got a job with a subcontractor that wired aircraft. However, our income did not increase as he sent most of what he made home to his mother and we had to live on my salary. I never knew for sure whether Amite quit or whether the work ran out, but within a few months, he was out of a job again. Winter had really set in by that time, and, unaccustomed to the snow and ice, I slipped and fell, suffered a miscarriage at three months, and found myself out of work.

Amite did not like the work he was being offered and said that since he was trained in telecommunications, he would not do anything else. He stayed at home a lot playing and practicing on his guitar, hardly ever looking for work. Amite is an excellent guitarist, knew more about classical guitar music than any of the people we encountered in the field and it was not long before we found out about a position for a music teacher at a school in a small town called White Plains. The school, however, wanted someone who could teach accordion as well. Amite didn't know how to play the accordion, but since I'd had piano lessons,

I felt I could easily learn. I told him to accept the position, enrolled in a class in Sedgewick, rented an accordion, took a week's lessons and knew enough to teach. We moved to White Plains, a town of twenty-five hundred people about a hundred miles from Sedgewick. The people of White Plains were happy to have us. We moved into a one room basement bachelor suite and I bought material and sewed a curtain to separate the place. We used a small unoccupied house as the music school. Things went quite well in White Plains for a while as the people were hungry for art in their lives, bought guitars and accordions and the number of students rapidly increased. We would drive fifty miles away to two other towns once a week and give music lessons there.

My oldest son, Amos, was born in White Plains. After a year, our employer decided to move to another town, because he did not feel he was making enough progress with the music school. We could have made more money if Amite had been certified in his field of expertise. However, in order to take additional music lessons formally, he would also have to take academic subjects, and since he felt academics were frivolous and unnecessary, Amite refused. About a year after arriving in White Plains, we moved to Cachet, a larger town about fifty miles from White Plains. While we still went back to White Plains to service our students there at the music school, we were unable to go to the students in the other towns since they were now fifty miles in the opposite direction. Of course, the people were more than a little peeved with us since many of them had bought guitars and accordions specifically in order to be able to take lessons from us. We stayed the spring and winter in Cachet until Amite grew tired of the man who was working with us in securing the students and he decided we should leave. The deal we had with the man was for accommodations and a cut out of the fees for the students he brought in. When everybody was signed up and there was no new influx of students, the man stopped paying us, and insisted on giving us moose meat as compensation.

On the worst possible winter day, Amite packed us up, put everything into the car, and left. We were lucky. We stopped to see Canadian friends who were about to embark on a holiday for two weeks and made a deal with them to baby-sit their kids while they were gone; they let us live in the house. During that time, Amite found an unheated shed for us to live in. We nearly froze to death. We had no furniture save a crib for Amos and it was one of the most frigid winters I recall during the ten years we were to spend in Canada. Amite and I slept in sleeping bags. The baby had to have milk so we bought a fridge. During the day, we used the box the fridge came in as a playpen for the baby, and it doubled as a table for us as well. Amite began to spend more and more time playing his guitar, saying that great artists had to practice at least eight hours a day. I got a job peeling potatoes at a residential college where I soon began to trade with the student residents. I would help them with their homework in exchange for their helping me with dishwashing and potato peeling. My supervisor was totally nonplussed by this turn of events. When I had applied for the job, he had refused me at first and said that he would call me back. I learned that he had done so in order to confer with the two workers already there—a thirty year old Greek woman who knew very little English and a sixteen year old illiterate from Grand Pierre—to see how they would feel about working with a black person. I was barely in the house after the fifteen minute drive from the school when he phoned to tell me I had the job. By the time I left the school, I had had my first experience in giving ESL instruction and had encouraged the sixteen year old to attend night school and improve her education.

Of course, my letters back home read: "Dear Papa, I am working at a college, etc., etc." Never once mentioning that I was the chief potato peeler and dishwasher! So while I worked at the college, Amite kept Amos. Amos had a healthy appetite even as a tiny baby. It was in Cachet that Amite began to complain about the amount of baby food the baby could put away and began to call him greedy. I would come home from work at the college and find Amite strumming his guitar with Amos in his crib soaking wet. There would be porridge on the table where Amite had heated it and left it to cool for the baby. However, he would soon forget it when he went back to playing his guitar. Day after day, I would come home to find the cold porridge on the table and the baby wet in his crib. From the time we were married, I would serve Amite breakfast in bed on Sundays. Once the baby came, he insisted upon the same thing, including my moving the dishes when he was finished, no matter if I were busy with the baby or not. We would have argument after argument about his refusal to remove the dirty dishes.

When we moved back to Sedgewick, Amos began to creep around and get into things, and the toilet bowl held a particular fascination for him. Amite would punish him, but Amos was too little to understand punishment so he continued. Creeping around on the floor of the unheated shed, Amos developed first bronchitis, then asthma, which the doctors referred to as asthmatic bronchitis, and which he still suffers from to this day. I would come home from work, and Amite would let Amos out of his crib and say to me, "Watch this." No sooner than he put Amos on the floor of the one room open space that was our house, the baby would head straight for the toilet bowl and begin to play. Amite would punish him with a spanking, the baby would cry, and he would put him back down and Amos would head for the toilet bowl again. One day Amite did it for at least ten times. I saw it as a form of torture; Amite said he had to teach the child a lesson.

Amos' eating habits remained a bone of contention with Amite for the rest of his life with him. Amos liked to eat and like any child, had favorite foods. Amite would not allow Amos to eat a little bit of each food at a time, but would instead, insist that he finished all the foods he didn't like before being allowed to eat what he liked. There was always a fuss at the table as a result, and one day, I simply got fed up with watching Amite torture Amos at the dinner table. It had gone on too long, I guess, and I was tired of trying to reason with Amite. I became so frustrated that I dumped the table on Amite, and was immediately frightened, scared, wondering what Amite would do to me.

He was very quiet, picked up all the spilled food, not saying a word, placed everything aside, cleaned up the whole mess. Then he motioned for me to come with him. At this time, my sister, Lena, and his brother had come from Bemi and were living with us, so Amite took me aside into another room. He had a strange look on his face, his usually gray eyes had changed to another color and I feared for my life. He looked at me, then said to me in a low, menacing voice, never raising it: "Don't you ever, as long as you live, don't you ever cross me in front of my children! Ever! I am warning you now, and don't you ever forget it."

I guess I had feared that he might finally hit me. I don't know what I thought, but I know I was scared. But the warning served its purpose: I stopped defending Amos completely, never outwardly defended him from Amite again. Lena and Wentworth never said a word. Amite and I went back into the room and the matter was over. One day, not too long after that, Lena asked me if I had to choose between her and Amite, who would I choose. Of course, I said Amite. It broke Lena's heart. Lena did not care too much for Amite anyway. She was engaged to Wentworth but insisted upon waiting until she reached twenty-one before marrying him. After they came, we had to have at least three bedrooms because both Lena and Wentworth had to have a separate bedroom. It was not easy for Lena. Although she loved Wentworth, wanted to marry him, she found Amite unreasonable and domineering, thought I was too docile, unwilling to stand up for myself. And she had a hard time with Amite. Though she would challenge him to stay out of her business, he would still call her stupid, have her in tears at times. She would remark to me that she didn't see how I stood it, and vow that she would never have anybody take over her life that completely, husband or no husband. It took Lena a long time to forgive me for telling her I would choose Amite over her, and to this day, though she understands why I would have said such a thing, she still teases me about it on occasion.

The next fall I enrolled in university and began to go to school full time. I got a job at a mental institution and worked the graveyard shift, eleven to seven, nights. I had classes beginning one hour later at eight. I would come home from school, try to cook, clean and care for the baby, rest a little, and go to work at eleven at night. Amite would stay home with Amos most days depending on his schedule. He had begun to form bands with other guys from the Caribbean and would bring in a little money now and then. Finally, I asked around at the hospital and he was able to get a job where I worked. However, Amite soon came into conflict with the authorities there because he wanted to leave early for his band dates. Since he was an orderly with a regular shift, it was not easy for the hospital to accommodate him.

I was happy to be in school, though, really going to university for the first time as I had promised my father I would. So although it was a strenuous, seemingly impossible schedule, I managed it anyway. Nothing was going to keep me from getting an education. Although it was unarticulated, my thoughts were never far away from proving to my father that he had made the right decision by allowing me to marry Amite. For that reason, no matter how hard things became, I never allowed even an inkling of the trouble I experienced in those first years to reach my father's ears. No, I had to prove to him, indeed to everyone, that I could handle things, that nothing was wrong in my life. Through all the moving around, both then, and in the years to come, I convinced myself that it was what I wanted to do and when the children came later, I made sure they saw it that way, too. Throughout any hardship, of moving, living a primitive lifestyle in remote places—whatever the reason—whenever we had to pull up stakes and move again, I told the children that we were going on holiday, camping out, taking an adventure. I made it sound exciting, something nobody else was doing—and indeed they weren't— so that the children would not feel deprived and carry around any stigma from it. Things seemed to be going well for us that second year until February when I became ill and had to enter the hospital.

The month before, I'd had my menstrual cycle on time as usual, but it never stopped. I bled for a month, passing a lot of clots every day. I didn't know what to make of it, but since I didn't feel bad, I continued to work, not even going to the doctor. Finally, I passed an unusually large lump one day, it frightened me, and I decided that I needed to see a doctor. Of course, they immediately put me in the hospital where they stemmed the flow of bleeding, and kept me for about a week. The doctors first thought I had had an ectopic—tubal—pregnancy, but later found out that I had not. They were unsure of what it could possibly be, but decided that I probably needed to have a hysterectomy anyway. I had been given minor surgery upon entering the hospital but not by my regular doctor. He had been otherwise busy and had turned the surgery over to another doctor who informed me that I would still need a hysterectomy. I was dismayed but figured that the doctors knew best, so I was prepared to go along with the surgery. Shortly after the doctor had told me I should have the hysterectomy, I was lying in the hospital bed half asleep, half awake, worrying about Amos at home without me, who was taking care of him, wondering how long this new surgery would necessitate my staying in the hospital. I opened my eyes to see a young Chinese man whom I recognized as a doctor, standing over me. At first, I thought I was still asleep, dreaming, but I shook my head, half sat up in the bed, and the man put his finger to his lips.

"Do not have the surgery; you don't need surgery. What you need is rest because it is psychological."

I started to say something, to ask a question, I suppose, but he quickly put his fingers to his lips again, smiled at me, and as quickly as he had come, he was gone. I now sat completely up in bed, and saw and heard the door close softly behind him. I didn't remember seeing him before but his accent had seemed slightly Bemijian, although he was obviously Chinese. Well, I took no more time to ask questions even of myself. I realized that the man was right, threw back the covers, got out of bed, walked over to the closet, found the clothes I had worn to the hospital, and within minutes, was fully dressed. Just as I finished and was preparing to leave, a nurse walked into the room, carrying a tray of medicine, prepared to give me some, I guess. Seeing me dressed, she quickly looked down at the medicine tray, then reached for my chart, hanging on the bed, while speaking to me.

"I didn't know you had been dismissed; but you haven't! Where are you going?"

I explained to her that I was going home, that I had to check myself out of the hospital right then, that I would not be staying any longer.

"But you haven't been dismissed by the doctor; you can't leave."

I told her I was going home. She rang the desk for the head nurse, but I was already in the corridor headed to the nurses' station myself. I went to the desk, told them that I was leaving. They were quite upset, told me that I had been scheduled for surgery and that they could not be responsible for me if I checked out of the hospital on my own. I told them OK, signed some papers, and took the bus home. I rested for a few days before going back to my job, the bleeding did not return and I never had the problem again. I thanked God that my grandmother had been right: I was born lucky.

18

Things did not go too well after that, however. I realized that I had to slow down, so I quit the job at the hospital that spring after I discovered I was pregnant again. I had only completed one year of my four year degree program and my hopes of continuing looked rather dim. Soon after that, Amite lost his job at the hospital. It appeared that Amite was under investigation for leaving his post early too many times to go to play with the band before his shift was finished, as well as for having slapped a patient who slapped him, a serious infringement of the rules.

We had been able to qualify for a house earlier that year when we were both working, and by scrimping and saving, I was able to come up with the down payment of nine hundred dollars when I received my scholarship money for school. So we now had a house note, and Amite was out of work again. By this time, Amite had taken an advanced course in welding in a bid to find more viable employment and to improve skills acquired in Bemi. Wentworth was a welder and had not been out of work since arriving in Canada, so Amite felt that learning welding was a good move. However, as soon as Amite finished the coursework, welding jobs slacked off and he had difficulty finding work. Around this time, even Wentworth was laid off, so they both journeyed to the north together to look for work, some one thousand miles away. Wentworth came back the next day saying that the work was indeed too far away and that he had decided to keep looking closer to Sedgewick, but Amite had decided to stay. He phoned me that night, told me to pack up, that he intended to stay and that he would be coming for me.

Amite had already tried out for a welding job in Sedgewick but been fired the first day. The employers felt that he worked too slowly, that he was only operating at about nine percent of capacity and that he would not work out. Amite came home that day crying and told me about it. We had had such high hopes for that job. I had taken much needed money from my baby-sitting salary to buy welding coveralls for him to use at work. Now I wondered what this new job would bring as it was also in welding. After many protestations on my part, because there was no university within a thousand miles from where Amite had taken work, (with Amite reminding me that he had lost a job once because I wanted to stay in school for my students) I gave in and we moved for the ninth time since we had come to Canada four years earlier.

Pregnant with my second child, I felt that Amite should allow us to stay put to see how the job would work out, but he insisted that he was coming for us. We left the house with Lena and Wentworth and headed north for the eighteen hour journey by car to a town called Kissimee. We settled in, bought a new car, secured housing and made a few friends. Most of the people were whites, but I managed to meet one Caribbean woman, the town librarian, who introduced me to black books. During my pregnancy, I read voraciously and talked to my unborn child. Yala was born in November. After about five months in Kissimee, Amite heard a rumor that the company was getting ready to lay people off from the job and he decided that we should go back to Sedgewick. I thought we should wait until he was actually laid off, but he insisted that he did not want to wait around for the inevitable so we sold the car and our furniture, and came back to Sedgewick after Amite promised that he would allow me to go back to school.

Soon, I enrolled in school again. I was determined to finish and since I had only done one year, I immediately went to my advisor to find out how much more work I would need for my degree if I planned to graduate the same year as originally planned. It was more than two years work, so I went to my advisors to ask for special permission to take two additional courses each semester until I could finish. At first, they refused, but I persisted and after evaluating my transcript, looking at the grades I had already made, they finally relented and let me take the extra courses, cautioning me that I would be watched closely. I passed all of my coursework with flying colors. Finally, in May, 1974, I received my degree in education.

With Amite's experience in welding, he was now more employable in welding and was able to secure a job at the same place where Wentworth was working, some fifty miles away from Sedgewick. They camped out there during the week so I and the children stayed home. Wentworth and Lena, who had kept our house while we had lived in the north, moved out to an apartment of their own. I settled in to going to school every day and taking care of the children. During the ten months Amite worked on the job out of town, we managed to put some money into fixing up the house, he bought a car for himself and a Volkswagen for me. Amos had started to attend a special school as we had discovered that he was autistic, so I would take him to school and Yala to the baby-sitter.

During the summers, I would work in order to be able to pay my school fees myself. That first summer, I worked in a Catholic hospital and later, took a job at the mental hospital where I had worked when we first came to Sedgewick. Weekends, Amite and I carpeted, painted, and fixed up the basement of the house ourselves. Although Amite made good money during those years, he did not feel that it was necessary to upgrade our standard of living. Everybody else, over the years, even the people who had come up from Bemi long after us, people whom we had given a leg up, gradually moved to the suburbs to single family houses. We remained in a low income area in our old townhouse. I wanted us to move up, too, but Amite saw no need for it, and criticized the others for doing so. Money ceased to be a problem for us after a while because Amite no longer had to send money home for his mother's maintenance. His brother, Wentworth, had taken over when he had gotten on his feet. In the old days, whenever Amite worked, even when we were scraping together our own living, he would send most of the money he made home and I would have to work to take care of our family in Canada. Amite handled all of the money throughout our marriage whether or not he was the one bringing it in. While I was in school I only worked during summers. Amite would budget the money, give me money for groceries, take care of my gas, and keep the rest. I had no money to call my own. Finally, one day, I pulled him aside, spoke to him about it. "Look Amite, I'm your wife and I need to have some money of my own. When you are budgeting the money, it is only right that you should include an item for me, even if it's just two dollars."

He protested that he did not see the money as either mine or his, that it was our money and that I could always feel free to take whatever I needed. He saw no need for it to be included in the budget.

"But, Amite, listen to me. The money is in your pocket, so I will still have to ask you for it. I think that as a wife, you should hand me some money, include it in the budget, so that I will have spending money."

He said he was sorry that I felt that way, but that he would do something about it. The next time he made out the budget, there was a line item: "$3.00—pocket money for Jaye." He said it was just a token to please me.

"You are free to take whatever you want," he reiterated.

***

Around this time, Amite had stopped playing in the band. He never seemed to be able to get along with the guys because they felt that he wanted to impose unreasonable discipline on them. It was similar to the band members' complaints in Bemi: No talking, practice, don't be late. The rules were too much for these rather laid back, Caribbean men flexing their muscles for the first time in the white man's land. Besides that, Amite had very definite ideas about the kind of music the band should play, ideas that were out of sync with what the situation usually called for. The band members knew the regular, old melodies that drew the Canadian crowds, what the Canadians wanted to hear, but Amite had all sorts of new compositions that, though they were beautiful and innovative, were not what the guys were used to playing, nor in the best interest of keeping the people coming. When he failed to sway the men in the band, Amite quit.

Around the same time, we met a Tanzanian couple at the university I attended. Bertha was a cleaning woman whom I had befriended and her husband, Martin, was a student at the university. We began to visit with them and they with us, and finally became like family for each other. Amite and Martin would argue during those first days about the value of education versus practical skills. Martin and I talked no end about more esoteric things—the university, our ideas, what was going on in the world. Martin extolled the virtues of socialism as Tanzania had gone socialist some years earlier and in those early days, Martin seemed to look forward to going back to help shape the country. Amite fell in love with socialism and Martin promised that if we ever decided to come to Tanzania, he would help us get set up. We were very happy with our new friends; Amite taught Bertha to drive, sponsored her with immigration so that she was eventually able to gain permanent residence in Canada.

I was now going to university full time, enjoying myself learning, taking care of home and children, working summers. We began to have money for holidays and vacations. My father came to Canada for holiday and was quite pleased with what he saw. Amite was working out of town, so Martin drove my father around a lot. It snowed early that year, so my father had a chance to see his first snow. We had lots of family gatherings, and he truly enjoyed himself. Newly arrived Bemijians still came to us for advice and assistance, so we had a large extended family. My father got a chance to see lots of Bemijians doing well in Canada. It was a wonderful visit. When he left, I felt a sense of accomplishment that things had gone so well, that I was in my last year of university, going to school as I had promised my father, and had a nice family to boot.

It was that year, however, that Amite began to resent my going to school. He had changed jobs again, was living at home, not working out of town, and he had a good deal of time on his hands. However, he refused to help me out even in small ways. He would not pick up after himself around the house, refused to take the kids to the sitter or to school, would not pick them up and said that my schooling was getting in the way of family life. Amite said that taking care of the family's needs was my responsibility and since I seemed to need help with doing my job at home, I should quit school and stay home. The school was taking away his time, he said, taking me away from him. I had no intention of quitting school. I was too close to finishing, so I began to figure out how to make the school less intrusive. To compromise, I would never do homework in his presence. I would finish supper in the evenings, take care of getting the children to bed or whatever their needs were, sit around or do housework while keeping Amite company, wait for him to retire. When he did, I would go to bed with him, wait for him to drop off to sleep, then get up and attend to my homework. Sometimes that meant waiting until midnight, getting into the car and going back to the library in order to finish assignments. Amos was not doing well in school at that time, and Amite said it was my fault because I did not spend enough time with him.

Bertha and Martin were still part of our lives and when Martin received a research grant to do graduate work in his field, he offered to hire me as one of two research assistants he'd received funding for, which meant that I would have to travel with him sometimes to other cities. Amite hit the roof, said it was just another example of my trying to shirk my responsibilities. After that, Amite became even more envious of anything I did on campus and it was not long after that when he asked me to quit school. Of course, I refused.

Family Secrets

That spring, I was studying for a final that I had to take on Easter Saturday. I studied all day Good Friday preparing for the upcoming exam, and on Saturday morning, Amite got up early, got showered and dressed and prepared to leave the house. I asked him where he was going, since I knew he was aware that I had to leave for the exams. I had hoped that he would stay home with the kids while I went out.

Amite had looked at me coldly, "I don't have to explain to you where I am going. I don't know where I am going, and I don't want to lie to you." I didn't say anything, bundled the kids up and dropped them off at a friend's and went to sit for the exam. I returned, picked up the kids and later on in the afternoon, I called Bertha. We chatted for a while and in the course of the conversation, she insinuated that Amite was there. I did not speak with him. Martin was out of town so I figured Amite had gone over to Bertha's to lick his wounds and complain about me and the university. The children and I spent a restless evening at home, finally eating dinner when Amite did not show up for it, went to bed. Next day, Easter Sunday, Amite came home around noon. We had made plans for Easter dinner at Lena's so we got dressed and went to their house. After dinner, Amite was playing records and since he was at the phonograph, I asked him for a special record I wanted to hear.

"Amite, play 'Whiter Shade of Pale' for me," I said, watching him rifle through the albums. When the record he was playing finished and he still did not play the one I had requested, I asked him again, thinking perhaps he had forgotten. He refused to comply three or four more times. Finally, I went over to the record player, put the record on myself. Amite grabbed my hand, flung me across the room. I was startled into anger, came back charging. We started to fight, I ran into the kitchen, got a knife and drew it on him. The kids started to scream and some of the adults broke up the fight. Amite got into the car, said it was time for us to go. I refused to get into the car in spite of the fact that he drove the car alongside me for the full two miles, with the kids hanging out the window begging me to get in the car. I walked home in the snow. When we got home, Amite began to talk about what had just happened, said he had been upset that I was neglecting the children and him with school, that he was simply too frustrated and he wanted me to quit school. I managed to appease him by pointing out that school was a backup for us in case anything ever happened to him, that I would have an education and be able to take care of the kids myself. He seemed to accept this for

209

then. That summer, I didn't work, stayed home, and took the kids on a month long vacation to Winnipeg to visit with Yala's Godmother, a Bemijian whom we had known during the five months we'd lived in the north in Kissimee. When I returned, Amite had changed jobs three times and was bragging to me about his ability to do so.

"I quit. I'm a man. If they so much as look at me too hard, I walk off their job. I don't need to take anything from them!"

I didn't say too much, was glad that he was still working, felt grateful that he had still been able to find work what with his cavalier attitude.

Besides Bertha and Martin, we did not socialize too much except with family. When we had first come back and gotten on our feet, and Amite was still playing in the band, the wives of the band members would congregate at our house. Soon, talk of husbands would arise, and the women would have a heyday. I usually kept silent during these talk fests, not saying or disclosing much about us. Our situation looked pretty perfect, I thought, so there was no need to share with outsiders whatever went on behind closed doors. The women had a saying that was used to ask the man to check his behavior and to express displeasure in a joking way whenever the husband got out of line. For instance, the man might be flirting or being inconsiderate in public. The wife would say, "Behave youself, buoy; I will cut you off." Everybody would laugh, knowing that it referred to bed and private life, the woman would have made her point without a big fuss, and that would be that. I thought it was cute, but I had never, ever said it to Amite. Once when we were together with friends, relaxed and having a good time, and I said it to Amite, he did not respond then but when he got me alone, he admonished me about it. "Don't you ever say such a thing to me again. That's prostitute talk, you know. Sex is not a bargain!"

Amite would refuse to take me to the Bemijian dances with him most times. However, on the few occasions when I did go, we women seldom had a chance to dance. We would sit and sit and sit and even if a husband danced with his wife, it was usually an obligatory, solitary dance for the evening. Then the man would proceed to dance with the hippie looking Canadian girls, moving among them to dance for the rest of the evening, never once coming back to the table to dance with any of the Bemijians who were unescorted, like they did with the Canadians. When I complained to Amite, he said that those women wouldn't dance with any of those guys if they were in Bemi, so why should they bother to dance with them up here in Canada. Finally, after much wrangling over this issue and getting absolutely nowhere, I convinced the women that we could dance by ourselves. We would get up, dance together and have a ball. But it was not the same as dancing with a man or your husband, especially when you were looking at Bemijian men dancing around you all evening with the Canadians.

Gradually, my relationship with the women began to deteriorate, however. Since I didn't talk about my home affairs as they did, and was quite busy with university and studies, they began to not like having me around as much. They said I had gotten different since I had gone to university. It bothered me because I truly liked being around my own people. But since I was going to school, had a different set of priorities, indeed, I found myself pretty much outside of their company after a while. The summer prior to graduation, I took the children to Calgary for a week's holiday, happy for the chance to be alone with them and without the stress and strain of school or work. About three days after we arrived, Amite called me about two o'clock in the morning to say he was having a problem with Bertha. She had come over to the house for a visit, drunk, and since Martin was out of town, Amite had put her to bed. In her drunkenness, he said, Bertha had wet the bed and he had tried to change it. When he did so, Bertha had made advances at him. What should he do, he wanted to know from me. I told Amite that there was not too much he could do except leave the woman alone to sleep in the sheets until she woke up a bit more sober. Forget it, I said. And if Martin heard about it and objected or wondered why, he had protected himself by calling me to let me know. Amite said OK and hung up the phone. I didn't think too much more about it. Twelve years later, I learned that Bertha was living in my house while I was gone, that she and Amite had obviously had an ongoing affair. I trusted Amite, though, and I never, ever, suspected.

Finally, graduation rolled around. Things were bad between Amite and me. He had continued throughout the whole year to berate me for neglecting the family for school, asked me to quit. By then, I could see the end in sight so I held out, but it was a miserable year. Martin was graduating from graduate school and had gone all out to participate in all of the end of the year activities. Bertha was with me one day and asked me about my cap and gown for the ceremonies. I told her that I did not plan to go to any of that. I planned to pick up my degree after it was all over. I had not ordered invitations to send out nor did I avail myself of any of the other amenities that accompany graduation. She thought I was silly. "But you deserve that. Martin is having a celebration even though it is his second degree. You have worked for it."

Amite heard us talking, queried me and hit the roof. What do you mean you aren't participating? Why not? I explained to Amite that I was tired, that all I really wanted to do was obtain my degree and forget about it.

"Oh, no, that will never do," Amite insisted. "You have been going to school all this time to get the degree. No way. We can't just ignore it. You have to participate. It is the only sensible thing to do."

I was flabbergasted. I had to look at Amite twice to make sure it was him talking.

He continued, "Who did you invite?"

"Nobody."

"Nobody? Well, we have to get busy." With just two or three days left before the ceremonies, Amite got on the phone, called our few friends and hordes of acquaintances, invited them all to the ceremonies. He then planned an after graduation dinner at a restaurant and invited the attendees to celebrate by going to dinner with us. He was a whirlwind of activity. I was a little numb, sat through it all, the graduation ceremonies—where I surprised even myself by being recognized during the ceremonies for placing in the top of my class—and later the dinner where Amite continued to floor me. About thirty people attended and we were seated at a long table in a private part of the restaurant. Amite made elaborate toasts to my achievements, talked about how proud he was of me, etc., and went on and on and on. Still, in semi-shock, I sat through it all thinking, not so much about what he was saying in front of all those people, but about the past, what I had just experienced. It was like a television screen with the story rolling by: I could see myself, out on the freeway with the car broken down, having to take the bus when the car wouldn't start in the mornings, scraping ice and snow off my windshield minutes after Amite had scraped his own and left, running to and fro to the baby-sitter's and to the school, preparing the five course Sunday meal Amite always insisted upon; baking the bread he insisted I make him twice a week; crawling out of bed at midnight tiptoeing around so as to not awaken him as I prepared to do my homework. Then I could see Amite: Playing his guitar, sitting in the middle of a mess in the living room, refusing to lift a finger to help me, telling me the kids were my responsibility and refusing to keep his children so that I had to take them with me everywhere I went, refusing to help with the extra care that Amos required. The images were vivid, and no amount of closing my eye or propping them open to try to look attentive to what was going on at dinner could erase the memories that were floating around there, imposing themselves on the unreality of the moment. It was a painful day for me. I sat through the well wishers, the speeches, toasts, hugs, and genuine expressions of good will from people who knew me, smiling as best I could—on cue—and hurting all the while, literally paining from the strain. When it was over, after nearly two and a half hours, I escaped to home and bed.

I got work immediately, subbing in the public school system that summer. I was offered a position in two schools for the fall. The Catholic school offered me employment and I took it. Our lives seemed to straighten out a bit over the next couple of years. Amite was working regularly now and he insisted on our putting my check into savings. I didn't mind because his salary was plenty for us to live on. Indeed, I was happy that we had done so when we got a proposition from my father about land being subdivided in Bemi, wanting to know if we were interested in buying. Amite said yes, and we sent money home to secure fifteen acres for us. The children were in school, I was teaching French still at the Catholic school, having gotten second and third year contracts. In November, however, there was an accident on Amite's job and he decided to quit. A man fell off a scaffold and was killed. Amite had heard about Largo from people we knew from there so he said we should go there. He had already bought ten acres of land there on one of his holiday sojourns. I tried to reason with him, reminding him that my contract ended in the spring, and I still had about six months to go. Couldn't we wait until then to leave?

Amite said "No. Give the school a month's notice. That is enough. That is when I plan to leave here. If you don't want to go, I will take the children and leave. You can stay here if you wish!"

Well, of course, I couldn't stay and let him take my children, so I reluctantly gave notice. The school was upset, justifiably upset for such a short notice and I left with the bad feeling that I would never get a reference from them should I happen to need one. By the time the month was up, before we left Canada, Amite had decided that we would go back to Bemi—home—instead of to Largo.

19

In January, 1977, after selling our house, furniture, car, and packing our household goods, we moved back to Bemi. Amos and Yala were nine and six years old respectively. The fifteen acres of land we had purchased was a fantastic bargain. A road ran between the property and there was eight hundred feet of beachfront with a beautiful view of it from across the road. On the land grew typical island foliage, including coconut trees and the like. Amite, the children and I cleared the land, and our relatives came to help us build a small one-room house on the land until we could have plans drawn for the house we planned to build.

We moved in and began to work the land, Amite planted a garden, grew vegetables and went to sell them in the marketplace, taking my younger brother along. My father was quite impressed with all this. In the old days, only the poor and unsophisticated sold vegetables. My father had always seen himself above this. Now, since independence, entrepreneurship was being stressed and people were encouraged to use the land and make it productive. In the meantime, I received a job offer from the American school of a major corporation on Bemi. It was a good package: $3,600 per month and a loan for a house along with many other frills. Amite rather liked the deal except for the house. The houses were in a subdivision near the school which was a half mile from our land. Amite did not want to live among the "rich" and vetoed the idea. I took, instead, an offer to teach at the local school which paid $2,400 per month. We proceeded to draw up plans for our house and went to an architect to have the blueprints done. Later on, when Amite returned to pick them up, he changed the plans, so that instead of having to pay the man $800 as originally agreed upon, we now paid $1600 for two sets of plans. Finally, after about three or four months of dealing with the plans, we had them sent to Town and Country Planning for approval to start building.

Amite went to Bonsai for Easter of 1978 and returned to say that we should delay building on our land in Bemi because Bonsai was so much prettier and he wanted to check it out. We had the little house the men had built so I didn't worry too much, continued to teach.

In August, Amite decided to go to Largo to check out the place, stayed three weeks, and returned in September. I was eight months pregnant with Nefertiti when we moved to Largo in April of 1979 after buying a truck and driving in through Mexico. Amite, having bought land on the earlier trip, took us to it in Mayonne and built a small, one-room, twelve foot by eighteen foot house. Nefertiti was born one month later in May, 1979. The people in Largo didn't take to us very well and unlike the return to Bemi had been, we found ourselves the object of much dislike. We owned a truck, a brand new one at that, so the whole town would try to go with us whenever we went out in it. The people would also send children to beg for money and to top it off, someone tried to frame us for burning down a ranch.

We stayed in Mayonne a year, working to build up the spot of land we had purchased, the children and I building a road that Amite insisted we would need when our house was finished. The road was about eight hundred feet long, led from the main road to our present small house, around and back to it and led up a hill where Amite planned to build a permanent home for us. We collected stones from a quarry and carried them by hand, laying them to build the road.

By the time the road was finished, Amite decided that we should go to Tanzania to take up the offer made long ago by Martin as he knew that Martin had returned home and from all accounts, was doing well. However, we first had to go to Bemi to collect monies tied up from the sale of our fifteen acres of land there. This time, we did not sell our house, but instead, placed it in the hands of a group of Mennonites, along with most of our worldly goods. We told them that if we did not return in three months, they were to auction if off at sale and send the money to an account we had set up in the States over which we had made Amite's older brother the caretaker. Included in those goods were still unpacked crates of household goods from Canada which I had not bothered to unpack when we had returned to Bemi.

We left, taking very little with us save our clothes. I had wanted to take Yala's doll, a beautiful, three foot tall, black doll that I had bought for her on a trip to New York, but Amite said it was too much to pack and he didn't want to carry it. We had to stay in Bemi for a month, longer than we had planned, in order to untie the money from the sale of the land. We contacted Martin and he said he would accommodate us.

We went to Tanzania in July, stopping in France and England for sightseeing and having a nice holiday with the children. It was June, 1980. Martin was indeed doing quite well back home in Tanzania. He and Bertha had separated, he had re-married, and had a marvelously big house with servants and the works, but he did not offer us a place to stay. Instead, he led us to a hotel where we stayed for a week, then contacted a friend and asked him to rent us a house. He asked another of his friends to go with us to shop for household goods. Amite was more than a little put out with Martin and to top it all off, Martin's mother died in a village four hundred miles away and he went home. In his grief, I suppose, he never contacted us again while we were in Tanzania. We had trouble everywhere we turned, even in trying to open a bank account. Besides, the friend whom Martin had recommended to help us appeared to be a bit shady and seemed to want to find ways to rip us off. He even started to undermine Martin.

I settled down to trying to make the house we had rented into a home, acclimating myself to the new country. By the time I had been in Tanzania for a few weeks, I realized that the reality of Tanzanian socialism and what Martin had talked about, were two very different things. I would watch the Tanzanians stand in line for a cup of flour for hours and hours, and when they finally got it, it would be filled with boll weevils and worms. I put out word that I wanted flour and because I had money to pay for it, I was immediately brought a fifty pound sack of flour. I had so much flour that the Tanzanians were coming to me for flour! One day, the water went off early in the morning. I waited and waited for the water to come back on but to my dismay, evening came and the tap was still dry. Finally, a child came with a bucket of water upon her head, curtsied, and said in Shikamoo, "Good day and my respects to you."

I responded, "Marahaloa," which means "It is acknowledged." The child put the water down and left. As time went on, more and more children came bearing buckets and containers of water on their heads, leaving it upon the verandah for me, so that eventually I had thirteen containers of water. I boiled the water and began to use it. No sooner than I put the empty pails back on the verandah, they would disappear, but for the life of me, I could not see anyone take the empty containers, try as I might! The women explained to me later that this was the common people's version of socialism: See a neighbor in need and try to fulfill that need.

The inverse happened with my clothesline. I only washed a couple of days a week, but there were always clothes on my line. I never saw anyone put them there and I never saw anyone take them away, although they would be gone by nightfall. When I remarked upon it, a woman told me, "The line is not a line without clothes upon it. They are giving your clothesline life. When you are not using it, it has no life. It does not exist. Only by someone hanging clothes on it does it have a life. It belongs to no one, has no purpose, does not even exist, unless clothes are on it. They're keeping your clothesline alive."

With this explanation, I forgot my initial consternation about some unseen intruder entering the yard and using "my" clothesline and became a little grateful that someone cared enough to help my line stay in existence. Tanzania was a new existence for me, but it was short lived. Amite, in his usual search for land, went to a village about a hundred miles from where we were staying in Dar es Salaam and began to look for land. The people thought he was a spy and Amite barely escaped being arrested. He came home saying that was the last straw, that we would leave Tanzania immediately. "But Amite, we have not even seen the place; give it a chance. How can you leave here now, just like that?"

Amite was intent upon leaving, though, wanted to pull up stakes immediately. I refused to leave without seeing Tanzania, and he finally relented, took two thousand dollars and we went on a week's tour of Tanzania where we experienced the most lavish and outrageously posh week of our lives, before returning to Largo in September.

The Mennonites had followed our instructions to the letter, and when we had been gone three months, auctioned off everything even the house which someone in their village had purchased, attached to a larger house and painted white. We had nowhere to live, no memorabilia from the past thirteen years of marriage save for a few souvenirs we had managed to collect in Tanzania. I had even been forced to leave my dictionaries in Tanzania as Amite said the freight on them was too much to consider bringing them back. When we were girls in school, my father had purchased encyclopedias for Lena and me and the dictionaries—a two-volume oversized set—had come with them. After we were married and away from home, my father, recognizing their sentimental value, gave them to us and Lena had said I could have them both since the two made the set. I had taken the dictionaries everywhere with me, but no amount of pleading would make Amite pay for the freight to bring them back from Tanzania. I finally donated them to the University of Dar es Salaam. Conversely, Amite's photography books, a virtual horde of them dating back to his earliest days in Bemi, continued to travel with us and made the passage back from Tanzania to Largo. About the Mennonite village in Mayonne, we saw most of our things, scattered throughout people's houses here and there, including the doll that Yala had loved so much. A Mennonite lady had bought the doll for her daughter and I offered her all manner of money to try to get the doll back, but she refused, saying that her daughter had become attached to it and no way was she going to deprive her of it. When we checked the bank account in New York, we found that most of our things had been sold for a mere pittance.

Undaunted, we moved in with friends, stayed for two weeks, Amite bought a used vehicle, the new one having been sold at a very large loss by the Mennonites at auction, and moved the family to Weeds, a small village near Tall Palms where we eventually wound up staying. In Weeds, we rented a filthy house from a Largotian man for fifteen dollars a month and set about the unpleasant task of trying to clean it up and make it livable. We bought mattresses, ordered new furniture a second time, and slept on the floor until it arrived. We stayed in Weeds for two years. I didn't work the first three months, but instead, stayed home with Nefertiti, who was a baby then. I should say I didn't go out for a job because I worked like a horse alongside Amite, clearing bush, and helping him to plant. I would get up, prepare food, bathe the baby, work in the field or bush, return to the house to prepare lunch, then back to the outside to work again.

Amite soon discovered a beautiful spot on the other side of a very large river that was known for its volatile nature. He would go there to work alongside several other people he had convinced that the land was worth clearing, and when those people gave up and went home, Amite hired others to help him. We spent fourteen thousand dollars clearing the land. Amite began to farm it, planting citrus, pigeon peas, and coco. The land produced well, but it was inaccessible, hard to get to, being, as it was, on the other side of the river. I would come home from teaching at Rivertown High, prepare food and other provisions for Amite and his workers, drive three miles into the bush, walk almost a mile to the river, hail Amite, put on my bathing suit, and wait for Amite to come and help me to navigate the river with the packages. We worked all weekends as well. The land was really in the jungle and walking along I would often see leopard stools along the way. Sometimes I would make two trips with the food. One day, when we were sitting by the side of the river resting underneath a tree, with the sky overhead clear and undisturbed, the sun shining brightly, I heard or sensed a noise. When I looked around, I saw that the river had flooded right where we were. Scrambling to our feet, Amite and I ran to the shallow place in the river where I usually crossed, to find that the tree that marked the place was almost completely under water. He grabbed a branch of the tree, told me to do the same. He eventually let go, and was pushed by the current to water that was shallower and he managed to get out. I was terrified, afraid to let go of the tree limb, but knowing full well that I would drown if I didn't because I could see a log coming towards me, bearing down in the swooshingly fast waters. I finally let go, and managed to scramble to shallow waters and safety. I prayed silently, thanked God for keeping me alive and we left the place.

In spite of my insistence that the place was too remote for us to consider developing further, Amite refused to give up. He wanted to tame the jungle, began looking for a place to reach the other side without crossing the river. However, after two or three other very hairy incidents in which I feared for my life in the jungle he was trying to develop, I refused to go there anymore. Amite eventually saw the futility and gave up himself. That was, of course, after we had spent fourteen grand.

We finally moved to Rivertown in 1981. Both Amos and Yala had passed common entrance exams and entered high school. It was in Rivertown that we met Gramps, a kindly Creole businessman who took a liking to us and tried to help us out, giving advice we could trust. He told us where there was available land, and helped us to get along. I didn't like Rivertown too much. We had no sea view and lived in a rather loud, noisy neighborhood of people. I went to work every day though, so I didn't have to deal with them too much. Being home more, Amite became friendly with the neighbors and developed the irritating habit of stopping each evening at the house two doors away to chat with neighbors—a man and his daughters. Most of the time, the children and I would have already waited a while for him to join us for supper. The children would be anxious and Amite would idle the truck there for at least fifteen minutes. I finally spoke to him about it and he was outraged. Told me that he would stop where he pleased and he didn't care whether I liked it or not. He implied that I was jealous of the girls, one of whom treated me like dirt, and that I was being silly. I never tried to stop him again but decided that I would no longer wait for him for supper. When the children and I got ready to eat, we did, whether or not Amite was there. Finally, with Gramps' help, we found a spot of land in Tall Palms, a community six miles south of Rivertown and we began to clear the land.

This time, I told Amite outright: "No more money for development until we build a house." If we took more money from the account in the States, it had to go into a house. Amite began to draw plans for the house. Then, we planted trees and otherwise tried to make the site hospitable. We eventually moved in one week before Hannibal, my fourth child, was born. The house was incomplete but I hoped that we had finally found home. That was six years ago.

20

It is ten o'clock in the air over Canada and I feel the plane descend just as the voice comes over the speaker and the "fasten your seatbelts" light comes on. The Yankee voice, nasal sounding in its unfamiliarity, comes on, speedily, rushing, it seems, jarring me out of my reverie.

"We have begun our descent into Toronto International Airport. Please note that the captain has turned on the seatbelt sign. For the remainder of our flight, please remain in your seats and return your seat backs and tray tables to their upright and locked positions. We will be landing in just a few minutes."

Landing? I look at the children seated next to me and across the aisle. Yala has chosen the window on the three seater with me, and Hannibal is between us. Across the aisle from me are Nefertiti and Amos sharing a three seater with the middle seat empty. Of course, Amos has chosen the window, so Nefertiti is next to me. Both of us are on the aisle. Now, she looks at me, raises her eyebrows in a quiet smile, eyes twinkling. I manage what I know must be a wry smile. What must I tell her? How much should she know about all of this? Surely, as time goes by, I will have to tell all of them something. What? How much can little children take? The flight attendant is moving down the aisle waking a few hard sleepers who are still in slumber with their seats reclined, completely oblivious to the impending landing. The attendant is gently touching each one, urging them to comply with the landing regulations. Seeing her in her crisp blue uniform with bow tie and name tag reminds me of what we will soon face on Canadian soil.

Bea told me this morning that when she called Elsie in Sedgewick last night, Elsie had said that someone from the family will be in Toronto when we arrive. I had been dismayed that we were routed through Toronto. I feel it will mean as it usually does, that Immigration is going to give us lots of trouble when we arrive. Besides, Toronto is over a thousand miles from Sedgewick, and it would have been so much nicer to arrive in Sedgewick and be cleared there. The flight from Miami has been over four hours long and I am tired, so tired, but I know that I am nowhere near being over the hump yet.

In Miami, we had the good fortune to be guarded while in transit by a Guatemalan security person and the familiarity of someone from our region had made what could otherwise have been an odious six hours much more bearable. He chatted with us about Central America and the Caribbean, put us at ease, so that as the time progressed, he had not seemed to be guarding us at all, and had even gone window shopping with us in what must have been every shop in the airport. But I had not been fooled. We were in the States—Miami International Airport— and I could not forget the adamant refusal of the American embassy in Largo to even consider letting us in. Besides that, when Therese's emissary had finally arrived at the airport, she had informed me that the Largo Rural Women's Group had had to pay an additional rather large sum of money for someone to guard us in Miami since we were in transit and had no U.S. visas or adequate documentation for getting into Canada. Nonetheless, it had been a pleasant time and the children had been convinced that I knew the man. Of course, I didn't, but his was a friendly, familiar face, and I had welcomed the opportunity to forget myself for a few minutes and chat about Caribbean food, weather, even politics, as the hours had progressed.

The children see me as someone devious, a liar, I had thought. Amite had begun to talk to me like that in the last year, treating me as if I were one of the children, confronting me in front of them, questioning my judgment and veracity, countering my discipline of the children, etc. It was small wonder that I had managed to get them on the plane even. Talking to the security guard had been a welcome respite from thinking about myself, the children, and the unknowable future. When he had led us to the gate to board the plane for Toronto, bade us farewell, it had felt much like we were leaving an old friend.

Now, here was Canada. What will we face here? I turn to look at Yala, and find that she is looking across at me. Ever since I had explained to her at the Largo airport that I would tell the Canadian authorities that I was bringing her in for medical treatment, she has appeared to cooperate, but I can't be sure of her. She is so much her father's child, catering to his every whim, even thoughts, I don't know what the stress of trying to get into Canada will do to her.

Family Secrets

The plane is rapidly descending now, and in a moment we will be on the ground. Nobody speaks right away. I mentally begin to gather up our things, but realize that there is indeed not very much to gather. Our sole possessions are in two suitcases. The bag, which could only be described as a "grip" which Sister Deer had brought to the airstrip in Rivertown to put the rest of our things in, and the one small bag which I had managed to slip out with Mrs. Orlando to Bea's on Saturday. Now I allow myself the liberty of a smile, thinking of Sister Deer's bag. Sister Deer must have brought it to Largo with her when she came twenty odd years ago! It was a black affair, with hard handles, made of vinyl and cardboard, similar to the one I remembered Grandpa having when he had arrived, sight unseen, at our door when I was eight, thirty two years ago. But there had not been time for being particular, and no matter what we look like when we arrive, we will be there, I think.

Amos now leans over to ask an irrelevant question. "Mom, who is meeting us here? Aunt Lena?"

I shake my head "no" without bothering to answer, look around at Yala again to see how she is doing. Her face is noncommittal, but at least it is not encased in stone the way it had been when we had removed her from the Rivertown hospital this morning. The plane is coming in for a very smooth landing, and only the feel of it rolling down the runway indicates for sure that we are no longer in the air. I look out—lights, darkness, noncommittal lights. What is out there? Passengers have roused themselves and are beginning to go into the overhead compartment for carry-on baggage. I pick up my purse, signal to the kids that we must get off now, and we head down the aisle amidst the passengers. A Canadian woman smiles at me, asks if we are on holiday.

"Yes," I respond, "holiday."

She continues, having nothing else to do but plague me, "Toronto?"

"No, Sedgewick."

Just as she purses her mouth to make some comment, the line starts out and I am mercifully relieved of making further small talk with her while I am trying to collect my thoughts for the authorities in Immigration. I feel my tote bag instinctively, making sure that the tickets, passports and birth certificates are still there. Surely, they won't deny me admission with my sick daughter, I think, so the five of us head down the aisle, with me leading the way, ignoring the perfunctory and insincere "bye, now" of the flight attendant standing in the doorway with the pilot. Now, it's follow the red line, find the line for nonresidents and stand in it, wait. We are all ill at ease. I start to remind Yala of my plans, then remember that there are always cameras in these places, watching. Promptly, I think better of it and am quiet. Whatever it is she is planning to say, she will say it, I think. No need to try to rehearse.

"The Lord is my Shepherd, I shall not want; my soul doth magnify the lord for he hath..." The litany has begun again in my head. Will I want for a place to lie our heads? Of course not. My sisters will see to that; that is my least worry. What will they say? What will the people here in Immigration say? Surely, we will be detained for a while, but how long will we have to wait? Will it be necessary for Lena or Elsie to come from Sedgewick to claim us, provide proof that we won't become a charge upon the government, bring bank statements and documents to prove they can take care of us? God, why didn't I plan this better? Because there was not time for planning: we had to go, today or never. But can I take it?

"He will not put upon me any more than I can bear." OK, Bea, you said it; I believe it. But what rights have we? Yala and Amos are already citizens. They won't have any trouble because their birth certificates will prove that. What of me? I was a permanent resident ten years ago. What of that? Will it count for anything? Maybe. But Nefertiti and Hannibal, they're Largotians. What about them? They are minors, my babies, wouldn't make sense to let us in without them. But what has to make sense where authority is concerned? They've got their rules. Will they believe me when I say this is an emergency? I have to get in now. It is an emergency, I think, and of the worst order, but will they think so?

I look at the people in front of me. That man, woman, and two children appear to be together. They look affluent, probably have all their papers in order. The man and woman behind them will be next, then that Slavic looking man, then us. It is not taking too long for them to pass people through, so maybe we won't have any trouble. But, of course, we will have trouble. All those people probably have better sense than to come to Canada without proper papers, so they are just routine. We are hardly routine, so how can I compare us to them? How much strength do I have left? Lots. We have come this far by faith. What can stop us now?

The All-American family has made it through to the other side. The man and woman approaching the cubicle look as if they don't have a care in the world, have begun chatting to the Immigration official as he looks through their papers. They will get through easily enough. Yes, they are thanking the man, leaving. The Slavic looking man is next. The official is saying "next!" in that unconcerned, impersonal manner with which all clerks seem to be born. What is the man saying?

"Next!"

"Next? I don't want to enter your country!" The Slavic looking man is speaking.

"Next!" The nervous clerk intones, now a bit anxiously.

"I want to go home! Next! Next! Next!" The Slavic man speaks the "next" himself again, mockingly.

The official is becoming flustered, people are looking around. I am scant feet away, we are so close to freedom. What now, Lord? Has the man gone crazy? Indeed, he has, I think, as I watch the flustered clerk press a button, looking frantically around for someone to come and restrain the man who has begun to fling himself around like a chicken with its neck wrung, moving in several different directions at once, but never approaching the counter and continuing to repeat the clerk's "next."

"Next! Next! Next?" he continues, looking at the rest of the nonplussed people in the line next to ours, peering into our faces, too. "Next! Next! What do I need to come here for? Next! Next! Next!"

The man has begun to slobber and it is now dribbling down his chin, his glazed eyes darting frantically from passenger to passenger. Security guards are moving in to restrain the man, take him away. The flustered clerk has gone, probably in fear of his life, I think, since he may feel that his "next!" had something to do with the man going off. The two security guards take the screaming man away, and another clerk has appeared behind the desk and is motioning for us to come forward. I arm myself mentally, take a deep breath and step forward, with the children in tow. The clerk is looking everywhere but at me, nervously scanning the area for any further sign of trouble. I pull out the envelope with the papers inside, empty the contents onto the counter. He reaches for them. The two Canadian birth certificates fall out first. He looks.

"You coming on holiday?" he asks, rushed, ready to finish.

I nod my head, "Yes."

He glances at the birth certificates again, "Thirty days?"

"Yes, I reply, holding my breath, the sound coming out in a

whisper. He picks up the papers, stamps everything, hands them back to me with the envelope, with a perfunctory, "Enjoy your stay," and we are in.

We are in? We are in! Is that it? I stifle the urge to cry, to laugh, to scream for joy. No sitting on hard plastic benches in the airport waiting for someone to come and rescue us. We are in! God is good. He will not put on me more that I can bear. The Lord is my Shepherd. He sent a mad man for me!

I grab Hannibal's hand, pull him along, trying to affect some measure of calm so as not to arouse suspicions here by being too happy to get in, head for baggage claim. The worst is over, but there is a long uphill road ahead of us.

"Well, Amite, you say I am dumb, don't know anything, but just look at what God and I can do!"

21

A niece met us in Toronto, and after spending a little time with her at the airport, we boarded the plane for Sedgewick and were met by my sisters, Lena and Elsie. We went to Lena's house to live. After explaining to them what had happened, we finally had a chance to rest. But, of course, I couldn't. I was still in too much turmoil, still had too much unfinished business to take care of.

Bea called to say that all was well in Largo, that Amite had met her upon the road the next day on her early morning walk, and talked to her until her eyes glazed over, about three hours. Of course, she told him nothing, but in listening to him, she realized that he thought we were hiding out in Largo. Good! She said she rested easier that he thought we were still in the country, knowing that he would not be in hot pursuit of us. He told her the whole story, said that he would not change his relationship with his daughter to suit me. She was to tell me to come home, not to have his children in the streets; he would live elsewhere if I wanted. "Jaye, he is really crazy," she said, "much worse than I imagined. Frightening."

Bea said she had finally gotten rid of him—he followed her to her house—by going inside and leaving him on the verandah while she cooked breakfast. He had finally realized that she wasn't coming back outside, he had come inside uninvited, talked a few minutes more, repeating himself, and before leaving, reiterating that he would never change his relationship with his daughter to suit me. "It may be against man's law, but it is not against Mother Nature, God, as you all would say." She said he said that several times.

She said little, beyond, "If I hear from her, I will tell her what you say," this in response to his insistence that she tell me to come home.

And what was his relationship with his daughter? I'm afraid we still do not have the whole story. We went immediately into therapy as Bea had suggested, and what Yala has so far revealed is this:

From the time that she was eleven years old, her father began to molest her often, progressed to intercourse when she was thirteen, out of high school, and at home with him every day. He insisted on sexual relations with her an average of three or four times each week, told her she was his wife. The worst times were when I would go away to other parts of the Caribbean to serve on the CXC examination team, she said. During these times, he constantly plagued her for sex. Even when I was home, he would get up out of our bed at night and bother her, she says, even insisting on sex when I was under the same roof. He maligned and distorted her view of me, Bea, my sisters, parents, and anybody I was close to, providing examples of my supposed uncaring attitude. He even insinuated that Bea and I were lesbians, citing an example from *The Color Purple* to show the kind of person Bea was. Some nights he would enter Yala's room while I slept; she would hear him coming and go into her closet in the darkness to get away. Amite would enter the room, stand in the darkness for several minutes while she held her breath in the closet. He would reach out and touch her lightly on the shoulder, turn around and go back to his room. My premonition about stealing her from the hospital when we did as being our last chance was right: Yala says that during the days when Amite sat by her bedside at the hospital, he had already asked her if she had enough clothes in the thatch roofed house in the bush to last her for a while. He planned to take her even further into the jungle, some three miles straight back to a spot he had found earlier and where he planned to build another thatch, situated where one would need an expert guide to escape from.

The Canadian authorities were extremely nice to us, providing first, extensions for our visas and finally reinstating my resident status and granting residency to the children. Yala went back to high school for a year in Canada, graduated with high honors, and received scholarship assistance to college where at this writing, she has begun her second year. The Canadians also provided free counseling and therapy for Yala and me for a year. My two youngest, Hannibal and Nefertiti, six and ten years old respectively, were tested for any signs of abuse and it was determined that they escaped. Amos, aside from an initial visit or two, has refused counseling and bounces around from job to job, mostly menial. He has dropped out of trade school twice, and is currently working at another menial job that he hates.

Family Secrets

After the year's counseling, during which time the Canadians informed me that ours was a rather classic textbook case of family incest, we received counseling for another few months free of charge from the therapist on her own time. For six months, now, Yala has not had therapy and seems to be regressing sometimes. Counseling is hard to come by, and terribly expensive, especially when coupled with all the other ancillary expenses we have had to face. Attorney's fees have been prohibitive, but necessary immediately, as I was advised to obtain a restraining order advising Amite that if he came on Canadian soil to try to see the children, he would be arrested. The five hundred dollar check from Bea which she slipped to me in the letter as I was leaving Largo, paid the retainer for the first lawyer. My sister Lena and Wentworth took care of us in their home for the first year, as I was only able to work as a substitute teacher with no regular salary coming in, and Elsie, too, provided financial and moral support.

I told the children what their father had been doing. Amos vacillated that first year between wanting to go back to Largo to kill Amite and accusing Yala of lying on his father. His relationships with women leave a lot to be desired. Although he says he never knew nor suspected anything about his father's incestuous abuse of his sister while he was there, he was with Amite and Yala at home during the last two years of our stay in Largo so I can only wonder. Hannibal drew a picture at school which showed a man and woman on top of each other in a bed, obviously having sex. When I looked at the picture closely, I realized that the curtain above the bed, meticulously drawn with flowers, was the curtain in my bedroom back in Largo. He obviously did not escape quite as easily as the therapist had thought.

I had also underestimated the effect of the situation on me. Two months after our arrival, I went to the lawyer's office to sign the papers for the restraining order against Amite, read the therapist's report attached to it for the judge's information, and broke down then and there. Seeing myself described was too much for me. Before reading the report, all the time I had been going back and forth from lawyer's office to therapist, to Immigration authorities, taking care of business, I had had it in the back of my mind that I would get the children situated and go back to Largo to try to straighten out my marriage. On reading it, I realized just how brainwashed I had been. Today, it is still difficult to sort out my own thoughts sometimes, because, I know now that for twenty-four years, my thoughts were for the most part, Amite's. He had had just that much control over me. My sisters say it was always that way. Everybody knew but me, but no attempts to tell me had ever been successful.

Elsie's daughter, Kathy, had her own story to tell about Amite. He had tried to molest her before he left Canada when she was twelve or thirteen. Luckily, she was a boisterous, Nefertiti-like child, and succeeded in rebuffing his attentions. Poor Wentworth had had the same relationship with Amite that I had with Elsie, and although he took us in, automatically assumed that I had blown the whole thing out of proportion. After we had been in his house two months, Amite found out where we were and called to ask for me. Wentworth answered the phone and on my instructions, said I wasn't there. Ten days later, a letter arrived from Amite in which he chastised Wentworth no end for dipping into the "little spat" he had with his wife.

"What kind of brother are you? If you are a man, you will give Yala this letter, etc. etc." Wentworth passed the enclosed letter to Yala. In therapy by then, Yala read each page, passed them on to me. The letter was raunchy, vulgar, referred to their relationship, and told her to figure out a way to get back to him. I passed the pages on to Wentworth. Amite had even joked in Yala's letter about conning Wentworth into giving her the letter by making him feel guilty. Reading Amite's letter to Yala was when Wentworth truly believed. He went into a bathroom in the basement and spent most of the weekend there crying by himself. It was a horrible, horrible thing to see happen to this wonderful, kind man who is my brother-in-law. Amite had insinuated in the letter the same thing Yala says he told her: that Wentworth would take her for his wife if she came to my sister's to go to school. This lie was to convince Yala that she might as well stay with Amite.

Bea left Largo some three weeks after we did, but not before she had a chance to talk to Sister Deer. Sister reported that Amite came to her with Taiji in tow to explain his relationship with Yala. He also let her know that he had been told at the hospital that Sister Deer had been with me when I picked up Yala. He inquired of her who else was involved and Sister Deer told him that Bea had been with her as well. Sister Deer listened to him, she said, but did not comment much beyond asking questions. Sister had been very angry that I had to leave, felt that I should have gone to the authorities to have Amite arrested instead. Knowing now that Bea had known all along, Amite did not come back to talk to her again. During the final stages of writing this book, Bea reported to me that her student in the States whom she advised not to marry the man who had wet dreams about beating his four year old daughter, called her and asked for help in escaping from him. She enlisted Bea's aid in taking her three year old daughter from where he'd stashed her, and fleeing into a shelter where she reported to the authorities what she thought was going on, both with her own daughter and the now seven year old stepdaughter. Fortunately, both children have been put into foster care while the mother tries to regroup and get her own life together after undergoing three years of mental, emotional, physical, and sexual abuse herself at the hands of the husband. Although she was adopted at age three herself, in therapy, the woman has begun to explore her own behavior and complicity in the matter, and now suspects that she may have been a victim of very early sexual abuse herself.

***

My relationship with Yala is rocky. Sometimes I feel good about it; but sometimes I despair. She loves me; she loves me not. And I understand it. I am trying to allow her the freedom of anger and accusation towards me, still trying to heal myself, and trying to watch my little ones for signs of trouble. Yala needs much more extensive therapy than she is receiving. So does Amos, Hannibal, and possibly Nefertiti. And so do I.

My divorce from Amite Peay was finalized the other day, and although there was no property settlement, a burden was lifted off my shoulders. Our family is beginning to find the God that Amite tried so hard to take away from us, and I plan to apply for an annulment through my church. It will, of course, have no legal ramifications, but spiritually, I need the release. I believe when the church sees this book that it will be granted. In the meantime, we persevere. *The Lord is my Shepherd; I shall not want. My soul doth magnify the Lord. He will not put on me more than I can bear. Allelujah!*

About the author

Billie Jean Young has made a commitment to telling the stories of her people through her poetry, plays, and books. In her book of poetry, *Fear Not the Fall* (New South Books, 2004), and her play, *Fannie Lou Hamer: This Little Light*, Young shines the light on a civil rights heroine—a poor, rural woman from the Mississippi Delta who was largely ignored until Young wrote and began to perform her story in 1983. Young's poems tell the story of civil rights in Alabama as Young herself lived it. In *Now How You Do* (Wingate Books, 2010) she shares her mother's letters to provide a glimpse into the lives of rural Alabama Blackbelt women. *Family Secrets* represents a declaration that it is time to break the chains of silence and heal from the abuse in our communities. Her next book, whose working title is *Phoenix*, is her own memoir. Billie Jean Young is artist-in-residence at her alma mater, Judson College, in Marion, Alabama.

LaVergne, TN USA
11 January 2011
211926LV00001B/1/P